Anglican Orders
and Ordinations:

Essays and Reports from the Interim Conference at
Jarvenpää, Finland, of the International Anglican
Liturgical Consultation, 4—9 August 1997

edited by David R. Holeton

W0009107

THE ALCUIN CLUB and the GROUP FOR RENEWAL OF WORSHIP (GROW)
The Alcuin Club, which exists to promote the study of Christian liturgy in general and of Anglican liturgy in particular, traditionally published a single volume annually for its members. This ceased in 1986 but resumed in 1992. Similarly, GROW was responsible from 1975 to 1986 for the quarterly 'Grove Liturgical Studies'. Since the beginning of 1987 the two have sponsored a Joint Editorial Board to produce 'Joint Liturgical Studies', of which the present Study is no. 39. Three titles are produced each year, and existing Studies are listed on page 64.

THE COVER PICTURE
is by Lyn Stone

First Impression December 1997
ISSN 0951-2667
ISBN 1 85174 362 6

GROVE BOOKS LIMITED
RIDLEY HALL RD   CAMBRIDGE   CB3 9HU

CONTENTS

THE CONTRIBUTORS

Paul F. Bradshaw is Professor of Liturgy at the University of Notre Dame, Indiana and currently Director of the Notre Dame London Centre.

Colin O. Buchanan is Bishop of Woolwich and a member of the Steering Committee of the IALC.

Janet Crawford is a lecturer in Church History and Liturgics at the College of St. John the Evangelist, Auckland, New Zealand.

Kevin Flynn is Incumbent of the Church of St. Stephen-in-the-Fields, Toronto and Lecturer in Liturgy at Trinity College, Toronto.

John St. H. Gibaut is Associate Professor of Liturgy at Saint Paul University, Ottawa where he also directs the Anglican Studies Programme.

David R. Holeton is Professor of Liturgy at the Hussite Theological Faculty of the Charles University in Prague and was Chair of the International Anglican Liturgical Consultations from 1989 to 1995.

Louis Weil is James F. Hodges Professor of Liturgics at the Church Divinity School of the Pacific in Berkeley, California.

1. Introduction

by David R. Holeton

When it was decided that ordination would be the primary topic for the Interim Conference of the International Anglican Liturgical Consultation to be held in Jarvenpää, Finland from 4-9 August 1997, the Steering Committee was conscious that it was following a pattern set by the most important multilateral ecumenical document of our age—the Lima Document: *Baptism, Eucharist and Ministry* [BEM]. Having prepared the statement 'Walk in Newness of Life' on baptism at its Toronto Consultation in 1991 and the 'Dublin Statement' on the Eucharist at its Consultation in 1995, ordination was the next logical focus for the work of the IALC.

Following its present practice of alternating Interim Conferences with meetings of the full Consultation—in which the Conference is preparatory for the Consultation—over forty liturgists from around the Communion turned their attention to preparing material that would serve to stimulate reflection and discussion throughout the Communion. The reports of the four working groups represent the week's work at Jarvenpää and they are provisional documents reflecting work in progress. They will serve as one resource for the 1998 Lambeth Conference, and for those who gather for IALC-6 in 1999 when a statement on ordination will be prepared.

During the Conference, participants discovered that there were some issues on which consensus was easily and quickly achieved. There were other areas which were more controversial and on which further discussion must take place before any consensus can emerge. There were also a number of areas that need discussion and, while noted by participants, yet remain to be addressed. The careful reader will see these different levels of development within the report of the working groups.

Areas where consensus was easily achieved included matters like the firm grounding of any reflection on ministry and ordination in a baptismal ecclesiology as well as the incorporation of an articulation of apostolic/historic succession within an understanding of the apostolicity of the whole church. Significantly, consensus in these matters would unlikely have been possible a generation ago, something that reflects a development within Anglicanism in several respects. This reflects a renewed baptismal theology that has become a part of Anglican life over the past quarter century as well as a broader understanding of the apostolicity of the whole church. The latter is an area in which Anglicans have been helped to re-think their theology of ministry, through both the reception of BEM and our bilateral dialogues with churches which do not claim to have the 'historic episcopate'.

The question of the restoration of the diaconate as a full and equal order, for example, was another issue around which consensus easily emerged. The corollary, however,—that this will only happen when the church ceases to use the diaconate as a transitional order for those who are soon to be priests—was a matter on which further discussion needs to take place.

There were a number of areas that were raised in Jarvenpää but which need much more extensive discussion. For example, there are questions of language: e.g. should 'presbyter' be preferred to 'priest' or the other way around? And, while the possible shape and content of ordination liturgies received considerable attention, much work needs to be done to move the series of questions found in § 30-38 of the working group reports into a statement that will be of use to those who are responsible for drafting new ordination rites in their Provinces. These issues will be sure to take their rightful place on the Consultation's agenda for 1999.

Along with the report of the working groups, this volume contains a number of other papers. Paul Bradshaw's chapter was presented as the keynote address of the Conference and did much to provide stimulation and direction for the week. His thesis that theory has triumphed over evidence in the development of ordination rites is one that challenges Anglicans to re-think a number of questions pertaining to ordained ministry, starting from basic principles.

Colin Buchanan's chapter is a synthesis of two papers he wrote as resources for the Conference's participants. Guided, in part, by the ecumenical concerns of our own age, he gives a perspective on the history of Anglican ordination practice that raises important questions about possible ways forward in our ecclesiology, our practice of ordination, and our ecumenical relationships.

John Gibaut's chapter is also a revision of work prepared as a resource for the Conference. It is of particular importance for IALC-6 as it provides significant historical background for the discussion of direct ordination. Anglicans should find it freeing to learn that the practice of the church has been much more pluriform than is generally accepted. Thanks to this chapter, we are given the possibility to re-think our present practice of sequential ordination in a much wider context. In preparing for IALC-6, Anglicans need to reflect on their rationale for continuing the *cursus honorum* rather than ordaining directly. It will be clear from Professor Gibaut's chapter that such a rationale will need to do more than simply appeal to 'tradition'—whether Anglican or that of the 'undivided Catholic Church'— neither of which will support it.

Several essays arose out of discussions at Jarvenpää in which it became clear that the context in which we were discussing ministry and ordination had evolved tremendously in the past few decades. In her chapter, Janet Crawford outlines the evolution of the practice of ministry in New Zealand. This is one example of a process that is going on in many parts of the Communion. A variety of factors have coalesced to raise serious questions about our methods of selection and preparation of candidates for ministry. The ordination of women, new patterns of ecumenically shared ministry, economic crises, the democratization of the church and the implication of civil labour codes are among many factors which have recast some of the basic questions surrounding our inherited practices as Anglicans. These will play an important role in any document on ministry for the coming millennium.

Kevin Flynn's chapter on the diaconate raises another important issue that must be faced in addressing questions of ordination. Partly because ordination has been seen for so long as a clerical preserve, there has been a gradual confusion of the theology of ordination with a clerical 'piety of ordination'. While it is laudable that the clergy have developed a 'spirituality of office', some of its dimensions do not stand the test of historical and theological reflection. The common confusion of many between the diaconia of all the baptized, the order of deacon, and the status and appropriate vesture of others exercising liturgical ministries that have traditionally been those of deacons needs considerable clarification. As they begin to untangle these issues, Anglicans would be helped to unmuddle their understanding of the order of deacon if they stopped engaging in the practice of dressing priests (and, occasionally, bishops) in the liturgical vesture of deacons. This practice, which is uncanonical in both Roman Catholic and Orthodox churches and a relative novelty within Anglicanism itself, frustrates attempts to restore the vocational diaconate and can lead to considerable confusion in our ecumenical dialogues.

Clericalism is a serious sin because it reflects a model of the church which denies the status we have been given in baptism. When Anglicans celebrate the rites of ordination, however, they often model a clericalism that belies our baptismal theology, betrays the general principles of liturgical reform to which our provinces are committed and flies in the face of what the ordination rites themselves proclaim about the ministry of the whole People of God. Such dissonance between what we say and what we do cannot remain unchallenged. Louis Weil's chapter addresses one dimension of this problem and serves as a very helpful starting point for a reflection on the celebration of ordination. Any attempt to reform our rites will fail to serve the common life of our Communion unless the visual clutter and clericalized character of the actual celebration of ordination is satisfactorily addressed. May the day soon come when the celebration of our ordination liturgies clearly proclaim who we claim to be as a baptized, priestly people where ministry is shared by all and not a possession of the clergy.

The Ministry portion of BEM was the most difficult portion of the statement to create and members of the drafting committee sometimes found themselves passing over some areas in silence because no consensus could be achieved. It should be little surprise that this initial discussion on ordination by the IALC also had difficulties achieving consensus in some areas and left others unaddressed. Reconciling our understandings of ministry is often a very painful process because it is on this very matter that churches have most often 'unchurched' one another, calling into question the validity of the ministry of one another and, consequently, their status as church. My own paper is an attempt to address some of these issues as they focus on apostolicity and 'historic succession' as they are coming to be understood within Anglicanism.

The Jarvenpää Conference made considerable progress towards an IALC statement on ordination. The areas where consensus was achieved were significant both for the Communion and for our ecumenical relations. It will be clear, however, from the report of the working groups and the accompanying papers that there are a number of issues which Anglicans must resolve among themselves if there is to be a coherent understanding of ordination within the Communion and if they are to present themselves with integrity in their dialogues with other churches. The Jarvenpää Conference was one step towards that end. It is to be hoped that the report of the working groups and accompanying papers will be read and discussed widely. It is important that those who attend the 1999 Consultation come with a sense of where the life of their provinces is on these matters and how the deliberations of the IALC on questions around ordination affect them.

2. Ordination as God's Action through the Church

by Paul Bradshaw

The history of the study of ordination rites more than amply demonstrates the dire consequences of allowing theory to triumph over evidence, of letting preconceived notions determine the outcome of supposedly dispassionate analysis of texts. For example, the decision to include ordination among the seven sacraments of the Church in the high middle ages meant that it had to conform to all the requirements of a sacrament that were laid down by the scholastic theologians, that a precise 'matter' and 'form' which effected the sacrament had to be found within the rites. One of the serious repercussions of this was that all attention became focused narrowly upon one part of the rite as essential, and the rest dismissed as merely ancillary. Because of the long running controversy with Roman Catholics over the validity of our orders, we Anglicans have been strongly drawn into this way of thinking, and even recent revisions of rites in various parts of the Communion have not managed to extricate us from it. Although ostensibly reverting to the idea of an ordination prayer accompanying the imposition of hands as constituting the heart of the rite, yet in reality we have remained wedded to the vital importance of the words of a particular formula being said while hands are laid on each individual ordinand. The theology that the performance of the rites reveals is that of 'consecration by formula', of a 'moment of ordination', whatever the actual beliefs of the compilers may have been.[1]

Even if we were to take more seriously the claim in the preface to the earliest Anglican Ordinals, that admission to any ecclesiastical office should be 'by publique prayer and imposicion of handes', we would not have completely succeeded in recapturing the concept of ordination held by Christians in the first few centuries of the Church's existence.[2] For them, 'prayer' referred not just to an ordination prayer alone, as it tends to do for us, but to the prayer offered by the whole gathered community, to which the ordination prayer as such constituted the culmination and climax. Thus, for them, the involvement of the people in an ordination service was no optional extra, with which one could if necessary dispense without affecting the character of the rite; ordination was not an essentially episcopal act to which friends and family might be invited, but a rite celebrated by the whole Church — bishop, clergy, and people together, each playing their respective and equally important roles.

Nor did they at first distinguish, as we now do, between what we would see as the preliminaries of appointment to ecclesiastical office on the one hand and the liturgical rite proper on the other, and regard the latter alone as that which made someone into a bishop, presbyter, or deacon. They would not have viewed how a person arrived at the liturgical occasion as being entirely incidental to the validity of the act, but instead seen election and

---

[1] See further Paul F. Bradshaw, 'The Liturgical Consequences of *Apostolicae Curae* for Anglican Ordination Rites' in *Anglican Theological Review* 78 (1996), pp.75-86 = R. W. Franklin (ed.), *Anglican Orders: Essays on the Centenary of Apostolicae Curae 1896-1996* (Mowbray, London, 1996), pp.75-86.

[2] English translations of all extant early ordination rites can be found in Paul F. Bradshaw, *Ordination Rites of the Ancient Churches of East and West* (Pueblo, New York, 1990).

prayer as two parts of the same whole. Indeed, the Greek word which we translate as 'ordain', *cheirotoneo*, originally meant 'to raise the hand in order to elect' and was only later seen as referring to the ritual gesture of laying the hand on the ordinand. Although some of the sixteenth-century Continental reformers did manage to recover the insight that election and prayer essentially went together[1], it is not one that has managed to penetrate into Anglican thinking on the subject, let alone make its mark on liturgical practice.

ORDINATION AS PROCESS

If, therefore, the insights and practices of early Christianity have something valuable to contribute to our own thinking about ordained ministry, we need to expand our field of vision considerably. We need to regard ordination as essentially a process and not merely a rite, a process accomplished over time and not just in a brief sacramental moment, a process that begins with the Church's discernment of God's call to an individual for a particular ministry within a specific Christian community, continues with the community's prayer for the bestowal of the gifts and graces necessary for the effective discharge of that office, and culminates in the acceptance by the people of the new minister's role among them, expressed in their assent to his or her performance of the liturgical functions belonging to the particular office.

Let me say a little more about each of these stages. First, the discernment of God's call may legitimately come about through a variety of means: election by the local community may have been the standard early Christian practice for choosing a bishop, but it is not the only way in which God's will can be made manifest. According to Acts 1, for instance, lots were cast to determine who should be the successor to Judas in the Twelve—though that is not a practice that I would particularly recommend for regular use today! But, however it is done, it is vital to keep in mind that it is God's call that makes someone a minister, and not the Church's liturgy. As the Church of South India's Constitution and preface to its ordination rites affirm, in all ordinations the true ordainer and consecrator is God. All that the Church can do is to discern and ratify the action that God has already taken. When the person comes to the ordination service, therefore, it is not in order to be made a minister but to have God's appointment recognized, and the rites need to make this clear in some way. In ancient Roman practice, for instance, it was expressed visually by the ordinand being presented already vested in the robes of the order to which he was being admitted, and not having them put on at the end as though the change had taken place during the rite. In Eastern traditions, it was—and is—expressed verbally by the proclamation of the result of the election at the beginning; in the Byzantine rite it reads: 'The divine grace, which always heals what is infirm and supplies what is lacking, appoints [the presbyter] N., beloved by God, as [bishop].' It is unfortunate that later, through misunderstanding, the imposition of hands came to be performed while this was being read, and still more unfortunate that western scholars took it to be the essential scholastic 'form' of ordination—another example of the triumph of theory over the evidence itself.

Secondly, we need to pause to note the expression 'a particular ministry within a specific Christian community'. The early Church knew nothing of the idea of ordinations 'at large', and one could not be ordained 'absolutely' as a bishop, presbyter, or deacon in the universal Church, but had to be appointed to a specific, vacant ministerial role within an individual

---

[1] See for example Paul F Bradshaw, *The Anglican Ordinal: Its history and development from the Reformation to the present day* (SPCK, London, 1971), pp.39-40.

Christian community.[1] The remnants of this tradition linger on in the idea of the necessity of an ecclesiastical 'title'. It is unfortunate, therefore, that many modern rites stress strongly the notion of ordination being to the Church universal, and some make no explicit reference at all to the place in which the individual is to serve, even at the presentation of the candidate, where it would be most naturally expected. Thus, for example, we commonly have the spectacle of two bishops bringing forward a candidate for the episcopate with the words, 'Reverend Father in God, we present to you N. to be ordained as a bishop in the Church.' This practice conveys the unfortunate expression that it is membership of the episcopal college rather than the service of a diocese that is the main point of ordaining a bishop, and offers infelicitous parallels to nomination to an exclusive golf club by two existing members. Thus it matters not only what is said at the presentation but who the presenters are: do they really represent those responsible for discerning the divine call of the candidate and the local church in which he or she will minister? Rootedness in a particular community is the very means by which an individual Christian is connected to the universal Church, and ordination rites ought to articulate this vision more clearly.

Thirdly, in the light of what we have said above, greater emphasis needs to be given to the prayer of the community in ordination rites. This is not to undermine the importance of the ordination prayer proper, but to recognize that such prayer should always be set within the wider context of community prayer, to which it forms the climax and conclusion. Prayer by the assembled community prayer is not a mere preliminary to the 'real thing', but as much a part of the 'form' of ordination as the ordination prayer itself. Whether it is conducted in silence, by means of a litany, in the form of a hymn of invocation, or any combination of these elements, it should be accorded its proper dignity within the rite, and introduced by an appropriately worded bidding that expresses the theological conviction that ordination is an act of God working through the whole Church and not just through the bishop alone.

Fourthly, attention also needs to be paid to the wording of the ordination prayer proper. It should be noted that in my definition of the process of ordination, I described the prayer as one 'for the bestowal of the gifts and graces necessary for the effective discharge of the office', for this is how it is in nearly all ancient rites. The idea that the prayer is intended to bestow the office itself upon the candidate, to make him a bishop, presbyter, or deacon, is scarcely ever found in the oldest strata of ordination prayers of the East or the West. The vast majority of ancient rites take the view that the person has already been made bishop, presbyter, or deacon through the process of election just completed, and that what is happening now is that God is being asked to endue the new minister with whatever is needed to enable him to fulfil his calling fruitfully. It is, therefore, somewhat analogous to the act of prayer and blessing in a traditional marriage rite, which follows—rather than precedes or effects—the joining of the couple in matrimony. Furthermore, the listing of the particular powers and functions of the office is similarly rare in ancient ordination prayers. Instead the minister's role is often defined by analogy with Old or New Testament types, and what God is asked to bestow are the appropriate spiritual qualities to equip him for the ministry which he has just begun.

This may be the point at which to say a word about the laying on of hands. As I indicated earlier, recent Anglican revisions have attempted to bring prayer and the imposition of

---

[1] On this see further Edward Schillebeeckx, *The Church with a Human Face* (SCM, London, 1985), pp.154-156; C. Vogel, 'Vacua manus impositio: L'inconsistance de la chirotonie absolue en Occident' in *Mélanges liturgiques offerts au R. P. Dom Bernard Botte* (Louvain, 1972), pp.511-524.

hands together once more, as in early Christian practice. However, because the imposition of hands is generally only done during one particular sentence of the prayer, and that sentence alone is repeated for each candidate when more than one person is being ordained at a time, the impression given is that it is this particular formula of words that effects the ordination, and not the whole prayer. Indeed, it often seems as though there are three prayers here rather than one: a prayer of praise, a petition for the Holy Spirit (repeated), and a concluding collect. This way of doing things has no ancient precedent, but first emerged in the Church of South India in 1958, was copied in the ordinal of the abortive Anglican-Methodist reunion scheme in England in 1968, and from there found its way into the rites of many Anglican provinces as well as into the British Methodist rite of 1985. Attention therefore needs to be given to ways in which this unfortunate appearance might be reduced if not eliminated. At the very least, the laying on of hands might be prolonged beyond the single petition for the gift of the Holy Spirit. And although it is probably a forlorn hope now to try to eliminate from Anglican practice the 'rugby scrum' that occurs as each bishop or presbyter present tries to touch the candidate personally, it is perhaps just worth noting in passing that in the earliest traditions of both East and West about which we know, it was generally only the presiding bishop who actually laid his hand (hand, singular, not hands) on candidates for both the episcopate and the presbyterate, the directions of the so-called *Apostolic Tradition* of Hippolytus not withstanding. For the others, simply being there was enough to express their concurrence in the action.

Just as the prayer of the people can be overshadowed by the importance given to the ordination prayer that follows it, so too the centrality of prayer in the rite can be diminished by the wealth of secondary symbolism that frequently follows the ordination prayer and thus, in performance if not in intention, constitutes the climax of the act. The handing over of Bibles, patens, chalices, vestments, and other insignia of office is reminiscent of so many other occasions in life—from Sunday School prize-givings to university degree ceremonies—where similar actions are the central feature, that it is difficult for people to avoid viewing ordination in the same light. But ordination is different from those occcasions. It is not the achievement of success, graduation, or promotion, and so once again resemblance to such events is unhelpful.

One of the strange consequences of this proliferation of secondary features in modern Anglican rites is that the oldest and most significant of them—the exchange of a kiss between the newly ordained and the Christian community—becomes lost within this wealth of later accretions, and often appears merely as the regular exchange of the Peace at the resumption of the eucharistic rite rather than as the highly symbolic conclusion of the ordination itself. In ancient practice it functioned as a 'sealing' of the whole process: the bishop initiated it by greeting the newly ordained with a kiss, and the rest of the clergy and people then followed suit, in order to give symbolic expression of their acceptance of the new minister, which is a vital part of the whole ordination process. This acceptance was further demonstrated by their sharing together in the celebration of the eucharist that followed, with the newly ordained performing the liturgical functions assigned to their order. Thus, in order not to overshadow the centrality of prayer, and to enable this greeting to stand out as the appropriate conclusion of the process and as the bridge to the sharing of eucharistic fellowship, most of the other ceremonies could be displaced to a post-communion position. There they could form part of a 'missio' unit, sending the newly ordained out to serve in their ministry, while any vesting could be placed after the greeting and before the eucharistic action began, so that it would be more evident that the purpose of assuming these garments was to perform the particular liturgical duties in the eucharist.

The scholastic definition of ordination as one of the sacraments of the Church that had to conform in all its essentials to the pattern imposed on the other sacraments was preceded several centuries earlier by another piece of imposed standardization on the diversity of orders within the Church. St Paul's image of the Church as the body of Christ had included the vision of all its members exercising different but complementary ministries within it. It is true that in 1 Corinthians 12.28 he accords a degree of precedence to certain of the ministries over others: 'And God has appointed in the Church first apostles, second prophets, third teachers, then workers of miracles, then healers, helpers, administrators, speakers in various kinds of tongues.' However, his aim appears to be to suggest not that some are more important than others—the whole context in which this verse is set suggests exactly the opposite—but that certain ministries carry within them a leadership role in the Christian community, principally those that involve the proclamation of the word in one form or another.

By the time that we reach the third century the range of publicly recognized ministries within the Church has undergone a considerable contraction since St Paul's days. And that, I believe, is to be regretted. Yet there still remains some sense of complementarity rather than strict hierarchy. Thus deacons might be elected directly to the episcopate without having to become presbyters first; and in the listing of ecclesiastical offices widows might still be granted an honoured place, and readers mentioned before subdeacons rather than after, as was the later practice. Gradually, however, influenced greatly by the social structures of the ancient world around, a fixed hierarchy of ministries became established, arranged according to the extent of their liturgical, and especially sacramental, functions. This development was accompanied by the expectation that candidates for the higher offices would always pass through lower ones first. As John Gibaut has shown in his fine doctoral dissertation on the *cursus honorum* (as this pattern is known),[1] the original intention of this arrangement was to ensure that they could receive a substantial period of testing and training in these less onerous roles before being exposed to the demands of the positions of greater leadership. But in the course of time, this practical purpose was forgotten, and it came to be thought that ordination to each individual order was absolutely necessary before a person could proceed to the next one above. In other words, with the different orders now being thought of as successive rungs on a single ladder, it was considered essential that candidates should tread on every single rung, however briefly, rather than only spending time on one of them. Completion of the ritual stages had taken precedence over the need to gain relevant experience. Theory had once again triumphed over practice.

We need, therefore, to recover a greater sense of the complementarity of the different orders of ministry within the Church, and of the distinctiveness of the role which each one plays within the whole. If we truly believe in three separate orders of ordained ministry, rather than three different degrees within one ministry, then we must cease to define everything in terms of the presbyterate alone, and we must not rule out the possibility of direct ordination to any of the orders. A deacon is not merely a trainee presbyter (though it may still be appropriate for many presbyters to serve as deacons first in order to gain experience) and a bishop is not merely a super-presbyter (though it will nearly always be appropriate for a bishop to have served as a presbyter first). This way of thinking arose in

---

[1] John Gibaut, 'The Cursus Honorum: A Study of the Early and Medieval Development of the Clerical Cursus and its Significance for the Contemporary Church' (Unpublished Ph.D. dissertation, University of Toronto, 1993).

the Middle Ages when ordained ministry came to be determined primarily in terms of its relation to the eucharist. Since the presbyter had received at his ordination the power of offering the eucharistic sacrifice, the *potestas in corpus eucharisticum*, he was thought of as possessing the fullness of ordained ministry. Hence most, though not all, medieval theologians concluded that the episcopate could not be a separate order from the presbyterate but only a *dignitas* or degree within the same order, having the power of rule or government in the Church, the *potestas in corpus mysticum*.

Remnants of this way of thinking linger on today, even among those who would not regard themselves as particularly high sacramentalists. It can be seen, for example, in the tendency to say that the reason why we need more priests is so that we can provide for the more frequent celebration of the eucharist in parishes. Or again, it can be seen in the tendency to robe lay people who assist with the administration of Holy Communion and to seat them in the sanctuary, but to leave lay people who read the lessons in their own clothes and to seat them in the nave—a clear if sometimes unintentional sign of the greater importance attached to sacrament than to word.

The ordained ministry, however, does not exist principally to perform sacramental functions for the Christian community, and the reason why we need more presbyters is not first and foremost so that we can have more eucharists. Ordination brings order, structure, to the Church, and the ordained ministry provides recognized and recognizable leadership to the body of Christ. Bishops and presbyters exercise that leadership at different levels within the Church. And it is because they preside over the Christian community that they preside over its worship (and not the other way round), and because they have the responsibility to preserve the community in truth that they are its principal ministers of the word. Once again, ordination rites need to articulate this vision more clearly than they tend to do at the moment. At the same time, they need to recover a greater sense of the distinctive character of the diaconate, rather than relegating it to the level of trainee presbyter or liturgical functionary. Although even the early Church apparently had problems in defining exactly what the role of deacons was, if we are to judge by the vague wording of its diaconal ordination prayers, yet the chief enduring characteristic of the diaconate has been responsibility for the Church's pastoral outreach, especially towards the poor and needy. Any liturgical functions which it exercises should flow out of this primary focus.

ORDINATION AND PRIESTHOOD

Not only is it important to recover the sense of the complementarity of the different forms of ordained ministry to one another, it is equally vital to reconsider the relationship between the ministries of the ordained and those exercised by the lay members of the Church. The clerical-lay divide is something unknown in the Pauline concept of Christian ministry, and it emerges only slowly in the life of the early Church. It receives its most decisive push, however, from the attribution of priesthood to the ordained, and to this development we must now turn our attention.

In the New Testament, as is well known, sacerdotal imagery is never attached to any particular ministry within the Church, but only to Jesus himself in the Epistle to the Hebrews, and to the Christian community as whole in passages in 1 Peter and the Book of Revelation. This usage was continued in the second century. Christians were thought of as constituting 'the true high-priestly race of God',[1] whose principal sacrifice was the

---

[1] Justin Martyr, *Dialogue with Trypho* 116.3; see also Irenaeus, *Adversus haereses* IV.8.3; V.34.3.

oblation of their whole lives, in line with such New Testament passages as Romans 12.1: 'I appeal to you therefore, brethren, by the mercies of God to present your bodies as a living sacrifice, holy and acceptable to God, which is your spiritual worship.' Within this offering of life, the explicit occasions of worship, both eucharistic and non-eucharistic alike, formed a particular focus. There Christians offered their sacrifice of praise and made priestly intercession for the needs of the world. This idea of the Christian priesthood persisted in the centuries that followed. Thus, for example, Tertullian[1] and other later sources interpret the post-baptismal anointing of a Christian in priestly terms, and the eucharistic prayer in the ancient text known as the *Apostolic Tradition* attributed to Hippolytus speaks of Christians as having been made worthy to stand before God and serve as priests. Similarly, both widowhood[2] and martyrdom[3] could be described as special forms of priestly consecration.

Alongside this, however, began to develop a quite different usage, the seeds of which can already be seen at the end of the first century. *Didache* 13.3 compares Christian prophets to high-priests in a passage concerning the offering of firstfruits, while *1 Clement* 40-41 cites the example of the assignment of different cultic roles to different ministers in the Old Testament Law as an argument against Christians transgressing the appointed limits of their respective ranks, and also uses the cultic expression 'offered the gifts' (44.4) in relation to Christian presbyter-bishops rather than the Christian community as a whole. But these passages are unique within Christian literature of the first two centuries, and in any case do not go as far as explicitly saying that Christian ministers are priests. It is not until the beginning of the third century that sacerdotal terminology starts to be used regularly and in a more literal manner to refer to ordained ministers, beginning with the bishop, and then extended to presbyters through their association with him, and in varying degrees to deacons also.

Thereafter sacerdotal language became standard in theological discourse about the ordained ministry in both East and West, though there are vestiges of some hesitation over the appropriateness of its adoption. Augustine, for instance, uses *sacerdos* more cautiously than his contemporaries, at least in part because of his need to insist on the unique priesthood of Christ in his debate with the Donatists.[4] Similarly, the ordination prayer for a bishop in the fourth-century *Canons of Hippolytus* omits all the high-priestly language found in its principal source, the *Apostolic Tradition*. The more ancient strata of other Eastern ordination prayers are also reticent in their use of cultic imagery, and it is only in later additions to these rites that priestly language appears. The classic Roman ordination formularies, on the other hand, stand in sharp contrast to this. Here the image of Christian ministers as the spiritual counterpart of the Old Testament cultic functionaries is primary to the texts.

The introduction of priestly language in relation to the ordained at the end of the second century marks the inception of a major change in the relationship between the people and their ministers within the Church: bishops and presbyters would eventually cease to be seen as the presiders within a priestly people, and become instead a priesthood acting on behalf of 'the laity'—a term already used in this sense in *1 Clement* 40.5. Although thereafter liturgical texts themselves might still carry the more ancient image of the common priesthood in which all Christians participated, both theological discourse and ecclesiastical practice instead viewed ordination rather than baptism as the decisive point of entry into the priestly life.

---

[1] *De baptismo* 7; see also *De oratione* 28; *Exhortatio castitatis* 7.
[2] Tertullian, *Ad uxorem* 1.7.
[3] Cyprian, *Ep.* 76.3.
[4] See, e.g., *Parm.* II.8.15-16.

Even the sixteenth-century Reformers did not entirely succeed in throwing off the vestiges of this way of thinking, in spite of their strenuous rejection of the attribution of any sort of priesthood to the ordained ministry. They still tended to regard the ordained alone as the ones who should exercise any sort of active ministry, with the laity as the recipients of that ministry rather as co-workers with it. The ordained were to preach the word *to* the laity and to administer the sacraments *to* them, to make public prayer *for* them and to exercise pastoral care over them—a priesthood in almost all but name.

The compilers of modern ordination rites therefore need to reflect carefully which model of priesthood should find a place in future texts—that of the royal priesthood of the Church, which the ordained ministers lead in their corporate mission, witness, and worship, or that of the ordained ministry acting on behalf of the people. By 'find a place' I am referring not only to explicit references to priesthood as such, but to the whole relationship between lay and ordained members of the Church that is inferred in the rites. How far are the ordained to minister *to* and *for* the laity and how far together *with* them? In this matter, prepositions are everything.

ORDINATION AND ECCLESIOLOGY

Yet even if we were to revise our ordination rites once again along such lines as these, we would not have finished our task. We would not have succeeded in putting ordination itself back where it really belongs within the ministry of the whole Church.

One of the major distortions of our traditional thinking about ordination has come about through divorcing it from ecclesiological considerations, and imagining that one could have a theology of ordained ministry that was to a large measure independent of a theology of the Church. This can be seen exemplified in such things as the recognition of the validity of ordinations performed by *episcopi vagantes*, as well as in the nineteenth-century efforts to gain recognition of the validity of Anglican Orders from Roman Catholics, which resulted in the reverse—their condemnation as invalid by Leo XIII in the bull *Apostolicae Curae* in 1896. It can also be seen in various schemes of reunion between Anglican and non-episcopal churches in the twentieth century. In nearly all these cases it was assumed that recognition of orders might precede the recognition of churches as churches.

To me, however, this appears to be putting the ministerial cart well before the ecclesiological horse. The ordained ministry exists to serve the Church, not the Church to serve the ordained ministry. As Edward Schillebeeckx has argued, what was considered essential in the understanding of ordination in early Christianity was 'the church's mandate or the church's sending of the minister, not the specific form in which the calling and sending takes shape.'[1] On such an understanding, recognition of orders cannot precede recognition of churches, but is intimately bound up with it, since it is the validity of a church's mandate that determines the validity of its ordinations, and not the other way around.

This is but another manner of stating what has been my principal thesis throughout this paper: that it is the Church that is crucial to the question of ordination and to its liturgical celebration, and we neglect that truth at peril of distorting the whole process. I believe that we are called, therefore, to rescue ordination rites from a narrow scholastic sacramental theology and from their relegation to an essentially episcopal and clerical preserve, in which lay folk fear to tread, and instead to restore ordination as an action of the whole Church— or rather as God's action through the whole Church.

---

[1] Schillebeeckx, *The Church with a Human Face*, p. 139.

3. Anglican Orders and Unity[1]

by Colin Buchanan

BACKGROUND THEORIES

I want to address two competing theories of the authority for orders—broadly classifiable as the Cyprianic and the Augustinian. The two come into currency long after the apostolic age, not only because the New Testament gives us very few straws about orders from which to form relevant theological bricks, but also because it is controversies arising later in church history, which cause a framing of more detailed statements. These theories arise from two particular episodes in the life of the Western (indeed in both cases the North African) church, in a period when the theories were enmeshed and expounded in relation to episcopacy. However, at root the two theories touch on an ecclesiological issue which is logically prior to the manifestation of threefold orders capped by episcopacy. Both are very suggestive in relation to the theme of this paper, for both arose from theological ways of handling the fact of schism. Whilst there certainly were schisms prior to the two episodes I want to consider, and while virtually all schisms have some implications in relation to orders, it is these two episodes which have parented doctrines of orders which affect our understanding of a visible church in multiple division to-day.

Cyprian in the mid-third century says orders cannot exist away from the fabric of the catholic church—and possibly thereby implies that (a) rebels and schismatics 'lose' (or 'forfeit'?) their orders; and (b) no orders can be conferred except within the catholic church. Eastern Churches to-day tend towards Cyprianism[2]; and so, *mutatis mutandis*, does classic congregationalism. The concept arises again—very interestingly—in connection with ecumenism.

Augustine, a century and a half after Cyprian, was attempting to reconcile the Donatists with (and to) the catholic church. Whilst generally no less denunciatory of schism than Cyprian, he has one olive branch to offer—Donatist baptism will be recognized as true baptism. This allows the principle that 'once-for-all-for-life' sacramental ordinances (such as ordination also has always been reckoned to be) can be truly conferred outside the catholic church—and are thus valid and should be recognized. (Augustine would, of course, argue further that such recognition is given with a view to reconciling those baptized (and ordained) in schism to the catholic church, and that only the 'character' (to use a medieval term) is conferred, without the cognate grace, as long as they remain in schism.) There is actually little evidence of Augustine himself applying the principle to ordination, but the principle has nevertheless become known as the 'Augustinian' theory of orders.[3]

---

[1] Part of this essay originates in a paper on the Anglican Ordinal which I prepared for the Meissen Theological Talks in England in March 1996—papers which are separately published by the Council for Christian Unity of the Church of England under the title *Visible Unity and the Ministry of Oversight: The Second Theological Conference held under the Meissen Agreement between the Church of England and the Evangelical Church in Germany* (Church House Publishing, 1997).

[2] There is unclarity in relation to Roman Catholic orders, for, whilst Orthodox and Rome are not in formal communion with each other, it seems that, on Orthodox premises, Rome can be recognized as a *part* of the *una sancta*. The problem comes when Rome claims to *be* the *una sancta* without, as it were, remainder. But Roman presbyters are known to transfer to Eastern Orthodoxy without re-ordination.

[3] Augustine *ep. Parm.* 2.13(28).

This 'Augustinian' theory has prevailed almost unchallenged in the West. It has certain obvious advantages—the main one of which is an initial certainty about who has been ordained and who not: simple recourse to the stud book and the line of descent of orders establishes who has the true dynastic descent and who not. And this in turn has toughened the concept of 'validity', with its concomitant linguistic currency of 'invalidity'; or, more normally, 'nullity'. It has also been of great practical advantage in respect of Rome's attitude towards the Eastern Churches. And it would of itself rule out most non-episcopal orders, simply because they do not have an historic origin of the right sort. It is clear that, with some qualifications, Anglicanism embraced (or sustained) this theory when the Church of England split from Rome in the sixteenth century, and the consecration of Parker, carefully arranged to be done by four pre-Marian bishops in undoubted succession, witnesses to that concern. Rome in turn found itself hoist with its own theological petard, as Anglican orders could not be condemned and nullified simply on the grounds that they had been conferred in schism. When the time for Rome came that it was proving expedient and strategically prudent to condemn Anglican orders, all sorts of other theological ruses had to be employed in order to reach the appropriate conclusion.[1]

CRANMER'S REFORMATION ORDINAL

It is a commonplace that at the Reformation 'these orders in Christ's Church; bishops, priests and deacons' were (as the same Preface to the Ordinal declares) 'continued'. It was almost inevitable that they would be, for the progress of the Reformation in both Henry's and Edward's reigns depended in large part upon the clergy using the offices they already held to promote it. Had the archbishops and bishops at any point called in question the propriety of their own ordination, they would have lost their own standing and forfeited their appointments. So this type of 'top-down' Reformation was bound to function with emphasis upon 'continuity'.[2] The orders (and offices and appointments) in the Church of

---

[1] A different embarrassment arose for Rome from the Old Catholic schism. Whilst the consecration of seven successive Archbishops of Utrecht between 1720 and 1742 was effected by a 'single bishop consecration' through an excommunicated bishop *in partibus*, neither the singleness nor the excommunication rendered him incapable of conferring true orders, and therefore, in relation to Old Catholic orders, Rome has always had to concede that validity as a 'given', when Cyprian would have totally delivered them. (They were nearly delivered it was, as, towards the end of the Napoleonic War, only one of the three Dutch bishops was still alive, and he fell into a freezing canal on a Winter night and was only kept alive, along with his succession, through the prompt action of his coachman.) The Old Catholic line spread its episcopate through large parts of Europe following the secessions from Rome after Vatican I, and the canal incident cannot now recur. Since the Bonn Agreement (1931) Old Catholics and Anglicans have recognized each others' orders as valid (on Augustinian grounds), and have shared in each others' episcopal consecrations—thus derivately raising the (casuistical) possibility that, from Rome's standpoint, despite the defects in Anglican orders in 1550, 1552 and even 1662, some true juice may in recent years have been injected into the Anglican line through that Old Catholic participation—and modern Anglican ordinals (untouched by *Apostolicae Curae* in 1896) may possibly be sufficiently near to Rome's criteria to sustain true orders in being once they have been (so to speak) injected into the Anglican succession.

[2] 'Continuity' is, of course, crucial to the Augustinian theory. The whole origin of it lay in the assertion that the Donatists could 'continue' an element of historic catholicity by mere historcal sequence, even if currently in separation from the fabric of the church and in heresy. The only test of 'validity' was historicity, and, by accident of contingent pressures (or, of course, by over-ruling divine providence), the 'continuity' in the Preface to the Ordinal apparently provided just what later generations reckoned they needed.

England duly continued, from the legal aspect and in terms of their places in the Church's structures, unchanged *faute de mieux*. By the time of Elizabeth's reign there was also the force of martyrdom—five bishops had been burned under Mary for their reformed faith, and they were being celebrated as martyrs in Foxe's *Book of Martyrs*, the next book after the Bible to be read in English homes till *Pilgrim's Progress* appeared a hundred years later. In the next century or so the matter of episcopacy became so entangled with monarchy that it was crucial for all royalists to leap to the defence—indeed sometimes the assertion of the necessity—of episcopacy for the safety of the throne. This is interesting (and doctrinally it was bound up with the divine right of kings), but it has, of course, to be recognized as rather different from some of the doctrines that have been wished upon the sixteenth century retrogressively since. And if you consult the text of Article XXIII, you will find that, at the point where the Lambeth Quadrilateral of 1888, or even the presuppositions of the Meissen talks, would have made some statement about the historic epicopate, there is instead the most general statement about ministering in the congregation, made in a form which would probably unite Anglicans and Presbyterians on the spot.[1] Other Articles do refer to bishops, priests and deacons, but none refer to the need of them! The way these orders were 'continued' was by means of successive revision of the ordination rites, which yet retained 'Bishops, Priests and Deacons', and ordained the candidates by the laying on of episcopal hands. The revised Ordinal (drawn indirectly from the pre-Reformation Pontifical, but more immediately from Bucer) was not ready in time to be part of the 1549 Prayer Book, but was instead a separate book of the three rites for ordaining deacons, priests and bishops (in that order) published by authority in 1550. Because the Ordinal arose separately from the rest of the Book of Common Prayer, it has traditionally not been a legal part of it (though normally bound between the same set of covers), so that the title page of the '1662 Book of Common Prayer' (the Book that is still part of the foundational documents of the Church of England) actually reads 'The Book of Common Prayer and Administration of the Sacraments and other Rites and Ceremonies of The Church according to the use of The Church of England together with The Psalter or Psalms of David and the Form or Manner of Making Ordaining and Consecrating of Bishops Priests and Deacons'. The Ordinal has actually, in both its 1550 origins and in its later binding into the covers of the Book of Common Prayer as above, a slightly separable history from the rest of the Prayer Book. Indeed it was apparently overlooked in law at the beginning of Elizabeth's reign when the BCP of 1552 was revived, but the ordinal was not mentioned in the 1559 Act., It appears that this is why Article XXXVI retrospectively affirms the propriety of the 1552 rites for ordinations, whether or not that is sufficient for legality! The Ordinal is cited as a separate Book in the Canons and in the Declaration of Assent, and has become therefore a separate leg on which the Church of England—and in turn the

---

[1] The text of Article XXIII runs as follows:

> *Of ministering in the congregation*
> It is not lawful for any man to take upon him the office of public preaching, or ministering the Sacraments in the congregation, before he be lawfully called and sent to execute the same. And those we ought to judge lawfully called and sent which be chosen and called to this work by men who have public authoruty given unto them in the congregation, to call and sed ministers into the Lord's vineyard.

This is remarkable for what it does not say (for it is fully compatible with, for instance, Presbyterianism), and the more so as Anglicanism was on the one hand taking its place as an episcopal church among a family of reformed churches most of which had a 'parity of ministers', and also because the Articles run to great detail in other areas such as the sacraments.

rest of Anglicanism—rests.[1] And it will be recognized that, just as with the universal use of Latin for worship in the Church of Rome for upwards of 1000 years, many features of church life ordered by authority in the sixteenth and seventeenth centuries may still be questioned and changed; and it is frankly unclear, from the mere fact of something being ordered by Act of Parliament in those centuries for universal observance, whether such requirements have the same doctrinal force as credal statements about the Trinity, or whether they are merely disciplinary, contingent and open to change.[2] To that extent the highest contention to be made for the episcopal system of the Church of England is that it is of the *bene esse* (perhaps even the *optime esse*) of the Church, and certainly not of the *esse* and therefore not *de fide*. This position, which is closest of all to the reticence of the Articles on episcopacy, is always agreed to be an allowable position to be held in the Church of England as a theory, but the Anglican Communion corporately has for a century or more been nervous of anyone acting on the theory. There is very considerable frustration in being so boxed in in practice by the opposite theory, a theory which goes beyond the doctrinal position of the Reformers and their formularies.

It is worth a further look at that 'continuity' issue. The 1550 Ordinal, the first revision of the Sarum uses, provided the terminology, where the actual word occurs in the Preface to the Ordinal: '. . . to the intent that these orders should be continued, and reverently used, and esteemed, in this Church of England, it is requisite, that no man . . . shall execute any of them, except he be called . . . and admitted, according to the form hereafter following.'[3] Vast edifices have been built upon the words 'that these orders should be continued'. Yet the words may be hardly doctrinal at all, but may be (a) asserting the propriety of the orders already held by ministers, and (b) exerting a discipline—both thrusts being designed to exclude sectarian upstarts rather than express a particular—let alone a conservative—doctrine about ordination. Cranmer is sufficiently unworried about tactual succession as to be ready to argue that, if in any Christian country a succession of bishops were to cease through failure to appoint or through an attack of the plague, the monarch has power in himself to appoint new bishops, without the participation of existing ones—and it is even arguable to the present day in England that the confirmation ceremony makes a man legally bishop of his diocese (at the monarch's command) even when other episcopal hands have not yet been laid on him!

THE DISCONTINUITY OF THE ANGLICAN ORDINAL

Even whilst the orders were being 'continued', they were being so completely re-modelled as to look like an almost new start. If there is a 'continuity' in titles and appointments and in episcopal ordination, yet there is a great 'discontinuity' in the contents of the rites: and those discontinuities deserve serious examination. For this purpose it is the ordination of priests which is put under closest scrutiny, not only because 'the parish priest' is the normal minister most lay-people encounter, but also because, in the light of the teaching on

---

[1] Though the Church of England (Worship and Doctrine) Measure 1974 defines the Book of Common Prayer as containing the Ordinal, and thus makes modern ordination rites 'alternative services' within the meaning of the Measure. (I should add that, in writing for an international Anglican readership, I am aware that I do not know whether or not other Provinces have treated the Ordinal in the same way.)

[2] A comparable ambiguous requirement in this category might be the wearing of the surplice, or the use of the sign of the cross in baptism—ceremonies which were not urged as of divine commandment, but were nevertheless imposed by strict church discipline.

[3] The full text of the 1550/1552 Preface should be set out with the 1662 text in parallel with it.

priesthood which marked the pre-Reformation church, it is in that ordination that the greatest changes are to be seen.[1]

The changes in the ordination of presbyters from Sarum to 1552 come in two stages, firstly from Sarum to 1550, and then from 1550 to 1552. Firstly, there is a totally new question of a totally reformed sort: 'Be you persuaded that the holy Scriptures contain sufficiently all doctrine, required of necessity for eternal salvation through faith in Jesus Christ . . . ?'[2] The pre-Reformation use did not include questions to candidates for the presbyterate. So this stems from Bucer rather than from any pre-Reformation question.[3] Secondly, the central task of the order was changed—it ceased to be 'to offer sacrifice for the living and the dead'; and it became 'to preach the word of God and to minister the holy sacraments'.[4] Thirdly, the subsidiary laying on of hands of the Sarum rite became the central act (the 'matter') of ordination, still retaining the words from John 20.23—retaining them as scriptural rather than to justify, let alone to make central, the Roman practice of 'Penance'.[5] It is often commented among scholars that Cranmer thereby lost the great ordination prayer which was the 'form' of ordination—and although there is a prayer preceding the laying on of hands, it is hardly comparable (and the rite for deacons includes no such prayer at all).

Finally, in two stages Cranmer completely changed the *porrectio instrumentorum*.[6] In the Sarum rite, the new priest received paten and chalice (with their respective elements) with

---

[1] The word 'priest' is, of course, an unfortunate hang-over from the pre-Reformation days, and, although its etymology in English is undoubtedly that it is 'presbyter writ small', its general use as the standard English translation of the words from the *hiereus* stem in the Greek New Testament makes it inappropriate as the translation of *presbyteros*. Nowadays there is a slow but steady recovery of the English word 'presbyter' and that helps stop the doctrine of ordination falling into unnecessary confusion. We are wise to use the word 'presbyter' ourselves. It is the word Newman used of himself at the beginning of Tract no. 1 'I am but one of yourselves—a presbyter', and it is officially into our formularies now in the modern ordination rites—the title of the relevant service being 'The Ordination of Priests (also called Presbyters)'.

[2] Cf. Article VI of the Thirty-Nine: 'Holy Scripture containeth all things necessary for salvation: so that whatever is not read therein, nor may be proved thereby, is not required of any man, that it should be believed as an article of the Faith, or be thought requisite or necessary to salvation . . .'

[3] The full eight questions should be included in any thorough survey.

[4] Cf. the 'notes' of the visible Church in Article XIX of the Thirty-Nine (Anglicans were criticized at the time for omitting reference to 'discipline'!). The sacraments, of course, had been reduced to two only, but that numerical factor is of less significance than their becoming second (in the order of describing the roles of the ordained ministry) after 'the word of God'.

[5] Cranmer makes clear in successive revisions of the Book of Common Prayer that there is no place for 'auricular confession' in the reformed Church of England, and in his treatment of two sacraments excludes 'Penance' from being a sacrament—a position confirmed in Article XXV of 1571. On the other hand he apparently saw no reason in the Ordinal to dispense with scriptural words, and must have long since concluded (and surely rightly?) that Jesus' commissioning of his disciples in John 20 was not, and could hardly be stretched to be interpreted as, a command to go and spread a network of confessional boxes across the world. It is indeed typical of Cranmer, as can be seen in many places in the eucharist, to preserve pre-Reformation biblical material and give it a better context. And it is fairly clear that he must have conceived of the John 20 passage as a highly personalized way of chartering the original disciples to proclaim a gospel of repentance (cf. Luke 24.47, a passage which reports the same evening) throughout the world. None of the above precluded private and confidential spiritual counsel, which is strongly commended by Cranmer in the warning exhortation in the 1552 communion service.

[6] The texts of the 'Porrectio' at the various stages, if set out in parallel columns, are highly illuminating. For the consecration of bishops, in 1550 there was still the laying on of a Bible on the neck, and the delivery of a pastoral staff; and in 1552 this became the delivery of a Bible (as with the ordination of a presbyter).

the instruction to offer sacrifice for the living and the dead. In 1550 the bishop handed over the actual sacramental symbols of a cup and bread, but added a Bible as well; and in 1552 the sacramental symbols disappeared, leaving the Bible alone as the outstanding tangible indicator of the character of the reformed ministry. Gone were not only the 'instruments' of the mass, but also the vesting of candidates, the anointing of their hands, and any possibility of 'concelebration'.[1]

HINTS OF CYPRIAN

We move on from the text to a wholly different issue. The Preface to the Ordinal prescribed episcopal ordination for the Church of England, but it did not proscribe those, in reformation Churches elsewhere, who were being ordained by other means (usually Presbyterian); and for a hundred years after the Reformation the Church of England was ready to receive them into the threefold order as presbyters as if they had been episcopally ordained.[2] Nor was it different when James I and Archbishop Bancroft insisted on the Church of Scotland becoming episcopal—for, although the first bishops had to be existing presbyters who came to London to be consecrated bishop in 1610, they were not at that point first episcopally ordained deacon and presbyter before being made bishop; and when they returned to Scotland they did not attempt to ordain again the existing presbyters, but recognized and accepted them as true presbyters in the Church of God. In other words, the existing presbyters were being recognized *as ordained in a true ecclesial context*.[3] Whilst the Reformers could not have held to quite the same concept of catholicity as marked Cyprian's polemics, yet they were saying, in effect, that a genuine church provides a genuine, that is, a valid, ministry.[4]

This latter loophole ceased at the Restoration. Charles II was called (or re-called) to the throne in May 1660. The restoration of the Prayer Book took two years and it was finally imposed by Act of Uniformity from 24 August 1662. Until that point there were, as a run-on from the Commonwealth, perhaps thousands of ministers functioning as parochial clergy without benefit of episcopal ordination. But the returning Royalists were Episcopalian to the core—though not so much because episcopacy guaranteed the form of the church, or provided an exclusive channel of grace, but because the monarchical throne of England, as they saw it, was settled upon a sub-structure of monepiscopacy.[5] Thus the heaviest possible

---

[1] The Roman practice of the newly ordained priest echoing the text and imitating the action of the chief 'celebrant'—the bishop—highlighted the sacramental role to which he had been ordained. All that was swept aside with the change in the text.

[2] Norman Sykes' book, *Old Priest New Presbyter*, works carefully over the evidence for this.

[3] This point is strengthened when it is noted that, in Canon 55 of the Canons of 1604, the preacher is required, before he begins his sermon, to pray 'especially for the Churches of England, Scotland and Ireland'. In 1604 the first and third of these were episcopal, the second presbyterian. But they rank together in their ecclesiality.

[4] If it is remarked at the same time that the Anglicans never withdrew recognition from Roman Catholic orders (despite what they viewed as horrifying errors in the Roman doctrines of orders and priesthood, let alone their being excommunicated by Rome), that must go back to the 'continuity' factor set out above—in other words there never was a point where the Church of England could draw a line across and say 'From now on, Roman ordinations will not be recognized'. Augustine still reigned supreme on *that* front—and the paragraph above is only a note of 'hints', no more.

[5] They only just returned in time to save the (Augustinian) succession. No bishops were consecrated after 1645, not because no bishops existed to consecrate them, nor even because no king existed to nominate them—both were available in exile. But what could not be provided was the legal requirement (still improbably in force in 1997) of an 'election' by Dean and Chapter of the cathedral of the vacant diocese. So the survivors who might provide a true episcopal succession were looking quite thin on the ground and sickly by 1660 . . .

re-imposition of episcopacy was basic to the Restoration Settlement, and by the terms of the 1662 Act of Uniformity the non-episcopal ministers, ordained by whatever method during the Commonwealth, were forced to leave their parishes or to submit to episcopal ordination as though they had not been ordained at all.[1] The Preface to the Ordinal was strengthened in an exclusive direction: '. . . No man shall be accounted or taken to be a lawful Bishop, Priest or Deacon in the Church of England . . . except he be called, tried, examined, and admitted thereunto, according to the Form hereafter following, *or hath had formerly Episcopal Consecration or Ordination'*.[2] These last eight words are italicized editorially to indicate that they were added in 1662. The door open previously to Presbyterianly ordained ministers was now shut, the existing Puritan ministers who would not accept (re)ordination were chased out of their parishes, and the episcopal framework was complete and without exceptions. The Cyprianic doors had been closed for what to-day we might well think were politico-religious reasons rather than purely theological ones—but one theological result, a purely Augustinian view of orders, now reigned supreme in the structural character of the Church of England.[3] It is an interesting question as to whether the Church of England, by design or perchance, left itself still some room to negotiate as to the theological necessity of the office of a bishop, even whilst its formularies required unvarying use of episcopal ordination.

PROBLEMS IN AUGUSTINIANISM

In the light of this vignette of a particular Anglican century of change, it is appropriate to re-visit the underlying theory—an Augustinian theory of orders, embodied in a threefold set of orders, claiming historical succession from the apostles. The most obvious snags in the theory are threefold:

(a) The theory, which in essence is an historical one, rests on no historical basis whatsoever. Tactual succession simply is not part of first or second century evidence—and later evidence not only does not plug the gap but is strictly irrelevant. There is an element of

---

[1] There was a very strong bias against them amongst the Royalists, and therefore the exclusive requirements of the Act of Uniformity are not above suspicion of a deliberate vengeful attempt to twist the Puritans' tails.

[2] The 1662 text in parallel with the 1550/1552 one could also be an appendix to this essay.

[3] Curiously, in the actual changes in the Ordinal made in 1662, the slightly vague opening rubric to the ordination of deacons and priests made in 1552 was clarified as follows: (i) *. . . there shall be a Sermon or Exhortation, declaring the duty and office of such as come to be admitted Deacons; how necessary that Order is in the Church of Christ* . . . (ii) *. . . there shall be a Sermon or Exhortation, declaring the duty and office of such as come to be admitted Priests; how necessary that Order is in the Church of Christ* . . . In the consecration of bishops, whilst a sermon has been added (which was lacking in 1552), it comes in the normal place in the communion service, and without any hints as to its subject matter. Perhaps that 'Order' was not quite so necessary in the Church of Christ! And I put 'Order' in quotation marks because it is not even absolutely clear that the liturgical books of the Reformation period treat the episcopate as an 'order' (and therefore do not 'ordain' people to it, but instead 'consecrate' them); but it can be argued that (as with Aquinas and the medievals) the Church of England at the time thought of the episcopate as an 'office' somehow within the presbyterate. Thus the Preface to the Ordinal only mentions 'these orders', and, whilst delineating 'Bishops, priests and deacons', does not use the enumerative 'three' anywhere; nor did the Preface say bishops are 'ordained' until 1662 (when the word must have been deliberately added—see the texts). But a more frequent view is that the Church of England was correcting the medieval pattern by making the major (indeed the only) orders bishop, presbyter and deacon, thus adjusting the pre-Reformation error of presbyter, deacon and sub-deacon.

fanciful superstition about these assertions of historical continuity, but without demonstrable historic continuity there should in logic be no theory. Yet paradoxically the theory, with a little liberal adjustment of its exclusivity, appears alive and relatively well.

(b) The theory allows a divorce between church and ordination, in such a way that orders may be conferred without any true ecclesial context. That, from Augustine's point of view, was precisely what was happening with Donatist ordinations. In a divided church this leads to overlapping or 'parallel' jurisdictions, sometimes 'in communion' with each other, sometimes not—exactly the scenario to antagonize a Cyprian. At its worst this doctrine of ordination leads to lines of *episcopi vagantes*. These fantasy bishop-figures, when thought to possess orders deemed 'valid' by Rome, have in turn been known surreptitiously to give 'true orders' to Anglican clergy who doubted the validity of their own succession. This in turn witnesses to an atomization of the doctrine of orders, in which individuals seek an individual validation of their orders from right outside their ecclesial frame, and in despite of the ecclesial claim to have conferred orders on them.

(c) It is worth consideration as to whether the Augustinian approach does not overweight ontology at the expense of function in the definition of orders. It has been interesting in my own theological pilgrimage to spend time in interaction with Eric Mascall who was re-exploring the ontology of orders in his retirement in the 1970s. Whilst he had no doubts about an ontological basis to orders, he was starting to interpret that ontology in terms of a relationship to the fabric of the church.[1] And that in turn might move the doctrine towards a Cyprianic definition.

(d) It is inevitable that Augustinian expositions should be 'catholic'—that is, the ordination rite claims to ordain to an 'order', which belongs in some sense to the universal church of God, and in effect calls for universal recognition. It is a noble, but often unsustainable aspiration, and may all too easily lose touch with reality in a divided church. Whilst devised to cope with schism and end it, it apparently denies that schism exists—or at least denies that it affects the doctrine of orders.

(e) In an ecumenical century, the theory apparently precludes any recognition of non-episcopal orders. It is a matter for guesswork how long such doctrinaire exclusivity can (without biblical justification) over-rule ordinary Christian charity and instincts towards unity. For Anglicans it has already reached a point of being virtually intolerable—if the theory will not serve the actual joining of the churches, is it not time we ditched it or at least modified it?[2]

If the theory we usually follow gives us problems, what about the one over the horizon? Predictably, the Cyprianic concept is not an automatic deliverance, but is open to opposite objections:

(a) Whilst there has to be a churchly context for the giving of orders, it is not at all clear at what point of the splintering of the universal church there cease to be true orders. Alternatively, the concept can be expressed quantitively, and then all denominations have partial orders (and perhaps need to 'top up' from each other[3]);

---

[1] [Reference to be checked]
[2] See the discussion by the 'Orders and Ecumenism' Group on pp.61-63 below.
[3] 'Topping-up' is dissected and discarded in Colin Buchanan, E. L. Mascall, J. I. Packer, The Bishop of Willesden (Graham Leonard) *Growing into Union* (SPCK, 1970) pp.193-207.

(b) There is a tendency in a disunited universal church to think that orders have only the authority of that proportion of the catholic church which stands behind their conferral.

(c) An historic succession of orders becomes a frill, and ceases to provide the substance of the enquiry. The ultimate logical outcome of that would appear to be that any group of people can constitute themselves 'church' and confer ordination

On this analysis, Anglicans hold to a strictly Augustinian theory of ordination. That implies that evidence of ordination in succession from the pre-Reformation church would be enough to put our orders on a par with Roman ones; and would invite Rome to recognize them as true orders *on her own terms*.[1] In fact of course Rome has not done so, but has denied the recognition—and it is instructive to see how she has had to apply her own terms in order to give that negative result.

We are to read the Roman Catholic condemnation of Anglican orders as a condemnation of the liturgical texts.[2] The major objection was 'defect of intention', which is a subtle shift from the standard enquiry into minister, form and matter of a sacrament. The stated defect was that the Edwardine Ordinal had not been intended (as it should have been intended) to make priests whose role was to offer the sacrifice of the mass. The underlying assumptions here are threefold:

(a) Orders are conferred in order to provide priests to offer the sacrifice of the mass;

(b) Cranmer's eucharistic rites had abolished all hints of the sacrifice of the mass;

(c) Cranmer's Ordinal therefore could not be said to ordain priests for that task (and the more so as it gave no hint in its own text that it did so ordain them).

Whilst *Apostolicae Curae* undoubtedly arose from English Roman Catholics manoeuvring to get the Pope to put Anglo-catholicism out of court, it needed refuting rather than merely dismissing. A robust Anglican answer would have been that we had never claimed that the validity of our orders rested upon any acceptance of (a), and thus it was unnecesary and even misleading to argue about (b) and (c)—points which, once (a) had been challenged, a good Anglican might well concede! It might however be argued back that what was needed was not robustness, but sensitivity—and that if any recognition by Rome were ever to happen (which was not what the Pope or the Cardinal Archbishop of Westminster in 1896 actually wanted), then the Roman Catholics would have to be convinced, on *their* terms, that Anglicans had retained a valid succession. This was how the Archbishops of Canterbury and York went about replying—their 1897 document, whilst profoundly and satisfyingly scathing of the Pope and his scholarship on most points of both history and logic, veered a bit near him on this point of the eucharist. It virtually allowed (a), denied (b) and thus dismissed (c).[3] But it is arguable that both the polemical needs of the 1890s and the Reformation formularies and a constructive laying of foundations for the future actually called for the 'robust' reply on this point, challenging the starting point of the two Archbishops.

---

[1] The theory has been half-observed in relation to splinters from Anglicanism itself—such as the Cumminsite schism in the USA (leading to the line of succession in the Free Church of England), the Church of England in South Africa, or the more recent 'continuing Anglicans'. It does not particularly matter that the ordinations of these splinter-groups have been conducted within relatively tiny groups—the dynastic impeccability of the transmission of the orders has been sufficient. The claim to ordain candidates as 'bishop/prebyter/deacon in the church of God' is sustained by the sheer fact of the ordaining person being a bishop in the historic succession.

[2] It included a statement that the orders conferred were not clearly identified in 1552, but that is (a) special pleading, and (b) likely to pull out the rug from early rites also.

[3] The crucial sentence ran: 'Primo enim sacrificium laudis et gratiarum offerimus; tum vero *sacrificium Crucis Patri proponimus and praesentamus*, et per illud remissionem peccatorum . . . impetramus.' (*Answer* para XI—emphasis mine). The question is 'What does "Patri proponimus et praesentamus" mean?'

There are other modern trends which need to be followed up, notably the rise of Catholicism in the Church of England; modern revisions of the Ordinal, and the ecumenical implications of these trends.

The first of these is well known. Keble insisted on apostolic succession in his Assize Sermon in July 1833.[1] The theological doctrine of apostolic succession, drawing upon the rubrical uniformity of the sixteenth and seventeenth centuries, then began to engulf Anglicanism in a way previously unknown (though perhaps adumbrated in the narrow sectarianism of the Non-jurors). It produced its own concepts of ministerial authority (with its concomitant clericalism), its own insistence on episcopal confirmation for true Christian initiation (with its concomitant Anglican exclusiveness), and its own magnification of the bishop's office in all accounts of ecclesiology (and thus of terms for inter-communion and re-union). It found its way in a modest form into the Chicago-Lambeth Quadrilateral. We need to note these effects—relatively new to the nineteenth century. Earlier evidence suggests that such insistence is neither integral to the gospel nor grounded in the Reformation settlement, but is a partisan and over-narrow view which has deeply affected and damaged our relationships with Reformed Churches.

Secondly, I come to revision of the ordination rites, which has happened round the world since the early 1970s. In my collection of the rites[2] I have traced their origins to the CSI rites of 1950, the Lambeth Conference document of 1958, and the Anglican-Methodist Ordinals of 1967 and 1968. Almost all of these have seen a shift from an indicative or imperative formula at the laying on of hands to a prayer of thanksgiving (indeed a 'eucharistic' prayer) within which or following which comes the laying on of hands.[3] It is a move sufficiently sharp as to raise the question as to whether we had a sufficient rite before![4] But *that* would be to open a retrospective can of worms . . .

What both Leo XIII and new rites have in common is a reliance upon Augustine. On the wider ecumenical front, however Cyprian starts to get a look in.

The concept of tactual succession, going right back to its origins in Augustine of Hippo, looks promising for the purpose of reconciling two episcopal churches, both of which can claim this historic succession and now need—for the sake of convergence or uniting—to recognize each other's church as a true part of the catholic church and its ordinations, and

---

[1] Similarly Newman wrote in September 1833 in Tract no. 1 '[when all else fails] There are some who rest their divine mission . . . upon their temporal distinctions. This last case has, perhaps, been too much our own; I fear we have neglected the real ground on which our authority is built—OUR APOSTOLICAL DESCENT'. And John Mason Neale wrote a hymn which is still to be found in *Hymns Ancient and Modern Revised*:

His twelve apostles first he made   So age by age and year by year
     his ministers of grace: this grace was handed on;
And they their hands on others laid   and still the holy Church is here,
     to fill in turn their place.   although her Lord has gone.

Further comment on this is to be found in my forthcoming *Is the Church of England Biblical?: An Anglican Ecclesiology* (DLT, 1998).
[2] COB (ed.) *Modern Anglican Ordinaton Rites* (Alcuin/GROW Joint Liturgical Study no. 3, 1987)
[3] This had been worked into the CSI rite through the participation of Edward Ratcliff, and it was then propounded strongly as a matter of principle in the 1958 Lambeth report (through the person of Leslie Brown, who had been on the CSI Liturgy Committee in 1949-50), and Ratcliff in turn affected the Anglican-Methodist Ordinal of 1968.
[4] I recall Arthur Couratin telling me in the early days of my time on the Liturgical Commission 'I never assist at an ordination in Durham cathedral without saying to myself "Invalid orders—defect of form".' Such was the power of the concept of prayer as the 'form', a concept brought into question by Paul Bradshaw in the opening paper above.

thus its ministers, as valid and beyond question. As it is primarily the historicity question which has to be handled, the size of the two churches and other similar questions can be set aside. There has, however, arisen a variant in respect of this in the Porvoo negotiations; for, quite apart from those churches, such as the Church of Norway, where a 'broken' succession has arguably been 'restored' by the participation in consecrations of bishops from other countries or provinces (Anglican, Lutheran or even Old Catholic) of impeccable vintage, in the Church of Denmark this participation had been wholly and deliberately excluded. There had indeed been a break in the succession in the sixteenth century, and ordination by presbyters had had to be employed to provide new bishops, and the current 'threefold' order stems from that event. The Danes proved unwilling to effect 'repairs' from outside their own country, but the negotiators reported that the continuity of the church in Denmark through the Reformation was such as to give a kind of alternative validation to the continuity of ordinations, albeit not episcopal, which had occurred. Whilst in the event the Danes have not subscribed to the Porvoo agreement, yet the Anglican Churches of Britain and Ireland, in their voting on the report, declared themselves ready to accept the Danes on the above terms. It is arguable that, in the process, Augustine was getting a small injection of Cyprian into his system. It is not quite so clear that the crossing of a watershed was registered by the participants, and the discussion in the report reads more like a seeking of an expedient to stop a gap.

The next interesting case arises in those situations where it is proposed to turn a church episcopal in order that its ordinations may be recognized, usually in the course of a quest for union of some sort. Such was the 1963/68 Anglican-Methodist Scheme in England, and such too was the proposed 'Covenant' of 1978-82. The recent 'talks about talks' between Anglicans and Methodists in England addressed a not dissimilar issue in their report, *Commitment to Mission and Unity* (Church House Publishing / Methodist Publishing House, 1996).[1] Of these the 1963/68 and 1996 plans for integrating or 'reconciling' ministries would appear to be nakedly Augustinian in their concept of orders.[2] So far they have come to nothing, though there exist slightly perverse mirror-images in the gaining of the historic episcopate by the Free Church of England (not then called that) in the nineteenth century, and by the Church of England in South Africa in the mid-1950s. These looked like sheer Augustinianism, but the episcopate was being adopted by those who had themselves little interest in theories of orders, and were adopting it in order to set themselves up as plausible rivals to existing larger (but less pure!) episcopal churches around them.

There may have been a step towards Cyprian taken amongst theologians when Oliver Quick suggested (? in the 1920s) that the church of God was in 'internal schism', and thus every part was conferring partial ordinations. It is unclear that any practical steps emerged from this, but at intervals his analysis has been quoted with approval, and it has a general tendency, as is obvious at sight, to favour Cyprian—though it was hardly issues of orders which originated or powered Quick's original analysis.

In order of logic the next phenomenon to consider is the formation of the Church of South India in 1947 (it reaches its fiftieth anniversary on 27 September 1997, just after the

---

[1] It has to be added that, at the time of going to press, the Church of England General Synod has accepted the principle of formal conversations with the Methodists, *without* building in this Augustinian feature of the earlier report mentioned above. As a participating member of the Synod's Council for Christian Unity, I can only rejoice at how the matter has moved on.

[2] The 1978-82 Covenant was more enlightened but abortive.

Jarvenpää gathering). This was in essence Augustinian in its approach to orders, but it qualified the existing limits of that approach in three ways:

Firstly, it allowed the recognition of presbyterally conferred orders as providing presbyters in the church of God, on virtually the same terms as the recognition of episcopally ordained presbyters—though now within an episcopal frame of church government.and authority.

Secondly, and by the same token, it recognized such presbyters as immediately eligible to be bishops.

Thirdly, it opened recognition to presbyters anywhere in the parent churches to enter into the ministerial ranks of CSI.

Whilst all these points are, in the strictest sense, issues of the historicity of orders, it has to be acknowledged that the overt philosophy of the participants was something like 'we as churches are carrying our respective ordained ministries into this united church, and the ministers are not being reconciled to each other one by one (as would have been the case with Augustine receiving Donatist presbyters into the Catholic fold), but are brought together by our churches coming together.' Therein, I suggest are overtones of Cyprian.

CSI was much attacked by the 'Catholic' hegemony of the Anglican Communion at the time; and not only were the non-episcopal ministers treated as no ministers at all, but the Anglican participants in the union were denounced for having gone into it, and for having given recognition to the non-episcopal ministers. Other countries considering such schemes were told by the Lambeth Conferences of 1948 and 1958 to 'reconcile the ministries' from the start. It is from these partisan reproaches that North India, Pakistan and Bangla Desh were directed towards the 'laying-on-hands-all-round' rites. These in brief provided for representatives of all traditions, but particularly and essentially bishops, to lay hands on all presbyters to commission them for their newer wider ministry within the particular united church. They are described in principle in Paul Bradshaw's book, *The Anglican Ordinal*, and I have generally dubbed them 'unificals', and have made well-documented pejorative reference to them in various places (most notably in the appendix to *Growing into Union* (1970)).

Part of the trouble these rites cause lies in their duplicity. The non-episcopal presbyters are assured their orders are being recognized, and the text of the rites does tend to include an element of affirmation of previous ministry. However, the moment the issue reaches an Anglican Church or province, the presbyters concerned are deemed by the Anglican authorities to have been episcopally ordained within the rite, and thus to fulfil the terms of the 1662 Preface to the Ordinal.

However, a more far-reaching problem emerges as relationships with parent churches are concerned. Once the 'unifical' solution has been adopted, it can never be dropped. No-one can be a minister of such a united Church unless he or she has either been episcopally ordained within that church or has been 'unified' on entry to it subsequent to ordination—*whether that original ordination elsewhere were episcopal or presbyterian*. The upshot is that, in order to have their orders recognized elsewhere from the start, the United Church founders have created a wall round themselves which means they themselves cannot recognize other people's orders (episcopalian or presbyterian) without the 'topping-up' of the unifical process. Of course that may not seem too serious when there are but few of such Churches on the earth's surface, but the long-term implications, especially if there were many such unions around, are such as to detract drastically from any concept of 'catholic' orders (which Augustine and threefold orders preserve *par excellence*). The paradox is that, specifically in order to defend catholic orders on the Augustinian theory, these arrangements come very near to providing merely local domestic ordinations, claiming recognition from others, but actually erecting barriers against others, and very specifically having to *name the locality* of the scope of the 'orders' within the rite. I suspect that this is covert Cyprianism, but skewed by overt Augustinianism.

My own hope would be that Anglicanism could be more open to an interchangeability with ordained ministers of non-episcopal churches. Such a provision would undercut these ambiguous expedients . It is a joy to see the four-sided agreement forged and now implemented in South Africa, whereby the presbyters of Anglican, Methodist, Presbyterian and Congregationalist Churches have become for most purposes interchangeable. Of course there is an element of the Cyprianic about it; it begins with a recognition of churches, and then treats the recognition and interchangeability of ministers as deriving from that.

Indeed, despite hesitations above, I suspect we need an element of the Cyprianic in all future deliberations. There is something ecclesiologically absurd about the *episcopus vagans* conferring costless and even meaningless 'orders' in a churchly vacuum, or ecclesial solipsism. Liturgists are rightly concerned with rites—but the definitions of rites have to include considerations of context, of canonical framework, of the qualifications of candidates and of the principle of universalizability. Only if we are sensible ecclesiologians will our rites correspond to God's reality and further it appropriately . . .

For the rest, I must cite myself from the Introduction to my collection of Anglican ordination rites 'What ordination is and does remains elusive'.[1]

---

[1] Colin Buchanan (ed.) *Modern Anglican Ordination Rites* (Alcuin/GROW Joint Liturgical Study no. 3, Grove Books Ltd., Bramcote, 1987), p.11.

4. Some Reflections on Apostolicity, Apostolic Tradition, Episcopacy and Succession

by David R. Holeton

Virtually since the nineteenth century beginnings of Anglican involvement in ecumenical dialogue, the historic episcopate has been given a place as one of the cornerstones upon which any scheme for Christian reunion was to be laid. The Chicago-Lambeth Quadrilateral lists 'the Historic Episcopate, locally adapted in the methods of its administration to the varying needs of the nations and peoples called of God into the unity of his Church' along with the Holy Scriptures, the Nicene Creed and the Dominical Sacraments as 'inherent parts of this sacred deposit [of the undivided Catholic Church], and therefore essential to the restoration of unity among the divided branches of Christianity ...'

It should be no surprise to note that, of the four cornerstones, the historic episcopate has been one of the great stumbling blocks in Anglican ecumenical dialogue. From early in this century, when long-standing conversations with the *Unitas Fratrum* (often called Moravians) broke off when it was discovered that their claims to the 'apostolic succession' were 'mythical' rather than historic, to some of the modern plans for church union (e.g. with Methodists in England or the United Church of Canada) discussion has foundered on the topic of 'apostolic succession' or the historic episcopate.[1] To be sure, there have been some examples where this question has been resolved much more successfully. The creation of the Church of South India and the dialogue with Lutherans in North America would be two particularly good examples. There are important lessons (both positive and negative) to be learned in both cases.

The multilateral document *Baptism, Eucharist and Ministry*[2] is an important milestone in finding a way forward on this matter. This is due, in part, to the fact that Anglicanism's polity and practice is both affirmed and challenged. Anglicanism is affirmed, in that the apostolic nature of the church is central in the document's ecclesiology.[3] It is challenged, in that the understanding of 'apostolic succession' is broadened beyond the common Anglican usage of the term in which it has usually been reduced to 'historic episcopate' that is 'tactile succession—*successio manuum*' often above 'succession of see—*successio sedis*' let alone in any articulation of the apostolicity of the whole church.[4]

---

[1] The 'sting' left after the breakdown of conversations when 'apostolic succession' is an issue is particularly sharp and of long duration as it effectively 'unchurches' one of the partners in the dialogue. Anglicans would do well to bear in mind the analogy to ongoing Anglican bitterness over the declaration of the nullity of Anglican orders in *Apostolicae Curae*.

[2] Faith and Order Paper No. 111 (Geneva, 1982).

[3] *Ministry*, IV.A.34. In the Creed, the Church confesses itself to be apostolic. The Church lives in continuity with the apostles and their proclamation. The same Lord who sent the apostles continues to be present in the Church. The Spirit keeps the Church in the apostolic tradition until the fulfilment of history in the Kingdom of God.

[4] *Ministry*, IV.B.35. The primary manifestation of apostolic succession is to be found in the apostolic tradition of the Church as a whole. The succession is an expression of the permanence and, therefore, of the continuity of Christ's own mission in which the Church participates.

With BEM's affirmation of the apostolic character of the Church as a starting point, Anglicans must certainly subscribe to BEM's vision of what constitutes the basics of apostolic tradition:

> Apostolic tradition in the Church means continuity in the permanent characteristics of the Church of the apostles: witness to the apostolic faith, proclamation and fresh interpretation of the Gospel, celebration of baptism and eucharist, the transmission of ministerial responsibilities, communion in prayer, love, joy and suffering, service to the sick and the needy, unity among the local churches and sharing the gifts which the Lord has given to each.[1]

The consequence of this broadening of our understanding of apostolic tradition beyond its common meaning of 'historic succession' is that it compels us to recognize that there are churches who bear all the marks of the *apostolic tradition* and, therefore, must in some way stand in the *apostolic succession* of the church even though they may have neither the historic episcopate nor even the order entitled 'bishop'.[2] For some Anglicans this may seem self-evident. We must not forget, however, that for many Anglicans over the past century there has been an almost unreasonable willingness to overlook the qualities of apostolic tradition in churches without the 'historic episcopate'.

The corollary to a broadened definition of apostolic tradition is that Anglicans must examine their own life and ask to what extent they, themselves, stand in the apostolic tradition. This, certainly, is an issue in our ecumenical dialogues when those who claim to be the principal transmitters of the apostolic tradition allow themselves to appear to be the principal opponents of what is commonly received to be the apostolic faith.[3] A willingness to recognize how we can fall short in our faithfulness to the apostolic tradition must certainly be an entrée in our dialogue with other churches in this matter.

That said, it is important to affirm the centrality of the sign-act of episcopal hand-laying in ordination and the rôle it assumes in the intention of Anglicanism as a whole to remain faithful to the apostolic tradition. As such, 'historic succession' is a rich sign, though not a guarantee, of the continuity and unity of the Church; and it is one which is increasingly accepted by churches without the 'historic episcopate' engaged in union negotiations as a sign of the apostolicity of the life of the whole church.[4] Any diminution of the value of the sign-act of the transmission of succession in the apostolic and historic tradition would, therefore, be a diminution of the importance of the tradition itself.

What is imperative, however, is that when Anglicans engage in ecumenical dialogue with such churches there be no imputation that the ecumenical partner is somehow unequal as a church because it wants for this historic sign. As such, any question of 're-ordination' in the case of any eventual scheme of union or full-communion must be out of the question.

---

[1] *Ministry*, IV.A.34.

[2] *Ministry*, IV.B.37. In churches which practise the succession through the episcopate, it is increasingly recognized that a continuity in apostolic faith, worship and mission has been preserved in churches which have not retained the form of historic episcopate.

[3] Different examples will come to mind for each reader and it is not the purpose of this paper to judge the belief of any particular bishop. There is, however, a serious question of public perception. There was, for example, a time when the most serious stumbling block in the Anglican-Orthodox dialogue was the question of an Anglican bishop having been reported to deny the resurrection in the press. While this is quite a simplification of what the bishop was actually saying, the point remains that the bishop was perceived by many to be explicitly denying something central to the apostolic faith and, thus, touching on the very core of traditional episcopal claims to be the transmitters of the apostolic tradition.

[4] Cf. *Ministry*, IV.B.38.

As churches move towards a mutual recognition of one another and their ministries the question of how becomes a growing one. Out of dialogue must emerge the willingness of both partners to recognize that the other stands within and bears the marks of the apostolic tradition.[1] Synodical affirmation of this is an assumed part of the process. Liturgical celebration of this, however, lies at the heart of any such recognition. It is here that great care must be taken.

The sign of celebrating together at the Lord's Table ought to be central and primary to any such act of recognition. Other sign-acts that take place should not detract from that. Mutual imposition of hands comes to mind as something that ought to be avoided. First, because it is a fundamental sign of the orderly transmission of the ministerial commission which each church has recognized the other to possess. Second, because it is too easily interpreted by some as a 'moment' in which something ('historic succession') possessed by one church is given to the other while the church 'without' the succession engages in an empty sign.

That there are churches which are willing to recognize one another and their ministries assumes that the members of both churches will participate in the ordinations of each church. This is particularly important in the ordination of bishops where the personal sign is provided in that bishops from both traditions, standing in the apostolic tradition, stand also as witnesses to the continuity and unity of the whole Church. Recognition of this mutual sharing in the apostolic tradition will be imperative in any such acts so that, again, it will not be interpreted as a moment when those who have give to those who have not.

It can be left to the actuaries in our midst to determine the date by which all those ordained in both churches will stand in the 'historic succession'. In the interim Anglicans face one pastoral problem and at least one anomaly. The pastoral problem is that, for a long while, many Anglican pastors have taught that without the 'historic succession' a church has neither real ministers not real sacraments and have believed they were being faithful to the teaching of the church in so doing.[2] We must go beyond a quick invocation of somewhat alien doctrines of economy or *ecclesia supplet* to get around what was a rather facile way of addressing more basic questions of apostolic tradition and its succession.

The anomaly, like much from our past, is that insistence on the historic succession has not always been at the forefront of Anglican consciousness let alone polity. The emphasis on episcopal ordination made after the Restoration of the seventeenth century was much more a matter of episcopal control and 'unchurching' dissenters than it was of sacramental validity.[3] This is underlined by the fact that the Church of England did not hesitate to

---

[1] It is important to recognize that each community falls short of complete faithfulness to that tradition and, in effect, acknowledges that at its Sunday celebration of the eucharist—particularly at the epiclesis in the eucharistic prayer.

[2] To this day, an inordinate number of confirmation sermons far too easily turn upon the bishop who purports to be the bearer of the apostolic tradition telling the candidates that it is at the moment of the imposition of his/her hands that they are being brought into communion with the whole church.

[3] The fundamental issue at stake was retribution against those who had opposed the central authority of the King during the Commonwealth. When appeal was made to the validity of priesthood the fundamental model was that of the Aaronic priesthood, and the relationship between king and priest with little interest expressed in ordination rites. I owe this observation to my colleague the Reverend Dr. David Smart.

Some Reflections on Apostolicity, Apostolic Tradition, Episcopacy and Succession 31

employ (let alone question the 'validity' of their orders) German clergy in Restoration London or German and Danish ministers as missionaries in India in the eighteenth and nineteenth centuries even though they had never been ordained by bishops in the 'historic' succession.[1]

SOME UNRESOLVED QUESTIONS

It was perhaps only when looking at the history of early Christianity through the rose-coloured spectacles of nineteenth century Anglican bishops gathered in solemn assembly that the historic episcopate could have gained such an unqualified place in an Anglican position on the unity of the church.[2] Such an insistence was a novelty to Anglicanism and not one that had played an central role in the attitude of Anglicans to other churches where legal establishment had traditionally played a more important role than had the historic episcopate in achieving Anglican recognition of that church. When it came to matters of ministry, for example, it would have been more natural (at least when looking at our liturgical formularies) for the Quadrilateral to have insisted on the three-fold ordained ministry of bishops, priests and deacons than on the historic episcopate.

Unfortunately, this has led to a certain episcopocentrism in our attitude to ministry, the ecclesiological consequences of which are grave. Perhaps most serious is the tendency to use the historic episcopate, rather than baptism, as the starting point for a theology of ministry. A discussion of ministry which begins with the historic episcopate, rather than the baptismal ministry of the whole People of God and the acknowledgement that there is no such thing as a baptized Christian without a ministry, skews our attitude towards ministry as a whole. Similarly, separating the episcopate from the other orders of ordained ministry has had the effect of presenting an unbalanced attitude towards the wholeness and mutuality of ministry in the church in which the assurance of the integrity of each order must be assured. Both Anglican attitude towards and pastoral use of bishops has too often valued 'historic' far more than *episcopé*. While an increaing number of bishops have managed to free themselves from the restrictions of seeing the totality of their ministry as confirming machines[3], Anglicanism still needs to respond to BEM's challenge to widen its vision of *episcopé*. The unity of the Church would be well served if the Quadrilateral were to be contextualized in an ecclesiology in which apostolicity was seen as a possession of the whole body and not dependent on any pipeline theory of the episcopate and the spurious episcopal genealogies to which it leads.

---

[1] We must leave aside the question of contemporary shared ministries in which Anglican willingness to recognize the ministry of those without the 'historic' succession often seems to be temporary (recognition appears to cease when a minister leaves the team) and driven by less-than-worthy economic motives in which Anglican participation in an ecumenical team often ceases when an independent Anglican appointment or parish can be funded.

[2] At the Chicago General Convention of 1886 the House of Bishops adopted the 'quadrilateral'; the House of Deputies (clergy and laity) incorporated it into a larger plan and referred it to a Joint Committee on Christian Reunion for study and action.

[3] See, for example, J.C. Fricker, 'The Bishop in Initiation,' in David R. Holeton ed., *Growing in Newness of Life* (Anglican Book Centre, Toronto, 1993) 193-196.

5. Synodical Government: Consequences for Ministry

by Janet Crawford

In the last thirty years there have been significant changes in ministry in the Anglican Church in Aotearoa, New Zealand and Polynesia (formerly the Church of the Province of New Zealand). Two aspects of Anglican tradition have remained unchanged: the three clerical orders of bishop, priest and deacon, and episcopal ordination. Recent decades have however seen the development of non-stipendiary ministry and ministry in co-operating (ecumenical) parishes, the ordination of women priests, the election and ordination of a woman diocesan bishop, the acceptance of non-territorial ethnic (Maori) bishops, new patterns of preparation and training for ordination, the emergence of a permanent or vocational diaconate and last, but not least, a growing emphasis on the ministry of the laity. Probably none of these changes are unique to this particular church but in some cases, such as the ordination of women and the appointment of ethnic bishops, New Zealand has been in the forefront of new developments.

Undoubtedly many factors, including demographic and economic changes, have contributed to new developments in ministry, but New Zealand's well-established tradition of synodical government has also been significant for it is through this particular form of church government that the Church has responded to changes in its context, seeking to provide ministry which is both consistent with the Anglican tradition and relevant to the needs of contemporary society. It was the General Synod of the Church which voted in 1976 for the ordination of women to the priesthood and which in a series of legislative acts first established the Bishopric of Aotearoa and then in 1992 accepted a revised constitution which formed a three *tikanga* Church (i.e. consisting of three cultural streams). It was a diocesan electoral synod which in 1989 elected the first woman diocesan bishop in the Anglican Communion.

The development of synodical government in the New Zealand church was largely due to the vision of George Augustus Selwyn who was appointed Bishop of New Zealand in 1841. Acting on his own authority as bishop and without traditional royal approval, Selwyn called together a synod of his clergy in 1844. At a second synod in 1847 Selwyn informed his clergy of the principle on which he exercised his authority, saying that 'neither will I act without you, nor can you act without me. The source of all diocesan action is the Bishop and therefore it behoves him so much the more to take care that he act with a mind informed and reinforced by conference with his clergy',[1] Although Selwyn still retained the right to make final decisions by himself, this form of synod was a significant innovation in a church which was understood to be dependent on the Church of England. Selwyn, a leading spokesman for colonial churches, was of course aware of precedents for synodical government in the Scottish Episcopal Church and the Episcopal Church in the United States and was in fact in regular contact with North American church leaders.

---

[1] Quoted in A.K. Davidson, *Christianity in Aotearoa: A History of Church and Society in New Zealand* (Education for Ministry, Wellington, 1991) 30.

Synodical government of the New Zealand Church was established in its Constitution of 1857. This set out a structure for a 'Branch of the United Church of England and Ireland in New Zealand', a church founded on the basis of voluntary association, governed by a General Synod and diocesan synods. Each synod would have three houses (bishops, clergy, laity), with each house voting separately and able to exercise a veto over the others. Although there have been significant changes resulting in the revised Constitution of 1992 this is essentially the structure which remains today. The 1857 Constitution, according to which the Church was governed not by episcopal decrees but by the authority of a General Synod of bishops in council together with clergy and laity, was viewed by some in England as a radical novelty but it roused considerable interest and made an important contribution to the debates on synodical government and lay participation which were then taking place in many colonial churches.

The involvement of laymen in the synodical process (women were not mentioned in the 1857 Constitution and it was not until 1972 that the first woman was elected to General Synod) was the result of pressure from a group of Anglican leaders in the new colony. They included the Governor, Sir George Grey; the Chief Justice, Sir William Martin; and the Attorney General, William Swaiman. These men wanted to take an active part in church affairs, particularly as the church was dependent on its membership for financial and other support, Selwyn having deliberately rejected state aid when it was offered. The principle of lay representation in church government was already accepted in the Episcopal Church in the U.S. and one of its advocates was William Gladstone, Prime Minister of Great Britain. Gladstone argued that it provided a necessary balance between the orders in the Church and meant that ecclesiastical laws had to be based upon the general consent of all the members. Grey, Martin and others presented a letter to Selwyn before he met in Conference with the Australian bishops in 1850. In this they argued for the establishment of a form of church government which 'by assigning to each order in the Church its appropriate duties, might call for the energies of all, and thus enable the whole body of the Church most efficiently to perform its functions'.[1] The Conference approved the principle of provincial and diocesan synods with full lay participation and this principle then became enacted in the 1857 Constitution of the Church in New Zealand. Ten years later the first Lambeth Conference endorsed the principles of synodical government as a way of obtaining the cooperation of all members of the body in Church action.

Synodical government is now a characteristic of all the churches of the Anglican Communion although it was not until 1969 that the Synodical Government Measure introduced it into the Church of England where it replaced a system of Convocations and the Church Assembly. There are however varying constitutional arrangements and structures reflecting diverse historical and cultural contexts and there is no one normative form of synodical government. What Anglican churches have in common is structures of governance based on the desire to recognize bishops' authority in some form as crucial and distinct while at the same time including representation from clergy and laity. Among those churches which retain the historic episcopate, Anglicans seem to have devised a unique way of balancing the collegial responsibilities of the episcopate with the full participation of representatives of both clerical and lay members of the Church.

In the Anglican Church in Aotearoa, New Zealand and Polynesia the system of synodical government means that episcopal authority is both retained and restrained. Bishops, clergy

---

[1] *Ibid.*, 30-31.

and lay people participate together in decision-making, meeting together for debate but voting in separate houses. The Church cannot take action without a majority in each house. This may slow the process of change as when the vote on Church Union at the 1974 General Synod was narrowly lost at the clerical vote, or when the 1980 proposal for unification of ministries was lost by one episcopal vote. On the other hand, it means that decisions such as that on the ordination of women are made only after full debate and with the consent of a majority of those representing the whole membership of the Church.

With regard to ordination, synods play an important role in forming policies as to who may be ordained and what patterns of ministry should be developed. Clergy, those who are ordained, and who may have, or have been seen to have, certain vested interests, do not have a monopoly in making decisions about ministry, the views and concerns of lay persons are equally valid and decisive. Yet in the end, no matter what policies may be decided, bishops and bishops alone have the authority to ordain.

The power of synods is not limited to legislation. Much of the ongoing work of the Church is carried out at both provincial and diocesan levels by various commissions, boards and committees, membership of which is usually appointed by the respective synods. A recent review of theological education, initiated by General Synod and carried out by a small commission which it appointed, has already resulted in the establishment by Synod of a number of principles to make theological education more consistent with the ideals of a three *tikanga* church. The General synod in 1998 will take steps to allocate the available financial resources in the light of these principles. As a result there are bound to be further changes in the patterns of ordained ministry in the Church.

Synodical government is not perfect. It still relies on a form of decision-making by majority which results in 'winners' and 'losers' and there is a growing interest in finding ways of reaching consensus agreements. In spite of efforts to make synod representation more inclusive of women who make up more than half the worshipping members of the Church, they are still a minority in synodical structures, and governance of the church remains male-dominated. Young people and various minority groups have little more than token representation.

It is not yet clear how the development of the three *tikanga* model may affect the traditional three houses of the General Synod. Certainly it is evolving new ways of working which at present rely heavily on caucusing in *tikanga* groups. What does seem clear is that structures will continue to change and evolve. One thing that is unlikely to change is the belief that representatives of the whole Church should be actively involved in discussions and decisions about the Church's ministry.

6. Sequential and Direct Ordination

by John St.H. Gibaut

INTRODUCTION

Any contemporary discussion on the renewal of ordination practice ought to include on its agenda questions around sequential and direct ordination. 'Sequential ordination' refers to the current process whereby candidates are ordained serially and sequentially through the various grades or orders of ministry (e.g. deacon, priest, bishop). Thus, all Anglican priests have been ordained to the diaconate, and all bishops have been ordained both to the diaconate and to the presbyterate. 'Direct ordination', known in the Western canonical tradition as *per saltum* ordination (i.e. 'by a leap') refers to an alternative process whereby a candidate for an order of ministry would be ordained directly to that order without having received or served in the 'lower' grades or grade. An example would be the ordination of a candidate to the presbyterate without ever having been ordained a deacon, or the ordination of a deacon (or lay person) to the episcopate without having first received the presbyterate (and diaconate).

HISTORICAL PERSPECTIVE

From the outset it needs to be stated that both sequential and direct ordination have ample historical precedent. There are instances of ministers having been ordained sequentially through one or more orders as early as the second century, though such examples seem to have been the exception rather than the rule. The evidence suggests that in the pre-Nicene period direct ordination was the usual, though not exclusive, practice of the church. The earliest extant canonical evidence of sequential ordination is Canon 13 of the Council of Sardica, AD 343. From the fourth century onwards bishops, councils, and canonistic collections all began to insist that ministers proceed sequentially through the clerical grades, minor and major. Since the fourth century, the expressed purpose for sequential ordination has not been to meet a theological or sacramental end but, rather, has been that it meets the more practical and pastoral ends of the selection, testing and training of the clergy— particularly priests and bishops. Nevertheless, canonical legislation as well as biographical information indicates that the practice of *per saltum* ordination continued in the Western Church until well into the tenth century. It cannot claim to be a universal practice until the late eleventh century, with the ordination in 1073 of the deacon Hildebrand as a presbyter prior to his episcopal consecration as bishop of Rome with the name Gregory VII.[1]

At the Reformation the Church of England retained the principle of sequential ordination for the major orders of deacon, priest and bishop, the minor orders having been abolished. From the first Ordinal of 1550 to the present, the rubric at the end of the rite for the 'Making of Deacons' has stated:

> And here it must be declared unto the Deacon, that he must continue in that office of a Deacon the space of a whole year (except for reasonable causes it shall otherwise seem good unto the Bishop) to the intent he may be perfect, and well expert in the things pertaining to the Ecclesiastical Administration. If he has been found faithful and diligent, and has satisfied the Bishop that he is sufficiently experienced in the

---

[1] For a summary of the historical evidence see my article 'Sequential Ordination in Historical Perspective: A Response to J. Robert Wright' in *Anglican Theological Review* 77,3 (1995) 367-391.

things belonging to the Ministry, he may be admitted by his Diocesan to the Order of Priesthood at the Ember Seasons, or on any Sunday or Holy Day.[1] Until the middle of this century (when its suppression was recommended by the bishops at the 1968 Lambeth Conference[2]) the final prayer in the earlier Prayer Book Ordinals for the ordination rite for deacons contained the petition:

[that they] . . . may so well behave themselves in this *inferior* office, that they may be found worthy to be called unto the higher ministries in thy Church; through the same . . .[3]

The *Constitutions and Canons Ecclesiastical* of 1604, the foundational body of Anglican canon law, reflect the same understanding of sequential ordination as the Ordinal. The relevant canon, Canon 32, states 'None to be made Deacon and Minister both in one day'.

The office of deacon being a step or degree to the ministry, according to the judgement of the ancient fathers, and the practice of the Primitive Church; we do ordain and appoint, that hereafter no bishop shall make any person, of what qualities or gifts soever, a deacon and a minister both together upon one day; but that the order in that behalf prescribed book of making and consecrating bishops, priests, and deacons, be strictly observed. Not that always every deacon shall be kept from the ministry for a whole year, when the bishop shall find good cause to the contrary; but that there being now four times appointed in every year for the ordination of deacons and ministers, there may ever be some trial of their behaviour in the office of deacon, before they be admitted to the order of priesthood.[4]

The intent of Canon 32 is to prohibit a candidate from being ordained both deacon and priest in a single day. Like the Ordinal, it reflects the understanding of the order of deacon as temporary, a 'step or degree to the Ministry' (i.e., the priesthood) for the purpose of testing and training. While citing the 'judgement of the ancient fathers and the practice of the Primitive Church' the canon fails to take into account the practice of *per saltum* ordination in the ancient Church, mentioning that training and testing as the purpose of sequential ordination is consistent with patristic and medieval usage. In the end, although there have been notable exceptions, the diaconate has generally used been by Anglicans as a means of final testing and preparation for the presbyterate.

The question of direct ordination (and the vocabulary of *per saltum* ordination) has been part of Anglican discussions since the seventeenth century, notably around the ordination of four presbyterian ministers to the episcopate in 1610, as part of James I's initiative to restore episcopacy to the Church of Scotland. Of particular significance is the mid-seventeenth century work of the Restoration polemicist Peter Heylyn (1600-1668), *Aërius Redivivus, Or the History of the Presbyterians.* In an attempt to restore episcopacy in Scotland, James I ordered four presbyterian ministers to be ordained to the episcopate by bishops of the Church of England. In order to explain the episcopal ordination of those who had

---

[1] *The First Prayer Book of King Edward VI*, 1549 (Dent, London, 1952) 302. Cf. The Church of England in the Dominion of Canada, *The Book of Common Prayer* (CUP, Cambridge, 1918) 623; Protestant Episcopal Church in the United States of America, *The Book of Common Prayer* (1928), (The Church Pension Fund, New York, 1945) 535.

[2] Resolution 68. Roger Coleman, ed., *Resolutions of the Twelve Lambeth Conferences: 1867-1988* (Anglican Book Centre, Toronto, 1992) 162-163.

[3] E.g. *The First Prayer Book of King Edward VI 1549, 302;* The Church of England in the Dominion of Canada, *The Book of Common Prayer* (1921), 622; Protestant Episcopal Church in the United States of America, *The Book of Common Prayer* (1928), 534. [*Italics* mine.]

[4] Canon 32, *Constitutions and Canons Ecclesiastical*, 1604, qtd. G. R. Evans and J. Robert Wright, eds., *The Anglican Tradition: A Handbook of Sources* (SPCK, London, 1991) 192.

never been priests and deacons, Heylyn cites patristic examples of lay people ordained directly to the episcopate without ever having been ordained to any other order.[1] The (polemical) implication is that essentially four lay men were being ordained, rather than four ministers, reflecting the stance of the post-Restoration Church of England towards non-episcopal churches.

What is notable about Heylyn's somewhat forgotten work is his use of direct ordination as an interpretation of the 1610 consecrations, for it was later adopted by twentieth-century Anglicans as a way of understanding the ordination to the episcopate of non-episcopally ordained ministers in plans of union. For example, it was used by the Lambeth Conferences of 1908 and 1930 in the context of uniting churches involving Anglicans and non-episcopal churches. The Lambeth Conference of 1908 was the first to use the language of *per saltum* ordination, and it did so in the context of Peter Heylyn's account of the 1610 consecrations. In Resolution 75 the bishops stated:

> The Conference receives with thankfulness and hope the Report of its Committee on Reunion and Intercommunion, and is of the opinion that, in the welcome event of any project of reunion between any Church of the Anglican Communion and any Presbyterian or other non-episcopal Church, which, while preserving the Faith in its integrity and purity, has also exhibited care as to the form and intention of ordination to the ministry, reached the stage of responsible negotiation, it might be possible to make an approach to reunion on the basis of the consecrations to the episcopate on lines suggested by such precedents as those of 1610.[2]

A note within the body of the report (in Archbishop Davidson's edition) adds the following commentary: 'In so far as these precedents involve consecration to the Episcopate *per saltum*, the conditions of such consecrations would require careful investigation and statement.'[3]

The 1930 Lambeth Conference also employed the *per saltum* terminology regarding the ordination of non-episcopally ordained ministers in uniting Churches. The report on 'The Unity of the Church' states:

> On the question of Consecration *per saltum* [a footnote in the text elaborates: '*i.e.*, Consecration to the Episcopate without previous ordination by a Bishop to the diaconate and priesthood.'], our view is that while undesirable in the normal course of the Church's life, such Consecration is not invalid and in the special circumstances of the inauguration of the united Church is justifiable.[4]

Regarding the ordinations of bishops for these churches, the Lambeth bishops responded that ministers from non-episcopal churches ordained as bishops in united churches would be ordained *per saltum*. While the use of such language is open to question on ecumenical grounds—it virtually denies the validity of non-episcopal orders—its use by the Lambeth bishops indicates that direct ordination is at least a viable and 'not invalid' option. The inherited pattern of sequential ordination may be modified or simply disregarded in certain situations, as Anglican practice throughout the twentieth century in ecumenical schemes has reflected.

---

[1] Peter Heylyn, *Aërius Redivivus, Or the History of the Presbyterians* 2nd ed. (Robert Battersby, London, 1672) 382. N.B. The Aërius in question is a fourth century presbyter who denied the distinction between bishops and presbyters.

[2] Coleman, *Resolutions*, 43; R. T. Davidson, ed., *The Six Lambeth Conferences: 1867-1920* (SPCK, London, 1929), 336.

[3] Davidson, *Lambeth Conferences*, 432, n. 2.

[4] 'The Unity of the Church' in *Lambeth 1930* (SPCK, London, 1930) 128.

There are two main issues regarding sequential ordination which Anglicans face today. The first is a reassessment of the current use of sequential ordination, primarily between the orders of deacon and priest. The second question calls for the abolition of sequential ordination altogether and the return to the primitive practice of direct ordination; this question arises in the context of the restoration of the diaconate as a viable order of ministry.

Since the classical motive for retaining sequential ordination—especially the sequence between the diaconate and the presbyterate—is testing and training, ideally within the space of one year, it must be asked whether twelve months is an adequate length of time to prepare someone for the priesthood? It may or may not have been sufficient in the days prior to theological colleges. However, the advent of Anglican theological colleges and seminaries since the nineteenth century probably renders this period as far *too long*, given the many years of anterior preparation and probation. Today, if a bishop is not sure whether a candidate is suitable or properly trained for the presbyterate, is he or she really likely to ordain such a candidate to the diaconate in the first place?

A related and perhaps more serious predicament is the many instances in which the one year period in the diaconate is reduced, often considerably. One episcopal member of the International Anglican Liturgical Consultation is reported to have ordained some nuns in his diocese deacons on one day and priests on the next. In many provinces of the Anglican Communion (for example, some dioceses of the Canadian Church) six months has become the standard period of time in the diaconate. Two years ago in the diocese of Ottawa (where I live) some deacons were made priests within three months. Even more recently in Ottawa a former Lutheran pastor was a deacon for only three weeks prior to ordination as a priest. No doubt anecdotal evidence can be found from around the Communion of similarly reduced periods in the diaconate. Such abbreviated intervals in the diaconate may satisfy canonical minimums, but can in no way serve as a period of preparation and probation. One can only wonder about what rationale—theological, pastoral or otherwise—is used to justify such truncated intervals between the diaconate and the presbyterate.

On the other hand, the emergence of other forms of training for priesthood appearing more recently in the Anglican Communion—for example, locally raised candidates for ordination who no longer pursue training and testing in a seminary situation—may suggest that a one year period in the diaconate is far *too short*. It is interesting to note that in the patristic and medieval canonical sources, the time spent in the diaconate prior to ordination to the presbyterate was normally *five* years! If the primary reason for sequential ordination is training and testing, and, given the appearance of non-seminary trained clergy throughout the Communion, a return to the patristic and medieval interval of five years as a deacon could well be a far more realistic means of selecting, discerning, preparing and testing candidates for the priesthood. The longer period in the diaconate would correspond to the similar process whereby candidates for the episcopate are currently selected from among those who have been priests for a specified length of time.

Since testing and training are the historic reasons for sequential ordination, Anglicans clearly need to reconsider both if one year is an adequate period as well as the implications of reducing the time in the diaconate even further. In parts of the Communion, such a reconsideration has led some Anglicans to a critical reassessment of the current use of the diaconate as a preparation for the priesthood. They have pondered whether the diaconate ought simply to be abolished and candidates be ordained directly to the presbyterate.[1] Accordingly, the second and more substantial question posed today regarding sequential

---

[1] E.g. from the Church of England, *Deacons in the Church* (Church Information Office, Westminster, 1974) 22-25.

ordination is whether it ought to be retained at all. If the diaconate no longer serves as an authentic period of training and testing for the presbyterate, then why not simply ordain candidates directly to the presbyterate?

In recent years, especially in North America, advocates for the restoration of the diaconate as a 'full and equal order'[1] have argued convincingly that if the diaconate is to be recovered as a vibrant ministry in the church, it can no longer function simply as a final preparation for the priesthood. If the diaconate is to have any integrity as an order, then it must no longer be treated as 'transitional order', an 'inferior office', or as 'a step or degree to the ministry.' It is difficult to maintain the integrity of the diaconate as an order, advocates for the diaconate assert, while all candidates for the presbyterate are also routinely ordained deacons whether they have discerned the call and charism necessary to that order or not. Consequently, the restoration of the diaconate suggests that candidates for the priesthood be ordained directly—*per saltum*—to the priesthood, without ever having been deacons. As one Episcopalian has passionately contended:

> The issue of transitional deacons refuses to go away. Every ordination as a deacon of one intended for priest forces the issue upon the church . . . What does the transitional diaconate mean? At best it is polite fiction, at worst pious fraud. In almost every ordination of a person in transit, there exists a defect of intention. Transitional deacons don't intend to be deacons. They intend to be priests. Nor does the church intend them to be deacons . . . One must intend the order, and the church must intend it. Not for convenience. Not as a rite of passage into a new status in the church. But as a lifelong commitment to an order which finds its meaning in the imaging of service, the diaconate of Christ. Otherwise the sacrament exists only as a sham.[2]

CONCLUSION

If the classical patristic, medieval and Anglican understandings of sequential ordination—namely testing and training—remain valid, can a one year diaconate truly serve these ends? What are the consequences of shortening the period to a matter of months or even days? If testing and training are met elsewhere (selection committees, theological colleges and seminaries, etc.) what is the rationale for not permitting direct ordination? What does sequential ordination mean today, if its historic needs are effectively met elsewhere? Given the lack of correspondence between the current use of sequential ordination and its expressed intent, and given the negative effects sequential ordination may have on current efforts to restore and renew the diaconate, the time may well have come to recover the ancient practice of direct ordination in the contemporary churches of the Anglican Communion.

The current rethinking of the use (or misuse) of the diaconate as a means of training and testing candidates for the presbyterate must be seen within the earlier context of the reconsideration and modification of sequential ordination arising from Anglican ecumenical ventures. Lambeth Conference reports and resolutions in the earlier part of the twentieth century (as well as subsequent practice) have shown that sequential ordination can be modified or simply replaced by direct ordination if there is good cause. If it is possible in respect to episcopal ordination in ecumenical contexts, it must equally be possible with respect to presbyteral ordination as well. The renewal of ordination practice, the renewal of our understanding of holy order, the restoration of the diaconate, a reconsideration of the purpose of sequential ordination in light of other developments in the training and testing of clergy all clearly point to such good cause for a return to direct ordination at the end of the century

---

[1] From the title of James M. Barnett's estimable work, *The Diaconate: A Full and Equal Order* (Seabury Press, New York, 1981).

[2] 'Getting our orders straight: a defect of intention' in *Diakoneo*, 10.1 (1988) 1.

7. 'Once a Deacon . . .'?

by Kevin Flynn

The meetings of the International Anglican Liturgical Consultations, both full consultations and preparatory work, give us a useful indication of both current practice and promise for the future of worship in the Anglican Communion. The impact of the liturgical renewal within the Anglican Communion has, among other things, raised questions about what, if not 'The Prayer Book', will keep the Communion together. Some of the answers that have come from the IALC give much reason to hope. To say, for example, that '[i]n the future, Anglican unity will find its liturgical expression not so much in uniform texts as in a common approach to eucharistic celebration and a structure which will ensure a balance of word, prayer, and sacrament, and which bears witness to the catholic calling of the Anglican communion'[1] is to envision a supple, creatively interdependent organism that relishes the freedom of the Spirit. Over and over again, the IALC has found the source of that freedom to arise from the baptismal character of the Christian people.

The Boston statement of 1985 affirmed baptism as the sacramental sign of full initiation into the Church. Implications for the communion of children, communicant status in one part of the Communion to mean the same in another part, ecumenical dimensions arise from that affirmation.

Some may accuse liturgists at times of being overly hopeful about the effect that liturgical reform has upon the rest of the life of the Church. It has not universally been observed that the exchange of the Peace at the eucharist has necessarily transformed every parish into a hotbed of charity. But then the liturgical movement of the twentieth century has never seen the liturgy as an end in itself. What is at stake is the ability of the Christian Church to address itself to the world. Part of the renewal of Christian communities necessarily lies in the renewal of worship. The Brixen papers[2] point out the genuinely formative nature of worship. Again, the note of the baptismal character of the Church is sounded in many of the essays.[3]

Issues of inculturation, already raised by Elisha Mbonigaba at that gathering, received further attention at York in 1989. The baptismal community has a responsibility to respond deeply to its cultural context. Since '[t]he incarnation is God's self-inculturation in this world and in a particular cultural context.'[4]

The Toronto meeting of 1991, was dedicated to studying matters related to Christian Initiation. *Growing in Newness of Life: Christian Initiation in Anglicanism Today*[5] shows a

---

[1] David R. Holeton, ed., *Renewing the Anglican Eucharist: Findings of the Fifth International Anglican Liturgical Consultation*, Dublin, Eire 1995, (Grove Worship Series 135, Grove Books, Cambridge, 1996) 7.
[2] Thomas Talley, ed., *A Kingdom of Priests: Liturgical Formation of the People of God* [Alcuin/GROW Liturgical Study No. 5] (Bramcote, 1988).
[3] E.g., those of Robert J. Brooks, 'The Catechumenate' A Case History', Bryan Spinks, 'The Liturgical Ministry of the Laity'.
[4] 'Down to Earth Worship: Findings of the Third International Anglican Liturgical Consultation, York, England, 1989', in David R. Holeton, (ed.), *Liturgical Inculturation in the Anglican Communion* (Alcuin/GROW Liturgical Study 15, Grove Books, Bramcote, 1990) 9.
[5] David R. Holeton, (ed.) *Growing in Newness of Life: Christian Initiation in Anglicanism Today. Papers from the Fourth International Anglican Liturgical Consultation, Toronto, 1991.* (The Anglican Book Centre, Toronto, 1993).

Communion in the process of being transformed by a renewal in thinking about baptism. The koinonia that flows from the font is characterized by a diversity of ministries within the Church and to the world.

Discussions about the eucharist[1] refer frequently to the Church as the baptized who 'are called to participate in the great sign of our common identity as the people of God, the body of Christ, and the community of the Holy Spirit.'[2]

The preliminary conversations about ordination held at Jarvenpää returned regularly to the fundamental matter of baptismal ecclesiology. We appear to have learned that ordination depends upon baptism, rather than vice versa. Baptism initiates persons into the ministry of the whole Church. Thus, all Christians have a responsibility to exercise, for example, their liturgical ministry. 'In, through and with Christ, the assembly is the celebrant of the Eucharist.'[3] The implications of such an understanding are beginning to be seen in the way that planning is undertaken for liturgical celebrations, in the postures and gestures of the assembly, in the quest for more authentic inculturation, to mention just a few.

A baptismal ecclesiology assumes, too, that all members of the church are charged with the exercise of witness. If the Decade of Evangelism has taught Anglicans anything, it is that proclamation of the gospel by word and deed cannot be left to a few professionals. While some persons have particular gifts in testifying to the work and presence of Christ in their life, all Christians are called to make the same proclamation in their several ways. Finally, the appearance on the sign boards of some parishes 'Minister: the whole congregation' is but one indication of the realization that the exercise of *diakonia* does not belong to the ordained alone, but is a given of the baptismal covenant.[4]

The rediscovery of the diaconal calling of *all* Christians is among the chief factors urging a rethinking of our received notions of ordained ministry.

The newer baptismal rites of the Communion give heightened expression to this dimension of the Christian life. *Diakonia* is referred to in a variety of ways. Naturally, the Greek term itself does not appear, but its content is expressed. So, for example, in *A Prayer Book for Australia* the candidates are asks, 'Will you each, by God's grace, strive to live as a disciple of Christ, loving God with your whole heart, and your neighbour as yourself, until your life's end?'[5] Shortly afterwards prayer is offered for the candidates that they 'continue in the fellowship and service' of Christ's Church.[6] In the *Book of Alternative Services* of the Anglican Church of Canada candidates are asked whether they will 'strive for justice and peace among all people, and respect the dignity of every human being.'[7] In *A New Zealand Prayer Book* a 'Commitment to Christian Service' is a distinct section of the rite.[8] A similar expression of a call to service is found in the giving of a candle to the newly baptized,

---

[1] Summarized in Holeton, *Renewing the Anglican Eucharist* and *Our Thanks and Praise. The Eucharist in Anglicanism Today: Papers from the Fourth International Anglican Liturgical Consultation on the Eucharist, Dublin, August 1995*. (The Anglican Book Centre, Toronto, 1998).

[2] Principles and Recommendations, Dublin 1995.

[3] Principles and Recommendations, Dublin 1995.

[4] Can we hope that the idea of confirmation as 'ordination of the laity' has at last been laid to rest? Baptism is entry into the order known as *laos*.

[5] *A Prayer Book for Australia: Shorter Edition* (1995) 56.

[6] *A Prayer Book for Australia: Shorter Edition*, 57.

[7] *The Book of Alternative Services* (1985) 159.

[8] *A New Zealand Prayer Book—He Karkaia Mihinare o Aotearoa* (1989) 390.

so that they 'let their light shine before others.'[1] In addition to such prayers and actions, there will be the influence of preaching, hymnody and other music, and the whole range of formative experiences offered by way of catechesis. Experiments with various forms of catechumenal formation in different parts of the Communion usually include a community's commitment to help catechumens have significant experience in various forms of intentional Christian ministry. One begins as one intends to continue.

Being of service, striving for justice and peace, letting one's light shine, and so forth express dimensions of the New Testament's teaching about *diakonia*. New understandings of that term continue to be discovered. The work of John Collins, a Roman Catholic, is instructive.[2] He maintains that commonly understood meanings of *diakonia* display an undue reliance upon the narrow definition of the term in Kittel's *Theological Dictionary of the New Testament*.[3] In this view *diakonia* refers to active loving service of one's neighbour. Kittel and his antecedents stressed that *diakonia* referred originally to the humble service of table waiting. As a result, those who used the term as a referent for Christian ministry intended that everything done in the name of Christ should be characterized by a similar selfless service.

Collins enlarges our understanding of *diakonia* by pointing out that in the time of the early church the term also referred to the services of intermediaries or 'go-betweens', agents empowered by someone, commissioned to act on their behalf. This '*[d]iakonia* seems more concerned with apostleship than with our present understanding of the diaconate.'[4] At the same time, however, it must be remembered that a go-between is engaged in an act of service for another. Collins' work is a helpful expansion of a term which refers to a great many functions in the New Testament and the early church. A corrective on some of his emphasis, however, may be found in the study of James Monroe Barnett.[5]

Barnett discusses the variety of ministries within the early church as existing within an organic society. The Spirit is the empowering source of all the ministries within the church which was sent into the world with power and authority to save. 'All are sent for *diakonia*, for ministry, that is exercised foremost in service to others.'[6] This quality of service came to be focused in the specialized ministry of the *diakonos*. For Barnett the office of deacon was without pagan or Jewish antecedents, emerging rather from the nature of the Church of Jesus Christ, who came not to serve but to serve.[7] The history of the development and decline of deacons is traced in no little detail by Barnett.[8] This is the context in which to understand the church's diaconal ministry.

---

[1] Many Provinces include this option: Australia, Brazil, Canada, Papua New Guinea, Tanzania, the United States, Wales, the West Indies.

[2] John N. Collins, *Diakonia: Re-interpreting the Ancient Sources* (Oxford University Press, New York, 1990).

[3] Gerhard Kittel, *Theological Dictionary of the New Testament*, trans, and ed. Geoffrey W. Bromiley (Eerdmans, Grand Rapids, 1964-76).

[4] *Hanover Report of the Anglican-Lutheran International Commission: Diaconate as ecumenical opportunity* (Anglican Communion Publications, London, 1996) 7.

[5] James Monroe Barnett, *The Diaconate: A Full and Equal Order*, (Trinity Press, Valley Forge PA, rev. ed. 1995) 20-27.

[6] Barnett 27.

[7] Barnett 28-42.

[8] Barnett, chapters 4-6.

Current practice and understanding of the diaconate reflect the decline Barnett depicts. So familiar are we with the *cursus honorum* and sequential ordination and sequential ordination that we take it for granted that all to be ordained presbyters will first be ordained deacons. In practice, this is a 'larval' stage in which the prospective presbyter serves a kind of apprenticeship after a successful completion of academic training for ministry. Certain notions, too, about the indelibility of orders lead many presbyters to assert that they, in fact, 'continue' to be deacons despite the fact that their primary vocational desire was to be presbyters, that they do presbyterial work, that they function in the liturgy as presbyters and in any other respect that one can think of do nothing that could be considered to belong to a distinctively diaconal office. A slight nuance is needed here since some people, especially some Anglo-Catholics, do vest as deacons at the liturgy. The fact of 'still being a deacon' means that one has the right to dress the part. One has to wonder whether this 'continuing diaconate' is related to the desire to maintain the pleasing symmetry of three sacred ministers at High Mass, an ecclesiastical version of trying to find a fourth for bridge! A more significant factor, however, is that many presbyters do, in fact, engage in all sorts of *diakonia*. The fact is adduced to prove the reality of a continuing diaconate. Thus, for many, the restoration of a permanent diaconate seems moot.

Of course, it should not be surprising that presbyters carry out diaconal work. What would be surprising would be if committed Christians of any order somehow determined that they were free of the baptismal covenant's call to ongoing diaconia. The work of many of the ordained does in fact look a great deal like the work of what the Hanover Report offers as a 'general description' of diaconal ministers: 'Diaconal ministers are called to be agents of the church in interpreting and meeting needs, hopes, and concerns within church and society.'[1] The Report recognizes the fluidity and variety of forms that diaconal ministry has taken in the churches but notes that 'service typically forms the central emphasis of diaconal ministry.'[2] There are few presbyters who would wish to deny the service dimension of their vocation.

Yet even while presbyters give at least lip service to a baptismal ecclesiology and decry attempts to collapse into their own roles what is generally called 'lay ministry', there seems to be little collateral unwillingness on the part of the presbyterate to continue to claim to itself the entire ministry of deacons. Again, to be clear, *diakonia* is something given in baptism. To be a *diakonos*, however, is to be a focused ministry through which the church is able to give expression to its *diakonia*. While the active ministry of deacons inevitably varies, particularly as our understandings of *diakonia* continue to evolve, our common reflection on the nature of that ministry will be impaired if its liturgical expression is compromised by presbyters acting as deacons. To do so is to undercut the very sign value that is at the heart of our symbolic actions.

To insist on the indelibility of one's ordination as a deacon while yet living as a presbyter is to refuse to admit the implications of a baptismal ecclesiology. That ecclesiology refuses to understand sacraments in narrow terms of form and matter, of the particular 'moments' which 'make' the sacrament and ensure its validity, and, in the case of ordination, of a concentration on a static notion of order which persists regardless of its living connection to an organic body that gathers to celebrate and deepen its life. In the liturgy, we bless God, giving God thanks for the true nature of things that we receive at God's hand, and thus make them to be what they are. To abstract from the liturgy a notion like 'indelibility' is to reduce a sacramental action to one 'phenomenon'. When we do that we end up raising more questions than we answer.

---

[1] Hanover Report, Section 26.
[2] Hanover Report, Section 53.

By regarding the life of the church as fundamentally baptismal, we affirm it to be a mystery, hid with Christ in God. The liturgy points us beyond mere categories of functionality in this world to the coming reign of God, where *there is neither male nor female, Greek nor Jew, slave nor free.* Our world is not abandoned or destroyed, but rather taken up and transformed into the kingdom. In that fullness, the Church shines with the radiance of a multiplicity of gifts and graces, *some apostles, some prophets, some evangelists, some pastors and teachers* so that all achieve *the measure of the full stature of Christ.*

Part of the recovery of the kingdom dimension of the liturgy is found through the reverent use of the stuff of this world that becomes part of our symbolic action. Bread that corresponds to something recognizable as real bread is far more evocative of Christ as our true Food for both now and eternity. It awakens, too, the connections that must be made between that bread and the food or lack of it that is characteristic of human life now in this world. A taste of the kingdom stirs us to mission and justice now in the name of that kingdom. Similarly abundant water that can actually cleanse, refresh and even drown expresses vividly the entry into new life, and not simply life among human beings, but a life that has cosmic dimensions, in which our eyes are opened to see *this* life as being *in Christ.*

We call upon things of the material world to bear the weight of the glory of God for us. So too, human beings in the liturgy express that glory in divers ways. While the whole assembly is an icon of Christ, those in orders have particular ministries within the body which help sacramentally to express and deepen that reality. When the IALC in Dublin asserted that the 'liturgical functions of the ordained arise out of pastoral responsibility'[1] it was referring to eucharistic presidency. Nonetheless, the reality should hold true for the diaconate as well. Just what kind of sign, what kind of symbolic person do we think we are holding for the church when, too often, those who serve in the liturgy as deacons are either intending sooner or later to become presbyters, or are presbyters dressing up as something they are not?

The ordained, through a process of formation and the regular, committed practice of a particular way of life, undoubtedly find over time that their ordination has, as it were, 'taken', through the existential experience of repeated choices. When such persons participate in the liturgy people can see some congruence between the sign action they perform in worship and what they do in the rest of their lives.[2] Viewed from the perspective of the liturgy, the church can only be well served if those who are carrying out the liturgical actions of deacons arise out of their ministry apart from the liturgy. Without rehearsing all of the liturgical functions of deacons, let us recall some few that may help us to envision a church in which such dimensions of worship (*leitourgia*) and service (*diakonia*) are regularly experienced and witnessed within its life. The bidding of the prayers of the people (a crucial action of the eucharist and one generally needing much renewal) by the deacon is a privileged moment of bringing to the prayerful consciousness of the assembly the needs of the poor, the sick, the aged, prisoners and all who suffer. Those prayers would take on new life if they were regularly bid by those whose ministries are devoted to being the special agents of the church in humble service. Similarly, the reading of the Gospel by the deacon, like the proclamation of the Exultet at Easter, arises naturally from a ministry as servants of the church and witnesses to the world. The deacon as a symbolic person recalls the assembly to its own character as servants of Christ. The church has long known that we need symbols as a means to bring to expression our experience, and by so doing to enter into deeper discovery of the truth of our lives in God's light. We need to see and experience human lives that both express and are increasingly shaped by their ordination to ministries of service, so that we may all discover anew our own calling to the *diakonia.*

---

[1] Principles and Recommendations 6.

[2] This is not to say that one must be 'worthy'. There is always a gap between the ideal and the actual in anyone's life. Nevertheless, the church entrusts to some of its members the pain and privilege of living publicly with that gap.

8. The Practice of Ordination: Distinguishing Secondary Elements from Primary

by Louis Weil

It is generally agreed by all commentators that by the later middle ages the ordination rites of the Western Church had become extremely complicated and even confusing as to what was taking place in the rites at what point.[1] The simplicity of early patterns of designation for pastoral ministry, involving the presentation of candidates to the local Christian community for their approval, followed by the laying on of hands with prayer, had, by the ninth century, begun to show diverse ceremonial developments. The ordination rites became an amalgam of Roman and Gallican customs with the effect of ritual duplications which obscured the clarity of the early model. The insertion of new ritual elements, such as the anointing of the candidate's hands, the presentation of chalice and paten, and the clothing with the vesture and insignia of the order, further contributed to obscuring the primary aspects of the ordination rites.

One result of the excessive complexity of the medieval rites was an often intense debate among theologians as to what constituted the essential matter of the ordination rite. The primary focus of this debate was, not surprisingly, the rite of ordination to the priesthood, the order which theologians had come increasingly to view as to the highest order of ordained ministry, since the understanding of the episcopate as a distinct order had been generally lost.[2] Although some theologians maintained the ancient view that the essential matter and form were the laying on of hands with prayer, others taught that it was the delivery of the chalice and paten to the ordinand, and still others held that it was the anointing of the ordinand's hands.

Archbishop Thomas Cranmer's response in the first English Ordinal (March 1550) was to cut through the long debate by crafting rites which clearly place the laying on of hands with prayer in primary focus. In his revision of the Ordinal in connection with the 1552 Book of Common Prayer, Cranmer further clarified the focus by removing the presentation of vessels and the giving of vesture and insignia, leaving only the delivery of the scriptures. At this point, however, the bishop said the following words:

> Take thou Authority to preach the word of God, and to minister the holy Sacraments in the Congregation where thou shalt be so appointed.

The sacramental aspect of the new ministry of the ordinand was thus maintained, but seen in tandem with the ministry of the Word rather than as a distinct or self-contained ministry. Cranmer's Ordinal, in both the 1550 and 1552 versions, demonstrates that significant influence of the Strasbourg Reformer Martin Bucer (1491-1551), whose treatise *De ordinatione legitima* had served as a primary resource for Cranmer in his work on the ordination rites. Whereas the later Middle Ages had seen a loss of the sense of the primacy of the laying on of hands as the essential matter of ordination, Cranmer thus recovered the early tradition in his Ordinal. This was a bold clarification given the weight of later medieval

---

[1] See, for example, Bernard Cooke, 'Sacramental Ministry in the Middle Ages', in *Ministry of Word and Sacraments* (Fortress Press, Philadelphia, 1976) 574-90.

[2] As late as this century, in the Roman Catholic Church prior to Vatican II, the Code of Canon Law (Canon 949), stipulated that subdiaconate, diaconate, and presbyterate were the three major orders. Cf. *Lumen Gentium*, 21.

opinion, including the teaching of Thomas Aquinas, that the delivery of the chalice and paten fulfilled that role.[1]

It is interesting to note that this debate continued in the Roman Catholic Church until the pontificate of Pius XII in this century, when the pope promulgated the Constitution *Sacramentum Ordinis* (30 November 1947). The concern of Pius in this document was to end debate in the Roman Church concerning the essential matter of ordination by determining, from that time onward, that the *only* rite pertaining to the essential substance of ordination would be the laying on of hands with prayer. Whatever had been accepted opinions in the past, Pius wrote, the handing over of the vessels would in the future 'no longer be required for the validity of the sacred orders of diaconate, presbyterate, and episcopate.'[2] Although it was felt at that time by many Anglicans and Roman Catholics that this decree pulled the rug out from under the rejection of Anglican Orders by Leo XIII, the document had no significant ecumenical impact. But it did affirm the sacramental and distinct character of the episcopal order, and thus reclaimed the ancient pattern of the three-fold ministry as Cranmer had done in his Ordinal, as well as to unite the Roman Church to the otherwise general consensus that the laying on of hands with prayer alone constitutes the abiding tradition of the Church in ministerial ordination.

If, then, such consensus exists among the majority of Christians, what can be said about the secondary rites which have tended to accrue around the primary action? The late liturgical scholar Bernard Botte wrote concerning these rites that they serve an explanatory purpose, 'to render explicit in gestures and symbols what is implicitly contained in the essential rite.'[3] Thus we need to consider these secondary rites and to enquire whether they serve a useful explanatory purpose or else tend to clutter the ordination rite and to obscure what we claim—the laying on of hands—as the primary action. These rites are very distinct in their origins and intentions, and so a single judgment cannot address them as a whole. They include clothing the ordinand in the appropriate vesture of the order to which they have been ordained; the presentation of a bible, or New Testament, or even a book of the Gospels; the anointing of the hands of the ordinand, followed by the presentation of a paten and chalice containing bread and wine; and, in the case of an episcopal ordination, the presentation of regalia associated with that office.

At least in part, these secondary rites may be understood as signs of the gradual clericalization of the liturgy which began as early as the fourth century, but which had reached a very significant level by the ninth and tenth centuries. The celebration of the eucharist, which had been experienced as the action of the entire assembly by the early Church, had gradually come to be seen as the private domain of the ordained priest, with the laity increasingly seen as, at best, passive and non-essential observers of the sacred actions of the ordained. This perception of the eucharist had an inevitable impact upon the

---

[1] See the discussion of Kenan B. Osborne, O.F.M., in *Priesthood. A History of the Ordained Ministry in the Roman Catholic Church* (Paulist Press, New York, 1988) 204-16. The teaching of Thomas Aquinas on this issue reads: 'The conferring of power is effected by giving something pertaining to their proper act. And since the principal act of a priest is to consecrate the body and blood of Christ, the priestly character is imprinted at the very giving of the chalice under the prescribed form of words.' *Summa theologiae*, Supplement, q. 37, a. 5.

[2] *Sacramentum Ordinis*, 4

[3] 'L'ordination de l'évèque' in *La Maison-Dieu*, 98 (1969) 114.

ordination rites which became, for all orders of the medieval Church, explicitly interpreted with regard to their relation to the eucharistic celebration. Thus, in the case of the priesthood, the whole meaning of presbyteral ministry was focussed upon the priest as the offerer of the eucharistic sacrifice, and the ordination rite came to reflect that by introducing an anointing of the hands which would offer the sacrifice, and then placing into those hands the elements and vessels which would become the instrumental means of the sacrifice. In that context, all other dimensions of the earlier tradition of presbyteral ministry, such as pastoral care and mission, and the ministry of the word, were ignored.

It is not surprising that the reaction of the Reformers was to replace this focus with a renewed emphasis on the ministry of the word and preaching as offering the appropriate and fuller framework for the meaning of ordained ministry, and thus to substitute the presentation of the bible for that of chalice and paten. One cannot help but wonder if, in Anglican churches where the anointing of hands and presentation of vessels take place, there has been a conscious adherence to the underlying theology of these acts which is so alien to the priorities of the Anglican tradition. Again, it is a useful perspective to note how, in recent Roman Catholic documents on ordained ministry, a larger theological horizon has been reclaimed.[1]

The anointing of the ordinand's hands and the presentation of chalice and paten each raise important theological issues regarding the meaning of ordination. The anointing of hands implies, and in its origins was intended to imply, that in ordination the ordinand was receiving a higher dignity than that given in baptism. The custom was introduced at a time when the role of the laity in the Church was marginal at best and when ordination to the priesthood offered an intensity of identification with Christ which baptism alone could not give.[2] Given the significant recovery in this century of the fundamental role of baptism in the lives of all Christians, it would follow that ordination is not a higher dignity than that received in baptism, but is rather an explicit designation within the baptismal mystery in which the Church responds to the discernment of special gifts for pastoral leadership by ordaining those persons and thus publicly proclaiming God's call to them for ministerial service. In this perspective, ordination rites must be crafted so that no diminution of the baptismal identity is implied.

As we have observed, the presentation of chalice and paten became a part of the ordination rite at a time when the whole meaning of priesthood was defined in terms of the offering of the eucharistic sacrifice. It is also an example of the tendency throughout the middle ages to objectify the sacred in holy things rather than to recognize the holy dimension of sacred actions. The chalice and paten thus represented objectively what was understood as the central meaning of the eucharist. Is not the relation of the newly-ordained priest to the eucharist more fully embodied when the ordinand stands beside the bishop during the proclamation of the eucharistic prayer, and later, during the years of priestly ministry, in presiding at the eucharist as it is celebrated by the whole assembly of the baptized?

---

[1] Note the useful discussions found in: Jean Galot, S.J., *Theology of the Priesthood* (Ignatius Press, San Francisco, 1984) 129-53; and in: Osborne, *Priesthood*, 307-342. For a perspective on the origins of these customs, see Nathan Mitchell, *Cult and Controversy*, (Pueblo, New York, 1982) 86-90; 107-9.

[2] This view continues to have its defenders. Cf. Galot, 'The Priesthood of the Faithful and the Ministerial Priesthood' in *Theology of the Priesthood*, 105-28.

The clothing of the ordinand with the traditional vesture of the new ministry is a quite distinct custom. Most of the laity whom the ordinand will serve will not have been at their pastor's ordination. Indeed, the majority of laity have never attended an ordination. Vesture is thus an outward expression of the ministry which the ordinand has been called to fulfill, and, needless to say, that vesture should always correspond in the liturgical celebration to the real order the person holds in the community. Vesture should never be a kind of liturgical charade, with a priest pretending to the order of a deacon.

Yet questions remain about the vesting of the ordinand during the ordination rite. Sometimes the vesting is given so much time and attention that it seems to overwhelm the significance of the laying on of hands. Certainly if the vestments are to be blessed, this should take place, as the American BCP (1979) specifies, prior to the service. We must question, however, if it is appropriate for the ordinand to enter already vested, since that erodes the integrity of the central action of the ordination rite. The vesting, and any giving of insignia—such as the staff or ring to a new bishop—should be done with such simplicity that the laying on of hands with prayer is unrivalled as the primary moment of the ordination.

In the history of the liturgy, we may find many examples of an all-too-human tendency to overload and clutter our rites. Ordination has been a special victim of this tendency, and for the sake of a spiritually sound understanding of what these rites signify, it is crucial that secondary elements be clearly distinguished from what is primary.

9. International Anglican Liturgical Consultation

Conference on Ordination, 4-9 August 1997

Reports of the Working Groups

A THE NATURE OF ORDER

Ecclesiology

1   We affirm a baptismal ecclesiology as the proper context for understanding the nature of Christian ministry, as expressed in the ecumenical document, *Baptism, Eucharist and Ministry*.[1]

Ecclesiology: Baptism

2   We affirm the Toronto IALC statement (Section 2) that baptism is the fount of all Christian ministry.[2]

3   Baptism is a sign of the goodness of all creation and of the dignity of all human persons as created in the image of God. It manifests the birth pangs of the new creation and the new life of God's reign embodied in the baptized who are sent out in ministry with a mission to all creation. Baptism tells us who we are and who we are becoming.

4   As new birth through water and the Holy Spirit and participation in Christ's death and resurrection, baptism is a sign of the reign of God and manifests the radical change that is at the heart of the new creation. Baptism summons the whole church to identify with the costly self-offering of Christ for the sake of the world. Following his baptism, Jesus proclaimed his prophetic ministry (Luke 4.16ff). So through their baptismal anointing with the Spirit, the people of God are empowered to proclaim the liberating gospel to the poor and oppressed.

Ecclesiology: Mission and Ministry

5   The mission of the baptized is to summon the whole human race to their dignity and destiny given in God.

6   As the Toronto IALC statement concerning God's mission and the ministry of all the baptized says,

> Mission is first and foremost God's mission to God's world. 'As the Father has sent me, even so I send you' (John 20.21). This mission is made visible in the person and work of Jesus and is entrusted by him to the church.
>
> 'When the Advocate comes, whom I will send to you from the Father, the Spirit of truth, who comes from the Father, he will testify on my behalf' (John 15.26). The primary agent of mission is God the Holy Spirit, who brings into existence a community of faith to embody this mission and to make God's new order manifest in a broken world. 'You will receive power when the Holy Spirit has come upon you; and you will be my witnesses' (Acts 1.8; cf. John 15.27). The church needs the empowering of the Spirit to play its part in God's mission; it is called to proclaim the gospel, nurture people in the faith, care for the needy, and seek to transform the unjust structures of society.
>
> All that the church does is expressive of this mission, when it is true to its nature. This must be so of its worship. As the church remembers its calling and waits on God in prayer, it is empowered for mission. Baptism in particular declares the gospel of God's saving love in Christ, establishes the church as Christ's body, and marks the individual

---

[1] *Baptism, Eucharist, and Ministry* [BEM], [Faith and Order Paper No.111] (WCC, Geneva, 1982).
[2] *Walk in Newness of Life*, Section II: Baptism, Mission and Ministry, 9.

believers as those called to participate in the work of the kingdom . . .

. . . the whole church is formed as a participatory community, one whose members share life with one another, while at the same time being conjoined to the missionary purpose of God for which baptism calls the community into existence. Through the lens of baptism the people of God begin to see that lay ministry is important not simply because it allows an interested few to exercise their individual ministries, but because the ministry and mission of God in the church is the responsibility of all the baptized community.

'For as the body is one and has many members, and all the members of the body, though many, are one body, so it is with Christ. For in the one Spirit we were all baptized into one body—Jews or Greeks, slaves or free—and we were all made to drink of one Spirit' (1 Corinthians 12.12-13). Baptism affirms the royal dignity of every Christian and their call and empowering for active ministry within the mission of the church. The renewal of baptismal practice, with a consequent awareness of the standing of the baptized in the sight of God, therefore has an important part to play in renewing the church's respect for all the people of God. A true understanding of baptism will bring with it a new expectancy about the ministry of each Christian. It will also provide an important foundation for allowing different Christians their true and just place within the life of the church. This is of particular significance for categories of Christians who are marginalized by church or society. Baptism gives Christians a vision of God's just order; it makes the church a sign and instrument of the new world that God is establishing; it empowers Christians to strive for justice and peace within society.[1]

7   It should be noted that care for all creation, is included among the marks of mission identified by the Anglican Consultative Council.[2]

Order

8   The people of God in a place gather in prayer to proclaim the word, baptize and celebrate the eucharist. These actions shape the people of God as church. The church is a Spirit-filled community in which different charisms are given by God to every member. These gifts are for the building up of the body and the common activity of mission.

9   Within the Spirit-filled body, some are called to specific ordained ministries in order that the whole people of God might be a royal priesthood. God's call to ordained ministry must always be discerned within a particular Christian community. By ordaining these individuals, the church authorizes these persons to exercise their ministry in a particular community on behalf of the universal church (Ephesians 4.11-16).

10   The historic three-fold order serves as a way of symbolically ordering the people of God for mission. The Anglican tradition has always maintained this three-fold order, although the particular expression of these orders has been variously interpreted in different historical and cultural circumstances.

11   While this three-fold order is intended to serve the unity of the people of God in mission, the fact that some in the Anglican Communion do not recognize the ordained ministries of women has led to a situation of impaired communion within and among Provinces.

12   Within the community of the baptized, the three orders of ministry are called to reflect in different ways the self-giving love of Christ which all Christians are to manifest in the world.

---

[1] *Walk in Newness of Life*, Section II: Baptism, Mission and Ministry, 9.
[2] Section Report on Mission, Culture and Human Development in *Mission in a Broken World. Report of ACC-8: Wales, 1990* (ACC, London, 1990) 101.

13 Within our contemporary contexts, and in the light of a baptismal ecclesiology, these orders might be considered in the following manner:

Episcope is the focus of unity of the common life, worship and mission of the body of Christ, both in the diocese and in communion with the world-wide church. While this is often described as 'oversight,' it must not be understood in hierarchical terms. Episcope mirrors to the community the universal and inclusive nature of Christ. Within the church, the order of bishop seeks to ensure that all the gifts of the body work together to achieve its God-given purposes. There is no authority in the church except that which is service. As Augustine of Hippo said, 'When I am frightened by what I am to you, then I am consoled by what I am with you. To you I am the bishop, with you I am a Christian. The first is an office, the second a grace; the first a danger, the second salvation.'[1]

The presbyterate (commonly called priesthood), a shared responsibility exercised under the authority of the bishop, expresses Christ's ministry of reconciliation (2 Corinthians 5.18), and involves exercising episcope and proclaiming the gospel so as to forward God's mission in a particular community. This office includes various ministries and pastoral relationships which are focused in the act of presiding at the eucharist.

Diakonia is the servant ministry of Christ which the whole people of God are called to enact in their daily lives. This diakonia is given particular focus in the order of deacon, although all ministers, ordained or not, must address and engage personal and social need. In parts of the Communion, the order of deacon is being revived as a distinctive office to which one is ordained without anticipating subsequent ordination to the presbyterate. A helpful discussion of this renewal of the diaconate is contained in the 1996 Hanover Report of the Anglican-Lutheran International Commission: *Diaconate as Ecumenical Opportunity*.[2]

14 As the Anglican Communion embraces a baptismal ecclesiology, Provinces may need to review their constitution and canons and other ways of structuring their common life so that these more fully reflect an understanding of baptism as the basis for the church's life, worship, ministry and mission.

Order: Cultural shaping

15 The way in which the church, the people of the new creation, orders its life for mission and takes up the symbolic order of the historic or catholic tradition is profoundly affected by culture.

16 Culture refers not simply to styles of celebration, performance, greeting, etc., important as these are. It is a complex and evolving symbolic system that arises as a people pursue their life within, and are shaped by, God's creation in a particular place. Cultures involve social style, conceptual and material symbols, the technologies that sustain life and the media of communication. They include the way people are present to themselves and to each other in community. Equally they are expressed in the way in which leaders emerge within communities, are acknowledged and exercise their relationships and role.[2] In the Anglican Communion it is common for structures of decision-making and styles of leadership to reflect, at least to some extent, the parallel structures of society.

---

[1] *Sermon* 340,1. *PL* 38, 1438.

[2] Anglican Communion Publications: London, 1996.

[3] For example we heard that in the church in Melanesia a retiring bishop hands over his pastoral staff to the incoming bishop during the liturgy as a sign of the transmission of *mana*. According to Mircea Eliade, in many Polynesian languages *mana* is the state of being that is enjoyed by those who benefit from a strengthening divine influence. A primary mark of *mana* is outstanding effectiveness in action.

17 Cultures, despite other impressions, are not intrinsically static or isolated. They are subject to influence from the past (see the section on historical legacy below) and also to the impact of other cultures. Particularly important for many cultures in the Anglican Communion is their memory of a colonial era. Also significant is the way cultures respond to the powerful technological and economic culture which originated in industrial and post-industrial societies.

18 Young people and their culture, as well as the educational institutions that form them and the economic factors that shape their involvement with—or exclusion from—society are important. Patterns of selection, formation and ordination of deacons and presbyters that do not take this cultural dynamic into account fail the church as it seeks to relate to changing culture.

19 The moves in many Provinces to ordain local or community priests have the potential to engage more directly with culturally accessible styles of leadership. Ambivalence about traditional formational institutions needs to take account of two factors. First, they often have the task of remedying defective initial or catechumenal Christian formation. Second, the complex history of Western institutions on which they are often modelled combine at least two strands: an ancient and wide-spread tradition of being formed in apostolic discipleship by membership in a community engaged with the holy scriptures, and a more recent tradition of education based on the supremacy of reason and technology as an instrument of personal and social advancement. Churches need to evaluate for themselves the impact of these different modes of formation for ordained ministry.

20 Many Provinces of the Anglican Communion are situated in cultures where society is perceived as a religious body permeated by a sense of the God or gods by whom the life of the community is sustained. This will influence the form of corporate acts of the faith community and will interact strongly with their modes of liturgical celebration. Such cultures may also have strong traditions of how leadership is expressed and may view their leaders as personally embodying the well-being of their people (and even their relationship with the sacred). Great discernment is necessary in evaluating how the gospel embraces and challenges such patterns. For example, it should not be assumed that the informal style of address common in Western post-industrial culture arises from gospel values or should be normative for other cultures. Styles of leadership, and therefore of recognition and appointment, need to respect as well as redeem culture.

21 Western post-industrial (and post-modern) culture poses different dilemmas for the cultural embodiment of the ordering of the Christian community. In a fragmented society many are tempted to live within a self-defining community without recognizing or valuing broader community narratives or realities. Particular care should be given to honouring the Gospel vision of the new creation in which many cultural realities together form the body of Christ, the people of God in a place. 'Place' itself needs to be understood partly as a mechanism of social organisation which may ignore or screen out unwanted social reality, such as the poor on the doorstep.

22 One of the factors that is reshaping the way in which ordained ministry is embodied is the desire to liberate the community of the baptized for their mission. Another is the operation of financial and other resource constraints. Churches need to discern when such pressures reflect the voice of the Holy Spirit speaking through created reality, and when a more heroic and whole-hearted discipleship is needed.

23 The way in which the created reality of gender (Genesis 1.27. 'male and female created he them') is received in different societies varies and is characterized by particularities arising from life in that society and by distortions in which sin and oppression are incorporated into the social structures. Shifting patterns of the social ordering of gender can be the source of strong feelings, as can questions of how society or church relate to individuals who do not conform to the received gender patterns. This is reflected in the strong emotional reaction to

both the ordination of women and also to the increasing recognition of gay and lesbian people within the ordained ministry. Interaction between cultures may further distort the humane reception of gender or may catalyse a move for human liberation. In any context the impact of the Gospel of Jesus Christ should affirm and liberate people's created humanity while valuing healthy communal life.

24 The rich and sometimes bewildering culture that emerges in the life of the church can both sustain and stifle the vitality of the church, as well as affect the way in which the church is perceived by those outside. This, in itself, needs to be reflected on in the consideration of order and the celebration of ordination.

Order: Historical Legacy

25 There are a number of aspects of past inculturations and configurations of the classic or catholic symbolic order which continue to influence current thinking and practice and so need to be evaluated. The list that follows is not intended to be exhaustive, and does not imply approval or disapproval:

a A canon of the Council of Nicaea (A.D. 325) lays down that a bishop should be ordained with the consent of as many bishops as possible and in the presence of at least three bishops. This was in contrast, for example, with the tradition of presbyteral ordination of the bishop which had previously operated in Alexandria. It had the effect of identifying orthodoxy and continuity of doctrine with a particular procedure for episcopal ordination and has shaped subsequent views of apostolic succession. It raises questions of how the continuity of apostolic community is ensured and expressed.

The Porvoo Agreement of the Anglican Provinces of Britain and Ireland with certain national Lutheran Churches in northern Europe, and also the proposed concordats in North America[1], have sought to broaden the understanding of apostolic continuity and so provide an important commentary on the idea of apostolic succession. It is also important to recognize that for some apostolic succession functions as a sign and guarantee of a broader commitment to a sacramental liturgical life.

b As the presbyterate emerged as a more independent office within the landscape of church order, presbyters were given charge of individual congregations and came to be experienced by increasing numbers of people as the normal presiders at the eucharist and significant and immediate trustees of the theological tradition. Some would also argue that a link between the presbyter and the passion of Christ was later embodied in eucharistic presidency.

c Gregory the Great's Pastoral Care, an influential exposition of the pastoral office (primarily episcopal), conceptualizes oversight as governance or rule. This document has left a powerful political and ecclesiological legacy. It raises the question of whether the concept of 'rule' may be oppressive rather than liberating.

d Most of the early medieval Western church adopted a style of administration modelled on the structures of Roman government. This had an impact on the style of office and established an ethos based on Roman law as a prevailing idiom for church life and for relationships within the church. It also introduced Roman conceptions of authority and jurisdiction.

---

[1] *Together in Mission and Ministry: The Porvoo Common Statement with Essays on Church and Ministry in Northern Europe* (Church House Publishing, London, 1993); *Toward Full Communion and Concordat of Agreement* [Lutheran-Episcopal Dialogue, Series III] (Augsburg: Minneapolis MN, 1991); *Commentary on Concordat of Agreement* (Augsburg and Forward Movement, Minneapolis MN and Cincinnati OH, 1994); *Concordat of Agreement: Supporting Essays* (Augsburg and Forward Movement, Minneapolis MN and Cincinnati OH, 1995).

These developments significantly re-shaped the style and role of the episcopate, with bishops adopting characteristics from the civil magistracy and other high political office as well as a publicly recognized guardianship of the poor.

e The reforms of Pope Gregory VII (Hildebrand) sought to preserve the spiritual authenticity of the Christian community from absorption into the culture by treating clergy as a separate group in society and symbolically locating the transcendent character of the church in the office of the clergy. This radical extension of a biblical theme (cf. 1 Timothy 3.2ff) represented a partial withdrawal of the clergy from the social order and has continuing implications—for example, in the widespread view that clergy should not be directly involved in the shedding of blood.

f A number of questions should be asked about the development of ordered ministry in the period from the 11th to the 13th centuries. Were some of the characteristics of non-ordained monastic life (which some call apostolic) conflated with those of the presbyteral office at that time? Was preaching increasingly associated with the presbyteral office, at least in official reactions to the itinerant preaching of the friars, laying the foundation of a later (Reformation) identification of the presbyter as pastor-teacher and creating a link between the presbyterate and learning which found some of its rich expressions in the Benedictine and Dominican orders? What contribution did the model of the Benedictine presbyter-scholar provide for the spirituality of clergy in general? Did the appearance of the friars and other itinerant clergy at the beginning of the 13th century strengthen or establish the notion of a presbyteral or priestly 'character' of the office inhering in the person alone?[1]

g The Reformation, for its part, attempted to clarify the church's understanding of itself as a community created by God and under the word of God. It contributed to a new relationship of church and culture—which can be portrayed as authentic inculturation, as compromised subservience, as the onset of social marginalization of the church, or all of these. Further, the Reformation strengthens the image of the presbyter as minister of word and sacrament, a function more modest and biblical than the medieval priest's daily offering of the sacrifice of Christ in the oblation of the mass, but one which distanced him from an embodied identification with the passion of the Lord.

h A number of features of the Book of Common Prayer and the Ordinal continue to influence or challenge present understandings. The central place the Reformers gave to the public reading of scripture empowers the laity. It finds expression in the ordinal's emphasis on proclaiming and opening up the word of God, as well as in the use of the vernacular, the development of an extensive lectionary, and the presentation of the New Testament to deacons and the full Bible to priests and bishops at their ordination. The continuation of the traditional church order of bishop, priest, and deacon is itself expressed in the details of the ordination rites where deacons are ordained by the bishop alone as the ministers closely associated with him, and priests are ordained with the college of presbyters who are themselves seen as the pastors or shepherds of the church which is conceptualized as Christ's flock. The rites are framed so as to make clear how the catholic symbolic order and offices are to be exercised in the particular cultural context of Tudor and Stuart England.

The Book of Common Prayer carefully avoids a sacerdotal understanding of the presbyterate. Some would argue that Cranmer's continued use of the term 'priest' reflects not simply the etymological link with 'presbyter' but a deliberate echoing of Old Testament usage associating priests not primarily with the offering of sacrifice but with teaching and blessing.

---

[1] Edward Schillebeeckx, *Ministry: Leadership in the Community of Jesus Christ*, trans. John Bowden (Crossroad, New York, 1981) 33-74 and *The Church with a Human Face: A New and Expanded Theology of Ministry*, trans. John Bowden (Crossroad, New York, 1985) 115-119; 161-194.

The role of the Holy Spirit in ordained ministry is articulated in the liturgy, not least in the vernacular use of the Veni Creator. From a contemporary perspective, both the Veni Creator and the Litany set the act of ordination within the context of God's saving concern for the whole of the social and created order.

i The 17/18th centuries saw the further assimilation of the episcopal and presbyteral offices to the social order of society. Amongst other things this continues to influence the symbolic conceptualization of the office of bishop, with a link to the aristocracy and institutions of government. This period also radically accelerated the transfer of the earlier tradition of care for the poor from the church to the government and other organs of society.

j As the Anglican Church moved beyond the British Isles, forms of synodical government developed that brought together bishops, other clergy and laity in council. This happened first in the United States in the 18th century and expanded to other places in the 19th century, due in part to the influence of the missionary movement.

k The 19th century saw several developments which continue to influence modern understandings of ordained ministry:

a renewed emphasis on the ancient symbolic order of the church through the impact of the Oxford Movement, often interpreted in ways that have been problematic to other movements in the church;

the use by the Oxford Movement of the tradition of apostolic succession as a strategy to rescue the episcopal office from what its leaders regarded as improper subservience to the state, and so to recall the church to its spiritual dignity and apostolic faith;

the appointment of 'missionary bishops' as a primary means of establishing new churches and a consequent commitment to the pastoral role of bishops;

the adoption in 1886-1888 of the Chicago-Lambeth Quadrilateral with its reference to the 'historical episcopate, locally adapted' as one of the four pre-conditions for reunion with other churches.

Further considerations

26 In light of these theological principles and historical and cultural factors, we draw attention to the following issues for further consideration:

'presbyter' or 'priest': the term 'presbyter' was received in the English language as 'priest'. Some would argue that Cranmer's retention of the term was a reinterpretation of 'priest' as a pastoral office. Other languages use different terms with different connotations to denote this order. Which term(s) can best express contemporary understanding of this office? Perhaps a diversity of metaphors is needed.

Culture: how does culture impact on styles and patterns of leadership, formation processes and liturgies of ordination?

Sequential/direct ordination: must individuals always be ordained in sequence, that is, first deacon, then presbyter/priest, then (for some) bishop, or can individuals be ordained directly to the presbyterate or episcopate when that is the order the church recognizes as their primary calling?

Lay presidency at the eucharist: some propose permitting non-ordained persons to preside at the eucharist for various reasons, including the absence of ordained persons to preside in particular communities. This clashes with the received Anglican tradition that the presider must be ordained.[1]

---

[1] *Eucharistic Presidency: A Theological Statement by the House of Bishops of the General Synod* (Church House Publishing: London, 1997).

New patterns of ministry: the need for ordained leadership is prompting new patterns such as 'community priests' and locally ordained presbyters/priests and deacons. The emergence of such patterns highlights the tension between ordination only in a particular community and representation of the church universal.

Impaired communion: the fact that some in the Anglican Communion do not recognize the ministries of women who have been ordained presbyters and bishops has led to a situation of impaired communion within and among Provinces.

Diaconate: the revival of the diaconate as a full and equal order has been strongly encouraged in some places and questioned in others.

Conclusion

27   The reign of God which is revealed in Jesus Christ and manifest in the baptized community in its mission and ministry is a sign of the gathering of all races, peoples, and nations into the new creation. In its engagement of mission and ministry, the church always lives between memory and hope. The tradition of ministry and the three-fold orders is a living tradition, open to being shaped by God's future.

B IMPARTING MINISTRY WITHIN THE CHURCH: SOME THOUGHTS AND QUESTIONS OFFERED TO PROVINCES IN THEIR CONSIDERATION OF THE STRUCTURE AND CONTENT OF ORDINATION RITES AND HOW THEY ARE CELEBRATED.

Introduction

28   During recent decades, many Christian traditions have come to a renewed understanding of the profound importance of baptism, not only as a rite of incorporation into the church but as the sacramental source of the church's ongoing life and mission. This recovery has far-reaching implications for every aspect of the Christian life, and raises significant questions about the ways in which ministry is understood, and more specifically how the ordained ministries relate to the common ministry of all the baptized. Some of the issues are:

a   Does a baptismal ecclesiology provide a better way forward for constructing ordination rites which value the ministry of the whole people of God and set the ordination to particular ministries within that context?

b   If baptism is foundational for our self-understanding as church, what might be the implications of that for addressing the clerical-dominant style in which many ordinations are celebrated?

c   How does the assembly at an ordination engage in the rite with the expectation that what is being fulfilled in the life of the candidate is itself a mirror to their own self-understanding as the people of God?

d   How might our theological concepts, which see scripture, baptism, and eucharist as foundational for the church's life and mission, help us to shape ordination rites that are congruent with that understanding?

e   In what ways should the distinctive character of the orders of bishop, presbyter, and deacon be reflected in the rites?

f   How do ordination rites communicate the nature and place of orders in the church? If each rite says something significant and different about the place of that order within the ministry of the whole church, is it not preferable to avoid combining within one service ordinations to different orders?

g   Location, choreography, and rubrical directions are important because they convey a theological perception about the nature of the ministry and how it is imparted. The way a rite is celebrated can negate the theological intentions of a text. What general statements applicable across the Communion should we make which indicate some of the possibilities and dangers of this?

h Should there be encouragement to include in the general notes to the rites something about the need for balance between word and symbol (including body-language, movement, posture, arts, dance, and music)?

i How should local culture be reflected in ordination rites?

j In Provinces where both women and men are ordained, how adequately do ordination rites reflect this reality?

Stages in Ministry and Rites

29 God calls people to different ministries in a variety of ways. However the call comes, and to whatever ministry, a process of discernment begins which engages the whole body of Christ. Sometimes this process might lead to a clear call to a ministry that does not involve ordination. For those called to ordained ministry, the ordination rites themselves mark stages within the process. A number of other stages, which will vary from Province to Province and from order to order, might be envisaged, such as:

community nomination to selection,

community sending for (or supporting during) formal training,

acknowledgement of training/field placement,

a variety of provisions for recognition/reception of deacons and presbyters into the local community. Some deacons, for instance, will be returning to the community which sent them, others going to a new community.

It might be desirable to mark some or all of those stages—or others—with specific liturgical rites, as a way of focusing the integration of the different parts of the process with the prayer of the community and of the individual.

a Would it be helpful to have some material which could be used in this way, and if so, would full rites or simply resource material be the best way of making this provision?

b How should some indication of this process be included within the ordination services?

c What should the relationship be between the ordination rite and the more 'domestic' welcome, e.g., episcopal ordination when followed by 'enthronement' or installation?

Gathering/Presentation

30 The opening moments of any liturgical celebration greatly influence the way in which the entire rite will be understood by all participants. For this reason, what is usually called the entrance or gathering rite has, at an ordination, an important role to play in revealing the diversity of the various members of the assembly in their relation to the ordination candidates and to the wider constituency of the diocese or Province.

a What is the best way to indicate near the start of the service,

that the congregation is composed of a wide number of different groups, and

that this is an ordination service and that these are the candidate(s)?

b What guidelines regarding the choice of particular presenters would ensure that the candidate's rootedness in a particular community is signified, and that the whole church, lay and ordained, is involved in this action?

Address (or Charge) and Declarations

31   It has been the custom in Anglican rites since the Reformation for the ordaining bishop to address the candidate(s) with a set text as to the fundamental matters of faith and commitment to the responsibilities of pastoral leadership, and to describe the ministry to which the candidate is to be ordained. In this way, immediately before the ordination prayer, the assembly hears in this public context the candidate's resolve to fulfil the duties which are being undertaken. The inherited lengthy character of the bishop's address raises questions for us today as to how most effectively this preparatory element might be accomplished. For example:

a   Are some elements of the address best dealt with at earlier stages of the rituals?

b   Is there a need to recapitulate these earlier parts of the address in the main rites?

c   Is it necessary for the address within the rite itself to be as full as in most Provinces?

d   Would it help to split the address into three sections, with questions about the vocation and responsibility of the whole church at the presentation (at the start of the rite), questions about belief, intention, and commitment of the candidate before the ordination, and, at the conclusion of the rite, questions about the way in which the task ahead has been modelled, and will be exercised in and with the local community?

e   Should the address be so worded as to be less didactic and more praise and prayer oriented at

> the presentation,
> the ordination,
> the sending forth?

f   Should there be fewer questions and answers? Should there be questions addressed to the congregation as well as to the candidate? And should anyone other than the ordaining bishop be involved in asking questions?

Ministry of the Word

32   The ministry of the word is a standard element in every Christian assembly. Some particular questions in relation to ordination rites might be:

a   What should be the relationship between the lectionary for the day and the propers in the service?

b   What would appropriately be included in a selection of readings for ordination rites?

c   Should ordinations of bishops be only on feasts of apostles (as in some Provinces), or does this imply that it is only the ministry of bishops that is apostolic? Would it be helpful for certain days to be prescribed for ordination to particular orders?

d   What factors should determine who should read and who should preach?

Ordination Prayer

33   We note the diversity within the Provinces of the Communion on how the prayer is treated. This section of the rite raises two principal concerns:

a   How can the involvement of the whole church in the ordination be made more apparent by the participation of the congregation in prayers related to or in close proximity to the laying on of hands?

b   How can the integrity and unity of the ordination prayer be maintained and any suggestion that ordination is effected merely by the recitation of a specific formula be avoided?

In relation to the first, an appropriate bidding together with one or more of the following might immediately precede the ordination prayer:

---

[1] See Paul Bradshaw, 'Ordination as God's Action through the Church' (pp. 8-15 above).

—a litany for ministry
—the hymn *Veni Creator Spiritus* or some other invocation of the Spirit
—other prayer in dialogue form
—silence,

In relation to the second, since the difficulty is raised most acutely when more than one candidate is ordained on one occasion, some would propose that never ordaining more than one candidate at one time be considered. Others would suggest that as much as possible of the petitionary section of the prayer be repeated for each candidate while hands are laid on him/her. The unity of the whole act might be further expressed by the repetition of a response by the people (sung or said) during the prayer, and by the candidates remaining in one place throughout and those performing the imposition of hands moving to each one in turn.

34   Further concerns are raised by the content of the ordination prayer itself: should it include an acknowledgement of the ministries of all the baptized as well as the particular order being conferred, and seek to relate the latter to the former? Should it ask God for the bestowal of appropriate gifts of grace on the candidate for the effective discharge of the office rather than for the bestowal of the office itself and its powers?

After the Prayer

35   How should the welcome by the bishop, into the order, by the people be marked, for example by expressing the new pattern of relationships immediately after the ordination prayer with the bishop greeting the newly-ordained, followed by the greeting and later the Peace with the others present?

36   What opportunities should be provided in the rite to enable the newly-ordained to exercise the liturgical ministry of their order?

37   It is customary in many places for the newly-ordained to put on the specific vesture of their new order during the service. As this can obscure the primary symbolism of the laying on of hands if done in too close a proximity to it, would it be preferable for any vesting to take place in a simple manner after the Peace, as part of the preparation for the celebration of the eucharistic action? Some have suggested that another option might be for the candidates to enter already dressed in the vesture of their order.

For the same reason, would it be desirable for the giving of other symbols of office to take place at the end of the whole service?

Sending Forth

38   The focus at the end of the service should be on sending forth the newly-ordained to exercise their ministry in church and world, as part of a local baptismal community. It is important that any giving of secondary symbols at this point be subordinate to this primary aim.

a   Should the range of secondary symbols be determined solely by local culture?

b   Should any of this handing over of symbols or gifts be left to the reception/welcome rite back in the parish?

39   Already a variety of different agreements exist in a number of Provinces. Three churches are
      in full communion with all Provinces: the Old Catholic Church, the Mar Thoma Syrian
      Church, and the Philippine Independent Catholic Church. There are also the United Churches
      of South India, North India, Pakistan, and Bangladesh. A fruitful outcome of these unions has
      been the production of new ordinals.

40   Anglicans in some places have been ready to recognize as truly ordained those who make no
      claim to an unbroken episcopal succession, as in the Porvoo Declaration, and also those who
      have been non-episcopally ordained, for example in the Southern African Covenanting
      Relationship. One outcome of these agreements is the mutual recognition of ordained ministries.
      This has been done, commendably, without ambiguous rites which could be open to
      interpretation as 're-ordination'. Furthermore, there are the numerous parish-based agreements
      allowed by canon in certain Provinces.

41   At the same time we are mindful of failed schemes in which Anglicans have participated. We
      realize that in some cases Anglicans have been the cause of breakdown.

42   We are also aware of our own internal impairment over issues of mutual recognition. This
      particularly arises over women presbyters and bishops. Such a situation within the Communion
      requires patience with mutual respect for all conflicting positions. We note the provision in
      the Church of England and the Church in Wales of extended episcopal care.

43   Some Provinces are approaching ecumenical unity by recognition of orders and then mutual
      consecration of bishops. This results in a parallel jurisdiction of two churches in ecumenical
      partnership, for example, Lutherans in Canada and the U.S.A. Situations of parallel jurisdictions
      exist within the Communion, some internal to a Province and some with churches in full
      communion, e.g., the three tikanga structure in the Church of Aotearoa, New Zealand and
      Polynesia, and the conciliar unity between the Church of North India, the Church of South
      India, and the Mar Thoma Syrian Church.

44   The participation of former Anglicans in the China Christian Council is of a unique character.

Regional Contexts: What is proposed?

45   We are aware of talks at various stages around the world though our knowledge is incomplete.
      We draw particular attention to the promising approach in Wales which may be implemented
      in the near future.[1]

Regional Contexts: Issues of Recognition

46   Provinces develop ecumenical relationships according to their own contexts. This process is to
      be encouraged by all. We recognize that this can produce tensions across the Communion; this
      requires loving respect and thoughtful prayer.

47   The intention of dialogue is 'reconciled diversity not uniformity,' though not necessarily at
      the expense of the goal of organic unity. We regret previous attitudes by some Anglicans of
      triumphalism in particular with relationship to the episcopate.

---

[1] In 1975, five churches in Wales entered into a covenant for unity, recognizing one another as ecclesial
communities with a common faith and common baptism. In East Cardiff, the Covenanting Churches
have now identified an area comprising over 50,000 people where, after some years of growing
together in union, there is need for specific episcopal oversight which each of the participating
churches will recognize. Accordingly, a proposal is now before the synods of these churches to
establish an ecumenical Bishop in Council, who will be ordained and authorized by representatives
of the five churches (including the Church in Wales); ministers currently serving in the area would
not require (re) ordination but would have their ministry recognized simply by virtue of its exercise
in communion with the bishop.

48 Significant ecumenical convergence has been reached on a variety of issues around ordination. These include:

a baptism as the foundation in which a theology of the ministry of the whole people of God is rooted;

b apostolic faith/tradition is fundamental to the nature of the church—'it is increasingly recognized that a continuity of apostolic faith, worship and mission has been preserved in churches which have not retained the form of historic episcopate'[1] Historic epicopate is a witness to but not a guarantee of a church's succession in apostolic faith/tradition;[2]

c different forms of ministry are based on different gifts (charismata) given by God for the mission of the church;

d in order to fulfil its mission, the church needs persons who are publicly and continually responsible for pointing to its fundamental dependence on Jesus Christ, and thereby providing, within a multiplicity of gifts, a focus of its unity. The ministry of such persons, who since very early times have been ordained, is constitutive for the life and witness of the church;

e ordination is always presided over by persons in whom the church recognizes the authority to transmit the ministerial commission by imposition of hands and prayer;

f ordination is accepted in most denominations to be for life;

g recognition of the true ecclesial status of other Communions precedes the mutual recognition of ministries.

Anglican consensus in these matters has been influenced by the multilateral document *Baptism, Eucharist, and Ministry*, is reflected in such dialogues as ARCIC, Anglican-Orthodox, and Anglican-Reformed, and has born significant fruit in such agreements as Porvoo.

Ecclesial-Theological Considerations: Issues Yet to be Resolved

49 This emerging ecumenical convergence presents Anglicans with a number of issues yet to be resolved. These include:

a Provinces find themselves at different stages in committing themselves to or acting upon this emerging consensus;

b the traditional Anglican position that the orders of bishop, priest and deacon have existed from the beginning; that all three are necessary to be recognized as a church and that only a bishop in the historic succession can convey these orders;

c the understanding of episcope in relation to the episcopate;

d the place of the diaconate as a full and equal order in the three-fold ministry;

e the complementarity of ministries, lay and ordained, as well as the relationship of each of the three-fold orders to one another'

f the full implications of the ordination of women for mutual recognition of ministry within the Anglican Communion;

g refusal to ordain solely on the basis of sexual orientation;

h the nature of the jurisdiction and the experience of episcope of non-territorial bishops such as ethnic, suffragan, assistant, episcopal visitors and some Primates of the Anglican Communion;

i the question of authority and the exercise of power in the church, e.g. the nature and function of the 'Petrine ministry'.

---

[1] BEM, Ministry IV.B.37.
[2] BEM, Ministry II.A.8

Proposals
50 In view of the above, we find it important:
   a to commend generally a methodological approach that has proven and is proving fruitful;
   b to signal some areas of concern or areas that we think need special or careful attention in regard to ordained ministry and church unity; and
   c to encourage further theological reflection and articulation of certain questions concerning the theory and practice of ordained ministry in the above discussion of regional contexts and ecclesial-theological considerations..
51 Thus, and in the order indicated:
   a Proposals for church unity will best begin with the mutual recognition of partners' sacramental baptism as set forth and practised in official liturgies. Ecumenical dialogue can then move to questions concerning recognition of the partners as churches, i.e., ecclesial bodies comprised of members sharing a common baptism. Thirdly, the dialogue can then move on from ecclesial recognition towards mutual recognition of ordained ministries, and, when that is in view, to their consequent interchangeability.
      i With respect to the Roman Catholic international or national dialogues this methodology would go far in moving beyond the impasse represented for both sides by the 1896 encyclical of Leo XIII, *Apostolicae curae*, and the official reply thereto by the Archbishops of Canterbury and York. Overcoming the impasse will also be helped by a mutual recognition of twentieth century convergences in sacramental theology.
      ii In dialogue with traditions featuring an episcopate without historic succession, this methodology will also prove most helpful in allowing the discussion to go forward.
      iii With non-episcopal ecumenical partners, the same methodology would free Anglicans from unnecessary impasses created by the sheer fact of commencing dialogues at the point of attempting to reconcile ordained ministries.
      iv With bodies having an episcopate of historic succession this methodology could very well encourage the partners to a mutual consideration of the nature and practice of their ordained ministries within their respective churches. They might also exhibit, on the basis of such discussion, a renewal of those ministries in their mutual life and mission through the relationship of full communion.
   b There are, however, a number of concerns raised by the members of this Conference that require attention or vigilance as ecumenical processes or proposals bear on questions of ordained ministry. In particular we note:
      i Intra-ecclesial and inter-ecclesial issues of jurisdiction (e.g., parallel jurisdictions; extra-diocesan or extra-provincial bishops);
      ii Clarity about the particular long-range or short-range ecumenical goal (e.g. unity by stages; full communion; organic union);
      iii Proposals concerning 'direct ordination' and/or the disuse of one of the three orders maintained by the Anglican tradition;
      iv The helpfulness beyond its specific context of the Anglican-Lutheran International Commission's 1996 Hanover Report. *Diaconate as Ecumenical Opportunity*, in addressing issues and questions surrounding renewal of the diaconate in ecumenical discussions between Anglicans and their dialogue partners.
   c Finally, we commend to all the need not only to articulate more fully the nature and practice of each of the three orders within Anglicanism, but to delineate also the complementarity of these orders within and for the church. We believe this task to be vitally important as a clarification for ourselves as Anglicans and as an important consideration for present and future partners in the ecumenical enterprise.

Jarvenpää   16 August 1997

Alcuin/GROW Joint Liturgical Studies

All cost £3.95 (US $8) in 1997—no. 4 is out of print

1987 TITLES

1. **(LS 49) Daily and Weekly Worship—from Jewish to Christian**
   by Roger Beckwith, Warden of Latimer House, Oxford
2. **(LS 50) The Canons of Hippolytus** edited by Paul Bradshaw, Professor of Liturgics, University of Notre Dame.
3. **(LS 51) Modern Anglican Ordination Rites** edited by Colin Buchanan, then Bishop of Aston
4. **(LS 52) Models of Liturgical Theology** by James Empereur, of the Jesuit School of Theology, Berkeley

1988 TITLES

5. **(LS 53) A Kingdom of Priests: Liturgical Formation of the Laity: The Brixen Essays**
   edited by Thomas Talley, Professor of Liturgics, General Theological Seminary, New York
6. **(LS 54) The Bishop in Liturgy: an Anglican Study** edited by Colin Buchanan, then Bishop of Aston
7. **(LS 55) Inculturation: the Eucharist in Africa** by Phillip Tovey
8. **(LS 56) Essays in Early Eastern Initiation** edited by Paul Bradshaw,

1989 TITLES

9. **(LS 57) The Liturgy of the Church in Jerusalem** by John Baldovin
10. **(LS 58) Adult Initiation** edited by Donald Withey
11. **(LS 59) 'The Missing Oblation': The Contents of the Early Antiochene Anaphora** by John Fenwick
12. **(LS 60) Calvin and Bullinger on the Lord's Supper** by Paul Rorem

1990 TITLES

13-14 **(LS 61) The Liturgical Portions of the Apostolic Constitutions: A Text for Students**
   edited by W. Jardine Grisbrooke (This double-size volume costs double price (i.e. £7.90 in 1997))
15 **(LS 62) Liturgical Inculturation in the Anglican Communion** edited by David Holeton
16. **(LS 63) Cremation Today and Tomorrow** by Douglas Davies, University of Nottingham

1991 TITLES

17. **(LS 64) The Preaching Service—The Glory of the Methodists**
   by Adrian Burdon, Methodist Minister in Rochdale
18. **(LS 65) Irenaeus of Lyon on Baptism and Eucharist**
   edited with Introduction, Translation and Commentary by David Power, Washington D.C.
19. **(LS 66) Testamentum Domini** edited by Grant Sperry-White, Department of Theology, Notre Dame
20. **(LS 67) The Origins of the Roman Rite** Edited by Gordon Jeanes, then Lecturer in Liturgy, University of Durham

1992 TITLES

21. **The Anglican Eucharist in New Zealand 1814-1989** by Bosco Peters, Christchurch, New Zealand
22-23 **Foundations of Christian Music: The Music of Pre-Constantinian Christianity**
   by Edward Foley, Capuchin Franciscan, Chicago (second double-sized volume at £7.90 in 1997)

1993 TITLES

24. **Liturgical Presidency** by Paul James
25. **The Sacramentary of Sarapion of Thmuis: A Text for Students**
   edited by Ric Lennard-Barrett, West Australia
26. **Communion Outside the Eucharist** by Phillip Tovey, Banbury, Oxon

1994 TITLES

27. **Revising the Eucharist: Groundwork for the Anglican Communion** edited by David Holeton
28. **Anglican Liturgical Inculturation in Africa** edited by David Gitari, Bishop of Kirinyaga, Kenya
29-30. **On Baptismal Fonts: Ancient and Modern**
   by Anita Stauffer, Lutheran World Federation, Geneva (Double-sized volume at £7.90)

1995 TITLES

31. **The Comparative Liturgy of Anton Baumstark** by Fritz West
32. **Worship and Evangelism in Pre-Christendom** by Alan Kreider
33. **Liturgy in Early Christian Egypt** by Maxwell E. Johnson

1996 TITLES

34. **Welcoming the Baptized** by Timothy Turner
35. **Daily Prayer in the Reformed Tradition: An Initial Survey** by Diane Karay Tripp
36. **The Ritual Kiss in Early Christian Worship** by Edward Phillips

1997 TITLES

37. **'After the Primitive Christians': The Eighteenth-century Anglican Eucharist in its Architectural Setting** by Peter Doll
38. **Coronations Past, Present and Future** edited by Paul Bradshaw
39. **Anglican Orders and Ordinations** edited by David Holeton

TRANSLATION:

TIHANA TAMINDZIC

EDITORS:

TOMISLAV NOVAK

ELIZABETH BAKER

I DEDICATE THIS BOOK TO MY WIFE ANA TENODI

AS ROCKEFELLER SAID, SPEAKING OF HIS WIFE LAURA CELESTIA SPELMAN:

"HER JUDGMENT WAS ALWAYS BETTER THAN MINE. WITHOUT HER KEEN ADVICE, I WOULD BE A POOR MAN."

...I AM GOING TO SAY ABOUT ANA:

WITHOUT YOU I WOULD BE A POOR VERSION OF MYSELF. THANK YOU FOR HELPING AND SUPPORTING ME TO BECOME MY BETTER SELF.

WELCOME TO THE

BE YOUR BETTER SELF PROJECT

A HANDS ON APPROACH TO BECOME WHO YOU ALWAYS WANTED
TO BE

Table of Contents

"Man is made and unmade by himself. In the armory of thought he forges the weapons which will destroy him. He also creates the tools with which he will build for himself heavenly mansions of joy and strength and peach. Between these two extremes are all the grades of character and man is their maker and their master."

James Allen, As a Man Thinketh

Introduction

Fight Club

You have probably seen the movie *Fight Club*. I don`t know how most of you experienced that movie, but I can certainly tell you that the movie changed the course of my life. I was 19 years old when I stood with my friends at the movie entrance door, waiting for the 8 pm projection. We didn`t know what to expect of the movie, we simply behaved in our normal Saturday movie night pattern. We used to wait for the people at the first showing to come out and we would observe their emotions. If we noticed a familiar person, we would ask for first hand impressions before actually going forward with it. The same situation happened this time, when a few familiar people exited the movie hall. We gathered them and asked: "What was the movie like?" They unanimously declared, "Horrible, ask for a refund, you will end up losing time, the movie is completely fucked up, give up while you still can." We looked each other for a while and eventually decided to go for it. During the next couple of hours, an impact on my whole belief and value system occurred. The movie was far from weird, stupid or terrible and those two hours I invested in watching *Fight Club* were the best investment for my 19 year-old mind.

In one scene, late at night, two main characters, Tyler Durden (Brad Pitt) and the narrator (Ed Norton) approach a gas station. Pitt's character holds a gun to the head of a convenience store clerk. He aims the gun and calmly talks to the young man.

"Raymond, you're going to die." He looks through the man's wallet, "An expired community college I.D. What'ja study Raymond?"

"Stuff..."

"Stuff? Were the midterms hard?" He smacks him on the head with the barrel of the gun, "I asked you what you studied!"

"Biology, mostly," the man cries.

"Why?"

"I don't know."

"What did you want to be, Raymond K. Hassel?" The clerk is sobbing and Tyler Durden cocks the gun. "The question, Raymond, is what did you want to be?"

"Veterinarian, veterinarian…"

"Animals! That means you've got to get more schooling."

"Too much school."

"Would you rather be dead?"

"No, please…"

Tyler unlocks the gun and tucks it into his jeans, "I'm keeping your license. I'm gonna check in on you. I know where you live. If you're not on your way to becoming a veterinarian in six weeks, you're going to be dead. Run on." He tosses the man his wallet and the man runs away without looking back.

Don`t you think that every one of us has a little voice inside our head just like Raymond? You know those situations when things seem too difficult? Midway through something you`ve started, you realize it`s not for you? That there exists an easier and better way—better things, better experiences. Everybody has had at least one experience like that, haven`t they? If we take the most difficult venture on earth, one so meaningful that we would hear our own Raymond and decide to quit, do you know why would we do that? The problem lies in too many options. Having too many options means having a way out. If somebody like Tyler Durden would point a gun against your head and say, "Either you do this or you`re dead," what would happen? What would be different? You would simply start performing and you would finish in the shortest possible time frame because you were out of options or better yet, you were left with just one. You`re not any smarter or more capable than you were before… but suddenly everything becomes simpler, everything becomes crystal clear and there is a clear representation in your mind where you need to be in order to avoid pain.

The bad thing is that most people don't decide to react before experiencing pain, because options still exist. Only when life deprives us of options do we decide to conquer those unimaginable things. Having too many options means having too many excuses.

A Buddhist saying states, "You never know how strong you are before being strong is the only option you have got!" (Raymond)

Everybody has a similar experience with avoiding pain—let me share mine. I was 22 years old and most of my friends were already seniors at that time. As a child I was deeply inspired by 'rags to riches' stories and I'd decided I could make it without a college degree. Furthermore, studying wasn't something I enjoyed, so the logical sequence of events was working and saving until further notice. Until the moment I would have an idea that changed everything (at least that is how it goes in most rags to riches stories). But, the years passed, nothing happened and I found myself working in a food factory. My job consisted of working on a conveyor belt, big freezer and from time to time, on a press container. I worked six days a week for a minimal wage, all the time waiting for the day that would change my life, the day I would reach the riches. And it came; only I never dreamed it would look the way it did. Before the very end of the shift, my supervisor asked me to come to the press container. A dozen returned goods pallets needed to be unloaded (goods that weren't sold or were past expiration date goods). Goods like carton milk, carton iced coffee and bottled yoghurt. Woolen mittens were my only protection. I leaned down to get the iced coffees and when I tried to lift them, the carton bottoms stuck to the pallets because of the mold, and the rotten liquid that used to be coffee, spilled all over my hands and my woolen mittens. That was an odor I had never experienced in my entire life! In a state of complete disgust, covering my mouth and nose with my T-shirt, I continued to quickly throw the rest of the goods in the press container. Filling it to the brim, I pressed the ignition button, which launched a grinding spiral that ground the waste toward the end of the container. Standing 6 feet from it, I watched all that rot getting milled away and after a few seconds,

I heard a familiar breaking sound from within. I knew from previous experience that there might be a possibility the rotten food could explode on me, as it had on multiple past occasions, so I decided to move away and took a safe distance of some 20 feet. A green wall stood behind me. Suddenly the container went wild.

It started making crackling noises that I had never heard before, followed by the BOOM of a big bang. In a split of a second I saw container particles raining down on me. Looking at my arms, my body...I was completely covered with rot and decay. I turned around and faced the green wall behind me. I saw what up to that moment I thought existed only in cartoons. There on the wall stood a silhouette of my body. Pausing then and there, looking at myself, at the wall, at myself again, I heard a voice inside say, "Man, do you really want your life to look like this in five years...or even worse, ten years?" That was the day I decided to enroll in college. People told me,"Enrolling at 22? Don`t be foolish! You enroll when you`re 18, straight after high school." And they were right. Luckily for me, I ran out of options.

The start of BYBS

Everything that occurred after that event is my real rags to riches story... ok, not everything, but the bigger part of it. I was never what you would call a brilliant student. I was successfully completing year after year, while working part time and from my junior year, on I managed to be financially self-sustaining. Working as an underground garage cleaner, I invested my free time in tree activities: my girlfriend, my friend, Nick who first introduced me with personal transformation methods and reading piles of books on the topic. My friend Nick was a great support before the college enrollment as his accelerated learning techniques additionally motivated me. Nick was a real mind-mapping master and I felt honored to be a pioneer in applied mind mapping, together with my mentor. Considering the fact that my time was completely consumed with lectures and work that left me exhausted, I realized free time is something I must create. But how could I do that? There wasn`t a thing I could leave out of the equation: the job fed, dressed and gave me a roof over my head, college was a necessity, I loved my girlfriend and I needed Nick because he rapidly updated me with the most interesting topics. I couldn't imagine leaving anything out of the daily schedule.

These weren't options, these were necessities. Soon a solution appeared! I found a speed-reading and accelerated learning techniques seminar flyer with a student discount. It left me thrilled! The logic behind it was simple: if I learned how to speed read, I would save a lot of time on a daily and weekly basis, which meant I would have more time for my girlfriend and Nick. But the story gets even better than that. The first day of the speed-reading seminar I tried to communicate with the lecturer. The intention behind it was to gain more information than what I able to gather through reading and talking to Nick. To find out, in a quick way, all the things I don't know I don't know. Unfortunately, the lecturer didn't see my intention the same way I did. After the first day, he had the impression I was provoking him and that I was tearing down his authority. Right after the class he asked me aside to have a serious talk. The first thing that crossed my mind was that he would kick me out of this seminar I so desperately wanted. I was wrong. He offered me a job. He offered me the opportunity to be a speed reading seminar lecturer for the following week. This seminar was scheduled to last for four more days, I didn't know how to speed-read yet and I had a chance to be a lecturer, wow! Doing the very thing that thrilled me, study learning strategies and teaching them to others! Perfect! Of course I was interested but I need to know how much money I would earn. It would have to be at least the same amount as what I got cleaning the garage. The offered salary was four times as much and the number of hours needed to earn that salary was three times smaller. Just in one night I achieved all of my outcomes and more.

After that night, I rushed my self-development into sixth gear. I worked three hours a day, I had a free weekend, I went to classes more regularly than ever, and enrolled in a very expensive neurolinguistic programming seminar...at least I thought it was expensive a month before. With the new salary, the criteria have changed. You know how it goes.

It was all too good to be true and it didn't last for long. Two months after that I got fired. And why is that? I enrolled into NLP without my employer knowing about it. They had a negative past experience with a former employer who practiced NLP and they viewed the methodology solely as manipulative. They were afraid I was going to use NLP methods. The thing that seemed like the end of the world at the moment turned out fantastic. Two options lay before me at that moment. Either I would do speed reading on my own or I would go back to the garage. Which one to choose? With the help of my family, I founded my own company and started teaching. It turned out that in that way I could earn even more money in a shorter period of time. The following year, I invested the money into further NLP education and became an NLP coach, in further expanding my company's activities. In less than a year I earned the money I could never have earned if I got a job immediately after college and worked for full four years not spending a single penny.

I have a job I once could only dream about, I earn the numbers I always wanted to earn, I work less than I ever thought it would be possible and out of all the mentioned circumstances I generate my belief that would later on cost me. That belief is: "Everything I touch turns to gold."

Dealing with success and failure

Soon outside influences began to penetrate my successful story. People said, "What is it that Sasha is doing? That isn't a real job! People work Mondays through Fridays and he only works weekends. How is this possible and why isn't he embarrassed? He just talks rubbish, it isn't palpable. I wanna see him roll up his sleeves and do a real job."

Later on I realized that the worst decision I could have ever make is one based on peer pressure. I wanted to show those people, I wanted to demonstrate my power to them; I wanted to prove to them that yes, everything I touch turns into gold. I opened a pizzeria, my second company. Business went great. There wasn`t a moment in a day with an empty seat. Now nobody could say I`m selling people a bill of goods. Look at me; whatever I do turns out to be a success. Continuously and for years I was implementing sentences like that one into my mind through autosuggestion. In every moment that other people wasted, like while riding public transportation or walking from point A to point B, I would train my mind telling myself the most wonderful sentences and instructions possible...and now it was all falling into place. "People are standing in queues to buy our pizza...we don`t even have time for a short break... The pizza place is the place to be in just 2 weeks...my first company is well established." The demonstration was completed. I was so proud, so powerful, and so important. Praise to me! ...Ok, and arrogant and cocky and insolent and self sufficient and full of myself.

In the state of utmost self pleasure, only a few months after the opening of what I thought would be a successful company, it turned out that it wasn`t all that successful. I was pretty inexperienced at that line of business and on top of that, I chose equally inexperienced employees. Somehow, even though business was going really good, we were operating at a minus. Then, suppliers to whom we were indebted, started calling: "Sasha, are you aware how much you owe us?" I used to reply, "Yes, I`m well aware. But you know, business is going so great that I`ll take care of those debts in no time." A week after the phone calls, it turned out that we couldn`t pay back all the debts in the speed I imagined we would. From then on, supplier phone calls started coming in one after another. I tried to convince them that all they needed to do was to give me some time and that I would sort everything out for them. Then came that horrible Friday night when the news announced the Brothers bank bankruptcy and the world crisis. But our income was steady, I thought it wouldn`t touch me. And yet again I was wrong. Monday morning, the pizza place turnover dropped 70 percent. At first I assumed it must have been a bad day, but the next day the story repeated itself. And the day after that. And the day after that. Fuck. If I wasn`t able to pay the debts with the great turnover I used to have, what was I supposed to do now?

Things seemed far from my "Everything I touch turns into gold" catchphrase.

I believed in a better future, I sincerely tried to believe in a better future, a better day that would come...but the future passed by and things didn't change. Not only that the things didn't change, but they also became even worse. There was a motivational incoming call ring on my cell phone, Van Halen's Jump. After two weeks of continuous supplier rings, that song stopped being motivational. It became disgusting. As soon as I heard Van Halen, I started to choke. I couldn't sleep, I was on the verge of crying, the moment I fell asleep the trembling of my body would awaken me. When I was sleeping I would constantly jerk my feet. I stopped shaving, I stopped dressing up nicely, and I stopped combing my hair. All of my self-confidence, motivation and zest were gone. What's more, I transferred all the first company's money to the second company so it was all gone. It took me two years to go from a garbage man to a two company owner. And only three months after I accomplished it, I wished it had never happened and I had still worked as a garbage man. Would I ever come out of this, and if I did, how long would it take me? Those were my ritual daily questions for a bad morning, for a bad day and for a bad sleep.

My girlfriend decided it was best for me to separate myself from this environment, even if for only a short while. We went to her seaside cabin. Turning off my cell phone, I tried emptying my head for three days. Of course I didn't manage to do so, but at least I was close. The insomnia still continued but we took strolls, we talked, watched movies and did all the other activities that distanced me in my head from the reality I need to return to soon.

On the way back home, I got sick. I got back to my place and emptied the car trunk. While I was emptying the trunk, I accidentally moved a rug covering the spare tire and found a book I haven't seen for years. *Think and Grow Rich.* I read it couple of years back and didn't like it. I had an impression it was too superficial or it was just one more self-help book in a row. A lot of pages, nothing I could put into practice immediately. Then again, the situation I found myself in that particular moment resembled a movie scene. I thought to myself, let`s give it a shot, maybe this "coincidence" turns out to be a good anecdote one day. You never know.

I threw myself on the bed and started reading. After the first few pages, nothing revolutionary or especially uplifting happened, but I did start feeling better. For the consecutive nights that followed I read Hill and by the time I completed the book, I felt happy and optimistic. The business situation didn`t change but my state of mind did. The next night I grabbed another "how to get rich" book, *The Richest Man in Babylon*. Going through it I stumbled upon a metaphor, a story from the book that triggered something big, something that resulted in a magnificent shift. That particular moment something was born. I didn`t know then it would manifest itself in a form of this book. I said to myself, "I know where the problem lies, the problem is inside! The problem is in me! And I am the one who let that problem enter me!" How does a problem get inside my mind? It comes from the outside. Daily, I let into my mind various inputs that created, as a result, states of despair, victimization and helplessness. That information diminished my motivation to feel better despite the situation. All that led me to ask the question, "What can I do right now to change my state? How can I change my state by myself?"

I`m not talking about autosuggestion or similar tools—I'm talking about the usual physical things. What could I do for my body and mind that would change the state in my body and mind as long as I couldn`t influence the situation outside? A plan was devised. I told myself, ' First thing you`re going to do Sasha, when you wake up is five pushups! After that you are going to shave, fix yourself up and put on a suit. Then we`ll see what can happen.' Already on the very first day the feedback was amazing. From employees to suppliers, people changed their way of communicating with me. Just a couple of days back, I was in a sweat suit, unshaved and sloppy and now I was wearing a suit. They suspected...he must have a good reason...and so they changed the way they communicated towards me...which consequently changed my state. I said to myself, "This really works! Such a little change makes a huge difference." What else could I do to alter my daily inputs? What pieces of information could I consciously implant into my mind in order to feel better? To cut the story short, don`t worry I`ll come back to it later, let me just tell you that the business got worse by the minute, heading towards a sure bankruptcy, but with only minor exceptions, I felt incredibly good.

I went bankrupt on September 1, 2009. The pocket in my jeans hid my last $200, one company was frozen holding no capital and the other closed with enormous debts towards virtually everybody!

One thing was sure, now I owned better strategies. I believed that despite the crisis, current debt situation and other phenomena, I could succeed in an unprecedented way. I firmly believed that because it was a thing I was made to do!

I had no starting capital, no job, and I was sending out job applications, my girlfriend was sending job applications for me, I was living nowhere, sleeping for 3 days at one friend`s apartment, and for the next 3 days at another friend`s apartment. And so on. One of my good friends tried to set me straight, "Find yourself a proper job because there`s no way in hell you`re gonna sell yourself and your learning techniques now, in a time of complete crisis." Considering the fact I respected his opinion and him as a wiser, more experienced and well intentioned person, I didn`t even dare to try. My girlfriend brought me food, my friends gave me shelter and everything stood static for three long months.

One night, my girlfriend came into one of the apartments I was currently at and said, "Sasha, I have some really bad news for you. I`m out of a job as of an hour ago and I can no longer afford you, let alone myself." What to believe at this point? I managed to destroy two companies in less than two years, lost everything, created debts, relied on my friends for months, and tormented my girlfriend. One thing was one hundred percent clear. All of my resources had been exhausted. Not a single person existed that could help me. I was out of options. To put it more precisely, there were two options. The first one was: If I didn`t come up with money in thirty days, I would be left on the street. I couldn`t stay at friends` houses any more. The second one was: Do just the opposite of that. I knew that this was the worst time to sell my services, and myself as my well-intentioned friend Tom said before, but at the moment, it was my only option!

From that day on and for the following 365 days, I`ve earned more money than all the dollars I`ve earned till the crisis moment put together. I didn't dream my emotional life could get so harmonious and tranquil. I ask you and myself also, "Do you know why?" The answer is simply because I had no other options.

Napoleon Hill used a very powerful metaphor in his book *Think and Grow Rich*, the book I completely wore off reading:

"A long time ago, a great warrior faced a situation which made it necessary for him to make a decision which insured his success on the battlefield. He was about to send his armies against the powerful foe, whose men outnumbered his own. He loaded his soldiers into boats, sailed to enemies country unloaded soldiers and equipment then gave the order to burn the ships that had carried them. Addressing his men before the first battle, he said: „You see the boats going up in smoke? That means we cannot leave this shore alive unless we win! We now have no choice, we win or we perish. They won...every person who wins in any undertaking must be willing to burn his ships and cut all sources of retreat. Only by doing so can one be sure of maintaining the state of mind known as a burning desire to win, essential to success."

Thank God I found myself almost out of a place to live. Who knows what would have happened to me if I gotten some kind of a job, some other option.

ABOUT BYBS

Learning better strategies

In this book you will read and work on all of those things I personally proved work, practicing on me and on others. Whatever outcome you might set to yourself, you will achieve it by using simple principles and strategies with which you`ll enjoy in the process of the strived completion with minimal renouncements and regardless of the state you`re in. This book will give you an insight into the way you organize yourself. Specifically, why you love doing the things you love doing, why you don't like doing the things you don`t like doing, why are you good at one thing and lousy at another? This book will show you where all the causes lie. Considering my starting platform is NLP, using uncomplicated language I`ll clarify the principles and strategies with which you`ll not only understand yourself and the decisions you made so far but also give you strategies on how to adjust, improve and change certain things. What this book doesn`t do is give you advice. I`ve learnt that the process is much more important that the content itself, so I`ll do my best to make sure you receive this process. The content of the book you wish to apply is for you to choose anyway, and as you`ll see reading through the book, who am I to tell you what is right or what needs to be done. You have been told that up to now, haven`t you?

Why is the book called BYBS?

I chose the title, *Be Your Better Self* because I believe that man is by nature good. That originally each individual has good foundations, only that they are considerably influenced by outside influences, mostly negative ones. I believe that walking the path of change doesn`t mean altering your (good) essence and I believe that we should stick to the principle: be yourself. That`s precisely what I used the keyword "better." By becoming "better" I mean polishing various strategies. We can`t generally say that one person is "better" than another. But what we can say is that there is a person that is better than somebody else in a certain field. And so there are people that are better in communication, in entrepreneurship, in relationships, in nurture, and all of that doesn`t imply they are better people. That only implies they use better strategies in those certain fields. At least better strategies than us. That`s why we see them as better in this respect. To tell you the truth, I thought of the title "Be Your Best Self", and based on experience, I opted out. Let me tell you why. Most people delay an activity because they are waiting for the right moment, for the moment when the situation will be ripe or they will possess the perfect strategy for accomplishing something...in other words never. The goal of this book is to give you ways or better yet, a process with which you won`t lose yourself, your essence, your identity but with which you`ll upgrade and build your personal strategies. Strategies that will assist you to step faster and more elegantly toward wanted states, whatever they might be.

UNDERSTANDING PERSONAL ORGANIZATION: WHY WE ACT THE WAY WE DO ?

Identity is the product of your environment

From the very beginning, I decided to go with the explanation and examples of how our identity, our value system and our beliefs are created. The most important topic for understanding the way we are organized as a whole will give us the answers to following questions:

Who am I and why am I?

What drives my behavior?

What brought me to the point where I am what I am...whether I am happy with it or not?

You`re probably familiar with the following story:
One day, a scorpion looked around at the mountain where he lived and decided that he wanted a change. So he set out on a journey through the forests and hills. He climbed over rocks and under vines and kept going until he reached a river. The river was wide and swift, and the scorpion stopped to reconsider the situation. He couldn't see any way across. So he ran upriver and then checked downriver, all the while thinking that he might have to turn back. Suddenly, he saw a frog sitting in the rushes by the bank of the stream on the other side of the river. He decided to ask the frog for help getting across the stream.
"Hellooo Mr. Frog!" called the scorpion across the water, "Would you be so kind as to give me a ride on your back across the river?"
"Well now, Mr. Scorpion! How do I know that if I try to help you, you won't try to kill me?" asked the frog hesitantly.
"Because," the scorpion replied, "If I try to kill you, then I would die too, for you see I cannot swim!"

Now this seemed to make sense to the frog. But he asked. "What about when I get close to the bank? You could still try to kill me and get back to the shore!"

"This is true," agreed the scorpion, "But then I wouldn't be able to get to the other side of the river!"

"Alright then...how do I know you won't just wait till we get to the other side and THEN kill me?" said the frog.

"Ahh...," crooned the scorpion, "Because you see, once you've taken me to the other side of this river, I will be so grateful for your help, that it would hardly be fair to reward you with death, now would it?!"

So the frog agreed to take the scorpion across the river. He swam over to the bank and settled himself near the mud to pick up his passenger. The scorpion crawled onto the frog's back, his sharp claws prickling into the frog's soft hide, and the frog slid into the river. The muddy water swirled around them, but the frog stayed near the surface so the scorpion would not drown. He kicked strongly through the first half of the stream, his flippers paddling wildly against the current.

Halfway across the river, the frog suddenly felt a sharp sting in his back and, out of the corner of his eye, saw the scorpion remove his stinger from the frog's back. A deadening numbness began to creep into his limbs.

"You fool!" croaked the frog, "Now we shall both die! Why on earth did you do that?"

The scorpion shrugged, and did a little jig on the drowning frog's back.

"I could not help myself. It is my nature."

Let's take this story as a basic illustration of the way we're organized and how we behave the way we behave and how come we are what we are. In other words, where does our behavior come from?

Note the following terms:
IDENTITY – I am...
VALUES AND BELIEFS – I like, it's important for me, I believe...
CAPABILITY – I can, I can't...
BEHAVIOUR – I do...
ENVIRONMENT –My environment supports/doesn't support...

How do we decide what to like and what to avoid?

For a certain pattern to develop, specific conditions need to exist in the environment. What does it mean? It means that it`s almost impossible for a person born in Ethiopia to become a professional skier unless two minimal conditions are satisfied: that he has a stupendous will for skiing and a millionaire father. For a person to stand on skis in the first place, certain environmental conditions need to be satisfied. Firstly, a ski slope needs to be available, and then the person has to be well motivated for skiing. Furthermore, there needs to exist ample financial funds for the endeavor. Meaning that every potential behavioral pattern needs to be supported by the environment, the setting needs to be encouraging so that it allows the development of a certain pattern. If there are no such conditions in our environment, we have only two choices: either change the environment or give up the wanted state.

Conditions create decisions

I`ll add a personality development example of a boy named Mark.

Mark was born in a neighborhood where there are a couple of soccer fields. After he became old enough, his parents decided to let him play with his peers in the playground without their supervision. Considering that his peers were always playing in that playground, Mark had no other option but to play in that particular playground. Soccer fields were situated nearby. One day, older children were playing soccer and all of a sudden their ball found its way next to Mark. At that moment Mark took a running start and kicked the ball towards the older children on the soccer field. His kick was so good that the recipients were stunned. One of them invited Mark to show them again how he kicked the ball. Mark obeyed. He was then welcomed to play with the older children in the soccer field.

The story continues:

Version 1

Mark started playing soccer and already in the first game, he scored two goals. His older colleagues rapturously greeted his every well-played move. After his first game Mark came back home and said to his parents, "Mum, Dad, I played soccer today…and I scored two goals! Everybody was so happy, I had a great time and I can't wait to play again!" The parents loudly stated, "Way to go son, we're proud of you!" And so Mark began visiting the soccer field on a daily basis, scored goals and got better and better at it. One day, listening to Mark's success soccer stories, the parents suggested giving it a go on a real soccer practice in a nearby soccer club. Mark agreed. After the first practice, the coach noticed Mark, approached him and let him know he wanted him and his rare talent in the soccer club.

1. Condition – ENVIRONMENT: for Mark to even play soccer there would have to be a soccer field and enough number of children to play it with. If there hadn't been a soccer field there wouldn't have been Mark's soccer talent.
2. Condition – BEHAVIOUR: If Mark hadn't demonstrated that good kick and he hadn't been invited to play and he hadn't been supported by his co players and parents, the story would have gone in a different direction. He would get a chance but not that fast.
3. Condition – CAPABILITY: As Mark trains; he becomes more skilled and raises the level of his capability as a potential soccer player.
4. Condition – VALUES AND BELIEFS: Seeing that Mark likes to play soccer, which he demonstrates with motivation to play it whenever he can, represents a considerable amount of value in his model of the world. And with the fact that he displays the capability of playing soccer and is praised all the time, Mark develops a belief: I play soccer really well.
5. Condition – IDENTITY: Marks' belief I play soccer really well + parent support, inspired Mark to try his newly acquired talent in a nearby professional soccer club. After the coach gives him feedback on his play and welcomes him as a club member with the hope he will one day play the big leagues, Mark creates an identity: I am a soccer player.

When each of the previous conditions is satisfied, the probability of crossing to the next level heightens. To sum it up, our behavior is developed provided that certain conditions in our environment are met. Conditions meaning not only physical ones but also people, i.e. the context contributing to it. ("Good job Mark, way to go! We`re proud of you Mark! That was a fantastic score!") All of those supporting environmental inputs motivate Mark to continue on and work a bit more on his capabilities so as to increase them. The more his capabilities are developed, the more Mark`s beliefs take shape. On the level of behavior: I know how to kick a ball well. I occasionally score goals. On the level of capability, day by day, Mark gets better and better. Month by month the beliefs become stronger: I`m really good at soccer, I love soccer (value: because I`m good at soccer). The higher the value is and the more developed the capability is, the belief gets stronger which ultimately results in an irrefutable confidence. And from that confidence comes new motivation (value): I want to try my skills in a professional club; (belief) with my capabilities/skills I can be admitted in a soccer club. After the admission, this whole set of behavior, capabilities, values and beliefs helps create something bigger. A person`s identity. From today I am officially a soccer player.

1. ENVIRONMENT: There is a soccer field, I could try playing soccer
2. BEHAVIOUR: I know how to kick a ball and occasionally score a goal
3. CAPABILITIES: I play soccer and I`m getting better and better at it
4. VALUES AND BELIEFS: Soccer is the greatest sport there is. I play soccer really well
5. IDENTITY: I am a soccer player

Version 2

After Mark got invited to play soccer, his team members decided that because of his hitting talent he should play in the position of a soccer striker. A few times, Mark found himself in front of the goal and because of the pressure he missed an empty goal. His team members didn`t react the first time nor the second. The third time they became mad and instructed him to go play the central midfielder. Mark listened and tried to play this position but he wasn`t handling it well. It was only his first time playing soccer and his team members didn`t seem to have any understanding. They were very tense and reacted harshly to his every mistake. Finally they put him to play defense, the position that he again couldn't handle. In the end Mark's team members decided they couldn't tolerate it anymore and gave him a choice, either he was to go and watch the goal or he was to go home. So Mark went home. Mark had two options at that moment: either he would continue to put in an effort and prove to himself that they were wrong or he would quit, the latter being a more probable outcome taking into account the number of negative inputs received during his first/last game.

1. ENVIRONMENT: There is a soccer field, I could try playing soccer.
2. BEHAVIOUR: I know how to kick a ball, I'm going to play soccer now.
   2.1 Pf, I can't believe I missed all those shots.
   2.2 Yes, I completely deserve to be put in the center/defense.
   2.3 It would be best I got off the field because this is embarrassing. They're yelling at me all the time.
3. CAPABILITIES: I'm not good at it, I'm not handling it well.
4. VALUES AND BELIEFS: There are better sports than soccer. What's the point any way of having just one ball on so many players? Soccer is stupid.
5. IDENTITY: I could be anything in life, just as long as I'm not a soccer player. Soccer players are stupid.

If we didn't succeed at something at first, the possibility of us not liking it is increasing dramatically, and we will never again give it a chance. The learning direction with which we acquire our behaviors, capabilities, beliefs and values is exactly that. One met condition opens up the next. But the way our mental operative system functions is exactly the opposite. Identity has the biggest value according everything we do. And identity is the thing that embraces all the beliefs, values, capabilities and taught behaviors simply because first there existed environmental conditions.
Our beliefs and values support our identity. Our capabilities as well as behaviors are a part of our identity.

The first scorpion story perfectly illustrates the concept of logical levels and how it works. The scorpion's life is threatened, and life is a value, it is forced to fight (value). Seeing that a crossing over the river doesn`t exist, the scorpion starts to beg (a behavior coming out of the value) the frog to save it`s life. The frog realizes the scorpion might sting and kill it but that wouldn't make any sense because committing that act, it would also kill itself (here, the frog relies on the value towards life and creates a belief that because of that there won`t be any stings). When the scorpion eventually does sting the frog, it doesn`t come as a surprise considering it came from an identity (I am a scorpion) and identity is hierarchically higher than value, therefore identity beats value. This story illustrates all of our past failed attempts to change. We wanted to somehow change a certain behavior and tried to influence what we are with a new behavior, which actually up until that moment didn`t exist, and of course we failed. Just like in the example with the scorpion, the hierarchically highest level – identity, beats the hierarchically lower level – value.

Let`s take the experience of the well-known Abraham Maslow as described in the book *Beliefs: Pathways to Health and Well-Being*, "The psychiatrist treated a patient who believed he was a corpse. Despite all the logical arguments the psychiatrist used in order to shake the patients belief, he was persistent in his starting belief. In a moment of inspiration, the psychiatrist had an idea to pose a question, "Do corpses bleed?" The patient readily replied that it was a ridiculous question and of course they don`t. The psychiatrist then took a pocketknife and cut his patients index finger. Dark red blood gushed as the psychiatrist was, evidently proud of his idea, waiting for a reaction. Completely dumbfounded and shocked, with eyes wide open and staring at his bloody finger, the patient looks at the psychiatrist and tells him," I`ll be damned, corpses do bleed."

Analysis

A man holds onto a belief: I am a corpse (IDENTITY, 5TH LEVEL)
The psychiatrist asks a question: Do corpses bleed? (BEHAVIOUR, 2ND LEVEL)
The man replies: No, corpses don`t bleed (BELIEF, 4TH LEVEL)

The end result is yet again the same. Identity is so strong that any belief exiting the frame of what we believe in is automatically disregarded.

The power of identity over lower levels can be illustrated with a person who created its identity: I am a soccer player. This identity will influence the behavior every time. Imagine the next situation. A chess player and a soccer player walk in a park. There is a walnut in front of them on the ground. What do you think will happen? Will the chess player pick up the walnut or will it stay on the ground? What is the most probable thing you think will occur? Behavior is predictable as long as we know what`s hiding on the identity level, isn`t it?

Undesirable behavior change

Now imagine a situation in which a person, who says to him or herself that he or she is a smoker, decides to stop smoking. This venture is doomed from the beginning if the person doesn't change the language on the identity level. If the person says to himself,"I am a smoker", this means he sees himself with a cigarette and it`s only a matter of time when he will succumb to an opportunity lurking in the environment.

The fastest way for a person to change or more precisely to change their behavioral pattern is to remove the environmental triggers that support the unwanted behavior. For example, if person A goes to a pub every day and drinks a number of beers and suddenly decides to change his or her behavior, the first thing to do is to decide it. But if the visits to the pub still continue, no matter if the order is a non alcoholic beverage, it`s just a matter of time when he or she will slip and order a beer, saying internally, "Oh it`s just one beer...I`ve been abstaining for such a long time." And that will trigger a chain reaction putting him right back in the beginning. The best way to persevere in a change is exactly to stay away from the pub for a while, which would mean that the environmental conditions that weaken the decision were eliminated. If we manage to do that, we made the first and most important step towards influencing behavior and ultimately – identity.

My clients often complain about their children. Something like: "My child spends too much time on the Internet, how do I solve this?" I always reply, "Then you must have a computer in the house, don't you!" Funnily enough, if the family didn't have a computer in the house, there wouldn't be a problem such as somebody spending too much time on the Internet, would it? Of course, at this stage I'm not offering a solution, I'm simply pointing out how many unwanted behaviors exist because of all the conditions met in the immediate environment.

Our behavioral patterns are so intertwined into all our identity levels that it's no wonder change is so difficult for us. We are used to being what we are so much that we're unconsciously sabotaging ourselves at every step. Trying to change a behavior without linking it to an identity is destined to fail. In order to avoid failure, or in other words, to achieve success, we must build an understanding about how the whole system functions and how the smaller particles correlate.

Before losing my 30 extra pounds, I didn't want to go on a diet. I wanted to be the person that I am now. I thought, "I'm not on a diet now, so why should I go on a diet?" My losing weight had to do with me becoming a different person in many ways. I remember a woman who said, "I quit smoking a lot of times, but I wasn't successful at quitting until I became a non-smoker. This is a valuable perspective shift that Dillts and other authors presented in the previously mentioned book, *Beliefs: Pathways to Health and Well-Being.*

The first and simplest step is choosing the person you want to be. Right now. For example, I want to be a person who regularly attends practice or the person who reads books. After you have narrowed down your goal, think about all the conditions in the environment that are distracting you from achieving your goal. That means, if you want to be the person who reads books, think about how the following habits support you in achieving your goal: turning on the TV immediately after entering the house, long hours surfing on the Internet, chatting with a friend, or cleaning a clean room, etc. You are the only one who knows what you are actively doing to avoid being what you want to be.

Be aware of the influence the environment has on behavior and think, does a smoker think about a cigarette when in a sauna? Of course not.

Change is a multilevel process. Level one: environment

Change really is a multilevel process, which is best explained in the Beliefs book:" ...first, changes happen in our environment. Changes in our behavior happen as a consequence of interacting with our environment. Then follow changes in our capabilities and the strategies with which we direct and guide our behavior. Furthermore, changes in our beliefs and value systems by which we motivate and reinforce our guidance systems and maps. Finally, changes in our identity from which we select the values and beliefs we live by. As a result, changes in our relationship to those things which are bigger than us, those things that most people would call the spiritual."

UNDERSTANDING PERSONAL MOTIVATION

Values: the place where everything starts

Values, alongside beliefs, come hierarchically second, right after identity. I mentioned before that values support our identity, the very thing we are, in a way that we gain a certain benefit with the help of the behavior we exhibit, whether we`re aware of this benefit or not.

Values are our life drivers, our primary source of motivation. We don`t have to be conscious of all our values in order for them to make criteria that will eventually mold our behaviors and beliefs. When our values are synchronized, we have a sense of contentment and harmony. If not, we feel dissatisfaction and frustration. The values we cherish are the best example of our subjective experience and they are most often in contrast with the facts representing objectivity. For example, two people can claim they possess the same values, yet again behave differently in different situations.

According to Maslow, all human beings exhibit a need for a stable and grounded self-evaluation in respect to their subjective feeling of self-respect, self-esteem or respect coming from others. Those needs can be divided into two categories. On the one hand is the need for strength, achievement, adequacy and self-confidence while on the other hand, is the need for independence and freedom. Whether we want to admit it or not, we all posses a need for prestige and reputation, or more precisely, for respect and acknowledgement in our surroundings. Fulfillment of the self-esteem need leads to a feeling of personal importance, strength, capability and the feeling of usefulness and being needed in one`s role in the society. Failing to meet those feelings leads towards feelings of inferiority, weakness and helplessness. The form and ratio in which the needs will be conformed with, vary from person to person, from culture to culture.

Basic physiological needs aside (ex. the need for survival), our personal needs for security, love, respect – and more precisely, the way these needs are met -- considerably differs from individual to individual. Things that are imperative to one person may not be of any significance to another. Even when two different individuals verbalize the same needs, wishes or goals, they most likely will not satisfy them in the same way or for the same reason.

Why do we fail?

Values apply to the things we want and to the things we yearn for. In simple terms, there are two strong sources of motivation coming out of adopted values. In order for us to be motivated towards any kind of action, one of the value criteria has to be complied with. One source refers to avoiding pain, removing fear, frustration and other painful states, provided a negative emotion is concerned. Negative emotion is born when we put ourselves in a state that is so frustrating or painful that we cannot cope with it any more. That is why it doesn`t take long for us to decide to act. The reason we call this kind of motivation negative is because the current painful state is motivating us to act.

The other source of motivation refers to a strong wish or yearning and it is born when we see something that`s absolutely irresistible. That is the case of a positive motivation, because we are drawn towards something.

If we take a person who enjoys alcoholic beverages on a daily basis, there are only two reasons or values why this person would decide to change. The first and more probable one can happen if the person`s health is severely damaged and if the person has an irrefutable medical diagnosis where evident consequences are imminent unless the person stops that behavior. Remembering that the importance of identity lies above the importance of value, we conclude that the person will change permanently; still there is a considerable possibility that he will put in an effort in order to avoid pain or death.

The second and less probable reason to change is also related to health. This outcome is possible only in the scenario where a person changes their lifestyle, for example, becomes a part of a macrobiotic consumer group or an environment that will motivate the person to integrate the values of the new group.

Still, the general rule applies: something has to happen to trigger the value for change. A new value doesn`t appear on its own. A pain generating an escape pattern has to appear or a magnetic delight which will draw a person towards a new outcome, a new value.

Let me give you an example of a negative and positive motivation in everyday life.

Negative motivation
 After a festive feast, I gained 17.5 pounds. I stood in front of a mirror and said, "You look disgusting! How could you let this happen?" At that point, because of a bad feeling towards my own body, I decided to do something to ease the current state of pain. I decided to watch my diet and became a member of a gym so as to lose the extra weight and feel pleasure. Therefore, the source of my motivation was dissatisfaction, which made my motivation a negative one, as I wanted to distance myself away from pain.

Positive motivation
Saturday night I was watching a movie where a famous actor had an impressionably chiseled body. I said to my wife, "Oh man, I wanna look like that!" to which she replied that indeed the movie star had a great body. I said to myself that Monday morning I was going straight to the gym and by summer I would enjoy my newly acquired look. The source of this motivation is positive because it is pointing towards the wanted state instead pointing towards distancing myself from the unwanted state. The wanted state is so appealing that I feel a burning desire to attain it.

In both cases I decided to change regardless of whether the motivation was positive or negative. Of course, every person is motivated from different sources in certain life aspects and we can`t generalize by saying a person exclusively acts on negative or positive motivation. If somebody enjoys reading books, the same person will steal every possible moment to read an exciting text which means this person will be led by positive motivation. To that same person, tidiness may be of no value and consequently, his or her apartment will be a mess and a reason for cleaning the mess up will appear only when pain also appears. In this scenario the pain can be: in about two hours company is arriving, I can`t just let them enter this chaos. In that case the motivation source is that the person doesn`t want to feel shame, and so, decides to tidy up the apartment before the guests arrive. Still, in both cases motivation does exist and the problem will be solved after the needed criteria are met.

Heaven and Hell hold an excellent example of positive and negative motivation. Heaven represents the positive side of motivation: if you lead a worthy and honest life, you will go to Heaven. Hell represents the negative side of motivation: if you lead a dishonorable and evil life, you will go to Hell. With its source of motivation or better yet offer, Heaven will motivate believers. Not all, but a considerable number. It will motivate only those believers whose motivation stems from a positive source: "I want that," while fear of Hell will be completely unproductive for that same group of people because it won`t motivate them as much.

On the other hand, the concept of Hell serves a group of believers who aren`t motivated by awaiting bliss, meaning that for them Heaven isn`t a good enough reason to be leading a worthy and honest life. For that particular group, fear is a great motivator: if you will not be living righteously, you will burn in Hell. Using that strategy, both extremist groups are cunningly covered and both of them will be motivated to do good, only they will be motivated to do so for different reasons.

Work place motivation

Jack Welch demonstrated the same two sources motivation principle implementing a fear of loss and a wish to progress model in General Electrics. As Jack explains in his book *Winning*, every year he would fire 10 percent of the lowest ranking managers, while he would reward the top ranking 20 percent in terms of bonuses, shares and other stimulations. No matter how much the company would prosper every year and no matter how much the employees would excel, the same percentage would always be rewarded and fired. That can hypothetically mean that if an employee was top ranking for two years in a row, and due to a general effectiveness rise of a

100 percent, that same employee could find himself, according to the evaluation criteria, in the last 10 percent ergo, discharged in spite of his former accomplishments. Adding a two direction motivation: fear of loss and wish to progress, Welch covered both motivational directions and the result of that, by some deemed an inhuman motivational model, in just a couple of years GE achieved a remarkable upraise.

In whichever direction a motivation pulls, it`s useful because it urges us to move and achieve a wanted change. What is important to emphasize though, is that negative motivation will influence an individual strongly at first in order to move him away from the undesirable source. However it`s highly unlikely that negative motivation will be a permanently sustainable state. On the other hand, a high desire or yearning for a certain object isn`t as strong a trigger, but maintaining that state is desirable if we`re dedicated to a long-term goal. In order for us to understand it better, we must be aware where exactly our source of motivation lies.

It`s known that a majority of self-made successful and rich people were born poor. The state in which they had been living was so unbearable and made them feel so unhappy that while still in childhood they made a resolution: "I don`t want this. I have to get out of this. I must be successful. My children won`t live the way I`m living and so I have to do whatever it takes for them to have a better childhood." These words show a negative source of motivation because the emphasis is on the thing the person wants to avoid: I want to avoid this kind of lifestyle for my children. In this case there is a clear definition of the UNWANTED thing while the definition of the WANTED thing is missing. The only thing that is actually defined is that the wanted state needs to be different from the present one, just that the person speaking doesn`t know what that state should look like. He or she only knows that it mustn`t be like the present one.

The word must points to an inner command, or more precisely necessity and exclusivity. Must is a negative word because it limits the possibility of choice to only one choice, that one choice being moving away from the unwanted state.

When we don`t know exactly what we want, we can`t expect a positive motivation. To state, "I want a better life." Is a somewhat positive statement because it translates: "I don`t want the life I`m having right this moment," but it doesn`t actually translate what kind of life it is that one wants. In this case, the person`s behavior is focused only on moving away, which can inevitably lead to detrimental consequences.

Let me give you an example:

A person says: "I want to be rich."
"How come you want to be rich?" – "Because I hate the state of poverty I`m in."
When the person says he wants to be rich, we can naively assume here lies a positive motivation, but as soon as we ask our next question, "Why do you want that or how come it`s important to you", we receive an answer, which includes negations and negative words. Those words imply a negative motivation, a motivation that strives just to move away from the present.

If that person answered, "Because I`ll have a more fulfilling, more beautiful and relaxed life," it would be the case of positive motivation because it clearly implies an aspiration towards something.

An answer to the 'why' question will determine if we`re on the right track. It`s a good idea to put it into practice in your own environment by asking your friends two questions. Since you know them, you can ask them questions concerning the things they love.
First question: "Why is it important for you to eat ice cream?"
Then listen carefully to what your friend will say. After that pose another question: "Why is it important for you to clean your apartment?"
When you have both pieces of information, compare the content. In what answer do you find negations and necessities such as: I must, it`s necessary, I have to. Are there negations and necessities in the answer to the first question? Most probably not because your friend likes ice cream and so you find a positive motivation, as opposed to let`s assume, cleaning the apartment, for which your friend is negatively motivated.

Why do self made millionaires often experience early failure?

Example: I want to be rich, successful, and thin

I don`t want to be poor, unsuccessful, fat – is a current state and a current source of motivation.

The example above shows a trajectory from the current state towards the wanted state. Before the wanted state is reached, the potential rich person who is born in poverty stumbles and comes back to the starting point – poverty. The reason for this is simple. If that person had a negative motivation: "I want to be rich because I can`t stand this poverty anymore," this means that his starting point is the state of poverty he wants to get out of. The person is at first extremely motivated with that escape and day by day achieves better results, but at one stage fails. The person failed because he distanced himself from the original starting point of motivation, the point in which the motivation is strongest. The more he distances himself from that point, the more the motivation will be weakening, eventually disappearing. This is the moment where our potential rich person makes his fatal mistake, unconsciously sabotaging himself. The reason he unconsciously sabotages himself lies in the motivation loss and falling back to the place where this motivation is the strongest, in order to recuperate. The closer he steps to the source, the stronger the motivation gets; the further he distances himself from the source, the weaker the motivation gets.

To further clarify, let`s play with my weight loss example.

I wanted to lose 17.6 pounds in a month so the first thing I did was meet with a nutritionist and a professional coach. After I dealing with my diet, I started going to the gym and took up running. In the gym I had a personal coach who additionally motivated me. After three weeks, I had lost 11 pounds and I found myself on the way to triumph. I want to point out that this was the case of negative motivation; that is I wanted to distance myself from the fatness. So after the loss of 11 pounds I still didn`t reach my goal, then again I distanced myself from the motivation source and the frustration slowly began to vanish. One day, at the gym, I stood on that treadmill and was running for about 5 minutes when a 350 pound man entered the gym and planted himself on an orbitrek next to me. As

I'm still running, my gaze falls on that man from time to time. I notice he's starting to sweat and that while wiping off the sweat from his forehead, he makes torturing noises that signal he must be killing himself. The next minute I hear a voice inside my head say, "What would that guy give to have a body like you!" That was my last trip to the gym; I dropped my outcome and the pounds returned.

Analysis
After I distanced myself considerably from my source of motivation by taking off 11 pounds, the motivation weakened and the overweight man came just at the right time to finish me off. The moment I compared myself to a person who found himself in a worse position than me, my motivation was completely destroyed. What would have happened if instead of the overweight guy, a Greek god look-alike showed up? Wouldn't my motivation be different? It most definitely would.

One other problem with which we're going to be dealing with is the issue of how to maintain motivation in that in-between world – the place in between the desire for pleasure and distance from pain. In order to consciously decide to change, we must understand what motivates us in a certain context. And that is our first step, our starting point.

Plant the seeds of motivation

One entrepreneur friend of mine hired a single mother of two, who was in the middle of a battle for survival. After a couple of months he wasn't satisfied with the way she worked and he tried to stimulate her. He didn't have the heart to tell her he wasn't satisfied, so he attempted to influence her behavior in the following way: "Dear Mary," he said, "If you put in an extra effort this month and if you produce more results compared to the previous month, I'll reward you with a 15 percent bonus." After a month, Mary had an even lower result than before the bonus was promised. My friend continued to engage himself in helping the woman, promising her things for her to react and still her results were dropping by the minute. How come? The answer is simple. Considering that Mary's biggest value was surviving, that value was met by the mere fact she had a job. She earns a fixed salary, a sure income that provides her and her children an adequate life. Trying to reward Mary with an extra bonus on her salary, in other words positive motivation, proved unsuccessful simply because her problem was already solved. This created an interesting dynamic. My friend didn`t want to lay her off out of pity so he transferred all of the responsibility onto himself. After he familiarized me with the situation, it was as plain as the nose on my face. If he wanted to motivate Mary, it`s imperative that he clearly state, "Mary, honestly I`m not satisfied with your work, and as I`m aware of your situation I`m ready to give you another chance. Unless you handle x number of clients in the next 30 days, that being the usual norm, your salary will decreased by 20 percent. If you fail to make the norm the following month also, our paths must part. The opportunity lies in front of you, it`s nothing personal but refers only to the contribution you`re making to the company. I imagine that you`ll surely find a more suitable company to work for if this proves too much for you." In the first 30 days, Mary handled more clients than in the two previous months. The key to Mary`s success was simple. Her employer threatened to shake her survival, the starting point of her motivation, which alternatively triggered the motivation itself.

Everybody can be motivated. We just need to be aware what the needs or values the other person holds dear. The high achievers verbalizing ambition will most surely be motivated with rewards, because rewards symbolize their personal value and to them success is a matter of self-respect. While people who verbalize security as their main value, on the other hand, can only be stimulated by fear of a possible security loss.

Imagine two situations. Your superior approaches you and says:
Dear xx, if you make us 10 percent more profit than the previous month, you`ll get a bonus of 20 percent.

Or

Dear xx, if you don`t make us 10 percent more profit than the previous month, you`ll lose 20 percent of your current monthly income.

Which sentence motivates you more in a job context?

The key in achieving a personal development shift or at least just one behavioral pattern shift, doesn`t lie in positive thinking. Instead it`s hidden in finding the right direction of personal motivation inside a certain frame. If you have already tried a few times to change a pattern and failed, it`s most probably a case of negative motivation direction and you`re finding yourself in a starting and quitting loop. When frustration peaks, value is triggered and as soon as you move away from this state, value calms down and disappears, leaving you out of the loop. Overweight people call this famous loop the "yo-yo effect". The lower yo triggers motivation through frustration and pain while the upper yo kills the motivation. When a person who wants to lose weight would have a stable lower yo starting point motivation, that person would consciously and constantly think about what to put in the mouth. Like with the macrobiotic example, the easiest way the person is to enhance his or her value, which will alternatively trigger the motivation, is for the person to become a total calorie-calculating-diet-tips-giving freak. Funny, true and most of all efficient. This kind of possessed approach works because here we have a certain identity addition or even upgrade. You probably know a person who smoked for 2-3 packs a day for decades, and when that person stopped smoking, he or she began to preach about how smoking is not only bad for your health, but also unnecessary.

Goal: Motivation development

Get to know your values and the direction from which they are triggered because it represents a crucial step towards the wanted state.

A simple motivation/value influencing strategy to use in the case you don`t have handy a person who would assist you by putting a gun against your head (Raymond). You will get values out of your mind by asking yourself these questions:

"What is important to me? What else? What else? What else?"

Most likely you`ll be defining your values with nouns. Those are words like: security, freedom, love, pleasure, relaxation and money, etc.

When you have all the answers, ask yourself a new question: "Why it is important for me to have security? Why is it important for me to have relaxation?"

You may notice a negative motivation pattern in your answers, such as: "Security is important for me because I want to feed all my children." Instead, define the action in a following way: "If I don`t do a, b, c on a daily basis, my children will be hungry." When you say the statement this way you`ll feel an immediate call for action.

If positive motivation is the case, say the statement in the following way: "I will do a, b, c to achieve security." Most likely in this case negative motivation will be involved, but make sure to check anyway by saying both sentences out loud. Your gut feeling will very clearly tell you which one motivates you more.

If the desired state/value is specific, like for example pass a test, clean the apartment, write an article or finish education, and somehow you`re not managing to motivate yourself accordingly, probably the sentence you`re saying to yourself is: "It would be good to pass a test/clean the apartment/write an article...or I should pass a test/clean the apartment/write an article."
Immediately reformulate the beginning of the sentence: "I must study for the exam/clean the apartment/write an article."

This should create a more serious internal state towards taking action. If it`s working, reformulate the beginnings of all the sentences you`re telling yourself beginning with: I should, it would be good etc.

The word MUST is a powerful trigger.

Take my motivation to finish college, for example.. As I started earning for a living I didn`t recognize any value for my future life in finishing college. Having been left with only a few exams more, for years I didn`t make further progress because no kind of motivation existed. I had found neither a positive or negative one. I wouldn`t be gaining a thing by finishing college because anyhow I wouldn`t choose to practice my profession. I wouldn`t be losing anything because I had already been earning good money and had been appreciated in what I do. In short, I didn't have a clear value. The value could have been credibility. My role would have been worth more if I became a teacher, but in my head that wasn't a good enough motivation until I found an extremely powerful pattern.

The pattern looks like this:

I would rather achieve **A** than live to see **B**

A represents that activity towards which I simply can't motivate myself, and **B** represents something even worse. You're already assuming what's happening here is enhancing negative motivation, and it really is working, since after that I've finished college in just a few months.

After that, just one sentence won't do the trick: I would rather achieve **A** than live to see **B**. Continue on forming sentences until the moment comes when you realize the worst thing that'll happen if you don't take action. For me and my decision to finish college, it took until **E**.

1st sentence: I would rather achieve **A** than live to see **B**.
2nd sentence: I would rather achieve **B** than live to see **C**.
3rd sentence: I would rather achieve **C** than live to see **D**.
4th sentence: I would rather achieve **D** than live to see **E**.
5th sentence: I would rather achieve **E** than live to see **F**.

Always go one step further than you think is enough. When you come to the worst possible outcome, let's say that's **H,** you will say the following sentence:
I would rather achieve **A** than live to see **H**!

There's no help for the person if this pattern doesn't immediately shake values and doesn't create instant and strong motivation towards a solution in the quickest time span.

My college example looked like this:
1st sentence: I would rather finish college than have my family constantly remind me of my unfinished task.
2nd sentence: I would rather have my family constantly remind me of my unfinished task than have the possibility of loosing credibility with my potential clients.

3rd sentence: I would rather lose credibility with my potential clients than get out of the business I love.
4th sentence: I would rather fail at my business than consider the possibility of failing to take care of my family.

I would rather finish college than even consider the possibility of failing to take care of my family.

Logic doesn`t have to be involved, all that`s important is that you - follow your stream of thoughts. To finish off with, we`re combining **A** with **E or F**.

Just try and be amazed with the results.

POWERFUL vs. POWERLESS PERSONAL BELIEFS

All personal breakthroughs begin with a change in beliefs

This section is about how our beliefs block us and how they can create new resources for us. All personal breakthroughs begin with a change in beliefs. Beliefs represent one of the largest behavioral frameworks. When you really believe in something, you will behave in congruence with that belief. I mentioned that beliefs and values are together located on the same level, right underneath identity and what`s also important to note is that beliefs and values strongly correlate.

Personal beliefs can limit us or create new resources

Beliefs are those tools that support our values and consolidate them. If we carry a value within us but we don`t believe that accomplishment of that value is possible, the negative belief will strongly influence the value in way that we will eventually renounce it. Values and beliefs have to be synchronized; otherwise strong frustration, neglect or renunciation of the value will occur. It`s also important to note that beliefs, if limiting – block our behaviors, if empowering – create our behavioral resources that in return lead us to achieving wanted goals. Let me give you an example that will illustrate the connection between values and beliefs and their influence on behavior.

Limiting beliefs that cost us money

A man owned a 70 m² business space, situated in a great city center location. He inherited that space in 1991. What he wanted to do - which is the targeted value for him - was to get the best rental price. His personal belief was: the rental of that space`s worth $1500 per month and I`m not giving it out for a cent less. The space was partially finished, without proper flooring, toilet, and plumbing. You could see only walls and lights. Business men who were interested would often come to see the place and as soon as they heard the starting price and approximate probable investments, they would leave. Of course, not without having tried to negotiate a better price with respect to the needed investments but without much success because the owner firmly stated that place is worth $1500 and not a cent less. His friends convinced him to lower the price just for one year, at least until the person puts everything into order. Later, they said, you`ll be able to get the price you`re aiming at, even more because the place will be fixed up. The man cold-bloodedly ignored this advice stating, "I know how much my place`s worth and I`m not lowering my price. I`ll show you I can find a person who is willing to pay the money (identity level belief)." Years go by and the place remained empty until the end of 2007. That year he managed to rent it out for the aimed price. You couldn`t imagine the owner`s response to his friends. He was thrilled, "I told you I could find a person who would take it into lease for $1500 per month!"

So, the space was remaining empty for 16 years and that didn`t stop the owner to lower his price because lowering the price would mean running over his identity based belief: "I will find XYZ." Can you imagine the very worst-case scenario where the owner leased out the place for free three consecutive years (1991-1994) under the condition it gets furnished? After that he could have asked a minimum of $1500 since he would have some kind of value to offer. And if we take this 16 year period from which three years were free of charge, we come to an amount of $234,000 for the whole time the place stood empty. Why didn't the owner consider this? Why didn't he lower the price and make financial gain while this way he was at a sure loss? The reason: Because it is of utmost importance to every person on this planet to be right than anything else. The owner was ecstatic 16 years later when he succeeded, according to his own standards. He was screaming, "I did it! I was right and you were wrong!"

Beliefs drive us – they can cause us to lose our mind, and this example vividly shows we often do. Personally I believe the protagonist of the above story never thought about my calculation, because the foreseen profit value was below the "I`m right" value, which the mentioned beliefs completely supported.

Beliefs cover very important parts of our mental set and consequently have a major impact on our lives. They are being formed directly or indirectly through experience and as you have had the chance to see in the previously mentioned examples, it`s very difficult for us to change them rationally. Beliefs represent our personal judgments and evaluations, both about ourselves and the world around us. Considering that a belief is a result of experience and it symbolizes the truth, it can only be altered if a person lives through an experience that considerably differs from the previous one. This line of reasoning leads us to believe that the truth is the thing we believe in. Our personal truth depends only on input gathered from the experience we've acquired up to now. Our beliefs about the world, economy, politics, ourselves, possible/impossible things substantially influence our daily efficiency or lack of it.

Response expectancy belief and behavior generator

A good example of powerful and powerless beliefs is a "four minute mile", described by Dilts in his book *Sleight of Mouth*: "Until May 6th 1954 there was a belief that four minutes is an insurmountable barrier under which a human body can`t run a mile. During the whole nine years before the historical event when Roger Banister surmounted the barrier, no other runner didn`t even come close. Only six weeks after that event, the Australian runner John Lundy managed to outdo Banister`s record for one second. The nine following years brought over 200 runners who successfully ran a mile under four minutes.

The conclusion is that beliefs are very powerful mechanism with which we form our framework. It`s difficult to get out of the frame unless we believe it can be done or, as in the four minute mile example, somebody proves it can be done. The moment a single person breaks the frame of impossible it creates a brand new representation inside our personal belief system. Placebo effect holds a remarkable place in the way beliefs influence body and mind."

Dilts continues: "Expectation that something good or bad will happen in the future comes out of a belief, more precisely, expectation is a belief. Response expectancy is expecting an event, regardless of the fact if it is a positive one or a negative one. The person believes that these events will occur as a result of actions taken at a certain point. The placebo effect nicely depicts the influence of response expectancy. Placebo effect manifests itself when there is a positive reaction to a psychologically negative medicine flour pill, a milk substance capsule, sugar pill or some other inert ingredient. The patient is brought a (placebo) pill and it`s emphasized that this pill will induce a positive effect, which very often it does. The placebo has an extremely high success rate. In average, placebo functions equally well as a real medicine in one third of the cases.

One study tried to approach the placebo effect from a different angle. In that particular study they had an intention to test in what extent does a group of respondent react to a placebo the same way as they do on a real medicine, in this case morphine. Study results showed that 95 percent placebo respondents reacted positively on morphine. For comparison purposes, only 54 percent test subjects who didn`t react to placebo reacted to morphine, the rest of them didn`t react to morphine at all. The placebo effect (person`s response expectancy) is a vital human behavior and behavior shift component. Many beliefs have a strong connection with outcome expectancy, in other words if you don`t believe you will achieve a started outcome/you don`t possess the required resources and values there isn`t the slightest chance that particular outcome be achieved." *(Beliefs: Pathways to Health and Well-Being)*

To additionally support the thesis, let me give you a personal example.
I was born and raised to believe in astrology and tarot. Ten years ago I was going through a rough period in my life. I was a teenager and from that perspective, life can seem difficult, can`t it? I felt like

nothing I do turns out right. I was in a relationship that was all but a relationship, which would complete me, so beginning in April that year; I decided to dial a tarot hot line. A very pleasant lady picked up the phone, she was full of understanding and I felt the lady was a professional.

I asked her a question, "What will become of me? What will become of my relationship? Will I find a nice girl if this doesn't work out?"

To all of my questions, the lady answered explicitly, "Sasha", she said, "the relationship you are currently involved in isn't good for you and this relationship will end mid May."

To my question of what would happen then she told me that for the following few months, nothing of significance would happen but mid June here would be a surprise waiting for me. I would meet a wonderful girl and engage in a relationship with her. That relationship would be everything I want and need but didn't have this moment.

I wanted to confirm so I said, "This is really going to happen?" to which she replied, "Yes, just wait and see." This is where our conversation ended.

I ended the relationship with my girlfriend on May 10th, just as the pleasant lady predicted. For the next few days, nothing of importance happened, mid June was slowly approaching and I was all the more excited because I knew: If she correctly predicted the break up and if she correctly predicted nothing important would happen in the months following the break up, then the third prediction must happen mid June. It was June 14 2000 in afternoon when I started calling up friends to arrange a night out. What happened next was something that never happened to me before. Not a single friend was willing to go out with me that night! Some of them I even called a few times, but all of them sabotaged me. I was left alone. That was the time when we would always go in groups of at least five and to up to a dozen people. The thing is, if there would be five party applicants, we would seriously consider going out and under that number we wouldn't cross. Four interested party applicants – no party. In that case we would simply postpone the party for some other time when more of us would gather. I don't know why, but it was always like that.

Authority: a powerful influence

The time went by and I still didn't find anybody to go out with. I was so desperate that I even called people I barely knew. It was no use. That day not a single soul budged. It was already 9 pm and I said to myself, "You mustn't miss this chance under any condition. If you don't go out now, even if it means going out alone, the opportunity will be wasted and what the pleasant tarot lady predicted won't happen. And if that doesn't happen today, it all goes down the drain." You know what happened next. Despite of all the limitations, I decided to go out alone for the first time in my life. I walked into a club and waited for midnight to come. Why midnight? Because the pleasant tarot lady said mid June and June 14th is not the middle. After the clock ticked midnight, I noticed a nice looking girl and approached her. Additionally this was the first time in my life up to that point that I approached a girl so confidently and boldly that I surprised myself. And why wouldn't I be confident when I know how the story ends? I don't have anything to be afraid of, do I? After that night followed a wonderful relationship with a wonderful girl. The pleasant tarot lady was right in everything. Only a few years later did I realize this whole experience was response expectancy.

The next example refers to power of the people we trust, authority power.

During my senior year in college, I did practical work in a correctional facility. The age span of the children was from 12 and 16. They were a group of the most hyperactive children I have ever seen. One boy was prominently hyperactive. He was perpetually on the move, thinking about his next prank. Not long after that, this boy got sick waking up with a temperature of 40 degrees Celsius. He spent the whole day in bed not feeling any better. Towards the evening, the facility's staff member brought the boy to his office to measure his temperature. I was also in that room and was looking at the poor boy sweating, red eyes and face, visibly exhausted from the temperature - I couldn't bear to see him looking like that. At that point I already knew a few things about belief magic so I decided to help him.

I approached the boy and asked him a question, "Do you know what some people call me?"

The boy shook his head.

"They call me the wizard," I replied "Do you want to see some magic?"

"Yes, show me!" the boy said

I wanted to confirm: "Are you sure?"

The boy was sure. I asked him, "Where does it hurt the most?"

"Inside my head," the boy pointed to his right frontal lobe with his finger.

Then I put my index finger on the opposite lobe. "Ok, now you`re going to transfer that pain to the place I just touched you with my finger. All right?" I stated this in an authoritative way.

The boy looked a bit confused because he didn`t understand what I wanted from him. I hurried him up with the same firm tone, "Did you do it already??"

"Ok, ok, I`m doing it, wait," he panted.

Standing above him, I kept talking by saying, "You have to do it faster. Faster."

"Just about finished," the boy was really trying. And after 30 seconds he said, "Did it!"

I look over: "Good. Great. Now what you`re going to do is transfer all that pain that you put in that particular spot into my finger. All right?"

The boy agreed. I urged him to let me know the moment when nothing, absolutely nothing of the feeling is left in his head.

After a few second the boy screams, "Did it!"

At that point I remove my index finger from his temple, position it right in front of him, snap my fingers and say with a smile," Disappeared! The magic worked!" I looked at the boy`s face and notice there`s no more redness, blurry eyes or sweat on his face. All of a sudden the boy stands up and said, "Wow, I feel better already, I`m healthy now. Thanks!"

What exactly did I do? Nothing special, actually. I just led him to believe I possessed the power to help him with my "I`m a wizard" sentence. In the case of the boy not accepting that sentence as the truth, no magic or recovery would happen.

Similarly, healing sessions are often carried out. People with health issues are ready to travel for miles and miles to be cured. In the end, results really happen to some extent. But did the designated healer really cure them or was it their belief they were going to be cured if they decidedly travel so many miles?

Miligram`s experiment

The Milgram experiment on obedience to authority figures was a series of notable social psychology experiments conducted by Yale University psychologist Stanley Milgram. This experiment measured the willingness of study participants to obey an authority figure that instructed them to perform acts that conflicted with their personal conscience. The experiments began in July 1961, three months after the start of the trial of German Nazi war criminal Adolf Eichmann in Jerusalem. Milgram devised his psychological study to answer the question: "Was it that Eichmann and his accomplices in the Holocaust had mutual intent, in at least with regard to the goals of the Holocaust?" In other words, "Was there a mutual sense of morality among those involved?" Milgram's testing suggested that it could have been that the millions of accomplices were merely following orders, despite violating their deepest moral beliefs.

The experiment
Three people were involved: the one running the experiment (authority), the subject of the experiment (a volunteer), and a confederate pretending to be a volunteer. These three persons fill three distinct roles: The Experimenter (an authoritative role), The Teacher (a role intended to obey the orders of The Experimenter), and The Learner (the recipient of stimulus from The Teacher). The subject and the actor both drew slips of paper to determine their roles, but unknown to the subject, both slips said "Teacher". The actor would always claim to have drawn the slip that read "Learner", thus guaranteeing that the subject would always be the "Teacher". At this point, the "Teacher" and "Learner" were separated into different rooms where they could communicate but not see each other. In one version of the experiment, the confederate was sure to mention to the participant that he had a heart condition.

The "Teacher" was given an electric shock from the electro-shock generator as a sample of the shock that the "Learner" would supposedly receive during the experiment. The "Teacher" was then given a list of word pairs, which he was to teach the learner. The teacher began by reading the list of word pairs to the learner. The teacher would then read the first word of each pair and read four possible answers. The learner would press a button to indicate his response. If the answer was incorrect, the teacher would administer a shock to the learner, with the voltage increasing in 15-volt increments for each wrong answer. If correct, the teacher would read the next word pair.

The subjects believed that for each wrong answer, the learner was receiving actual shocks. In reality, there were no shocks. After the confederate was separated from the subject, the confederate set up a tape recorder integrated with the electro-shock generator, which played pre-recorded sounds for each shock level. After a number of voltage level increases, the actor started to bang on the wall that separated him from the subject. After several times banging on the wall and complaining about his heart condition, all responses by the learner would cease.

At this point, many people indicated their desire to stop the experiment and check on the learner. Some test subjects paused at 135 volts and began to question the purpose of the experiment. Most continued after being assured that they would not be held responsible. A few subjects began to laugh nervously or exhibit other signs of extreme stress once they heard the screams of pain coming from the learner.

If at any time the subject indicated his desire to halt the experiment, he was given a succession of verbal prods by the experimenter, in this order:

1. Please continue.
2. The experiment requires that you continue.
3. It is absolutely essential that you continue.
4. You have no other choice; you must go on.

If the subject still wished to stop after all four successive verbal prods, the experiment was halted. Otherwise, it was halted after the subject had given the maximum 450-volt shock three times in succession.

Results
Before conducting the experiment, Milgram polled fourteen Yale University senior-year psychology majors to predict the behavior of 100 hypothetical teachers. All of the poll respondents believed that

only a very small fraction of teachers (the range was from zero to 3 out of 100, with an average of 1.2) would be prepared to inflict the maximum voltage. Milgram also informally polled his colleagues and found that they, too, believed very few subjects would progress beyond a very strong shock. Milgram also polled forty psychiatrists from a medical school and they believed that by the tenth shock, when the victim demands to be free, most subjects would stop the experiment. They predicted that by the 300 volt shock, when the victim refuses to answer, only 3.73 percent of the subjects would still continue and they believed that "only a little over one-tenth of one percent of the subjects would administer the highest shock on the board."

In Milgram's first set of experiments, 65 percent (26 of 40) of experiment participants administered the experiment's final massive 450-volt shock.

From Miligram's experiment we can deduce that despite personal moral from which our basic beliefs are based on what's right and wrong stem from, the influence from the environment and the white robe person representing authority, we're completely ready to believe we're doing the right thing.

Beliefs limit us in problem solving test

There is a test to demonstrate how our behavior and way of thinking are connected to our beliefs and problem solving strategies.

The task is to connect the nine dots with three lines. The lines have to be straight and they have to be made in one uninterrupted stroke.

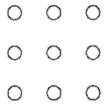

If you`re finding it difficult to solve this problem, the reason behind it isn`t intelligence. Instead, the reason is a belief that you`ve created long ago in your childhood and now that belief is stopping you from solving this problem. Think. And if you don`t come up with a solution you can find it at the end of this chapter.

Eradicate limiting beliefs that sabotage your desired state

You define a value. For example`s sake, let`s say your value is dancing. No matter if the value came from your wish to learn how to dance or other people`s expectations, like the case was with me. You must learn how to dance for your wedding day.

You may possess a value and yet on the other hand have a belief: "I can`t learn how to dance" or any other similar belief starting with the pattern: "I can`t XYZ."
You see, this belief is situated on the identity level ("I ") and with the strain of the best trainers in the world you won`t learn how to dance. Maybe you`ll learn the steps in the privacy of the training room, but you`ll never dare to use those steps in an actual public dancing

opportunity. The reason behind it is that your unchanged belief is stopping you. Limiting you. Even if that`s not the truth, **it`s your truth.**

A good trainer has to handle beliefs before anything else. The first belief he has to create is that the learning process is not only easy but also fun. Without that kind of conditioning, the wanted state and the wanted result will be missing.

There are a number of strategies on how to work on beliefs that limit our behavior that anybody can use without additional training. One of the easier strategies is autosuggestion. You`re probably familiar with Émil Coué`s statement: "Every day, in every way, I'm getting better and better." The principle is based on regular subconscious self-conviction that eventually works and in order to make this change, the statement must be specific. To get better and better isn`t specific enough because it doesn`t define the wanted state exactly.

If you have a belief that you can`t learn how to dance, the sentence, "Every day, in every way, I'm getting better and better" doesn`t cut it. For the sentence to have the desired effect, it would have to sound like this: "I am a person who is in the process of becoming a good/excellent dancer." Or "I believe that with my work, effort and training I become a person who enjoys dancing. With every next dancing training I become a more relaxed and better dancer."

***Notice that these sentences weren't written in the form "I am a great dancer" but "I am in the process of becoming a great dancer." The emphasis is on the process and here`s where people make the biggest mistake. If you believe you can`t dance and you suggest to your mind that you are a great dancer, your mind will automatically disregard the statement because at that particular moment it is simply not true. For that reason, instead of suggesting, "I am", the attention is directed to the process: "I am in a process/in the middle of becoming a XYZ."

Of course just saying the words and not acting upon it is a waste of time. To seal the wanted belief in your mind, it`s crucial to actively do something about it in order to connect it to a behavior or more precisely to a process. My personal development strategy learning path went on from autosuggestion and I can confirm they work. During my on process I discovered some additional strategies that also work and pretty quickly can dismantle old beliefs. The first strategy I personally use is a pattern with which I refer myself to the previous existing personal experience that already helped me to alter a belief.

My belief: "I can`t learn how to dance."

If we go from the self-convincing point of view, maybe one day we actually start to believe that we could dance, but for us time is of relevance. To achieve it, we choose the next sentence:
"Have I ever believed that I won`t be able to learn a thing and then I turned out surprised how fast I did it?"
"Have I ever believed that it`s going to take long for me to learn a thing and the opposite happened? I learnt it in x times less amount of time."

If the answer is still NO, which is almost impossible, let`s ask the next question:
"Have I ever made a wrong judgment?"

The answer here must be YES. And onto that yes comes:

"If I made a wrong judgment in the past, how can I be sure I`m not doing one right now? How do I know I can`t learn how to dance?"

One of my clients is an educational center owner. He was lucky enough to try out in practical sales environment the belief-altering pattern immediately after a two-day training on personal beliefs. A lady that previously signed up to one of his seminars called him and wanted to drop out. My client posed her a question. He asked, "Why would you like to cancel your participation?"
She replied: "I surfed a bit through the forums, talked to people I know and came to realize that this seminar is going to be too difficult for me. I don`t believe I could handle all the knowledge presented in your seminar." (An identity based belief)
"Let me ask you just one question", it was my client`s turn. "Have you ever before believed something is too difficult for you to handle and in the end it turned out to be easier than you imagined?"
The lady replied, "Yes, as a matter of fact I have."
His next question was: "If you already experienced that, how can you be sure you`re not experiencing the same thing now? I personally

believe that you can handle all the knowledge presented in my seminar."

"You know what? You`re right - I can handle it. I decide to go to your seminar. Thank you very much for motivating me, sir."

My client later gave me another feedback. They have a habit of sending a reminder for the seminar one week before it starts. From the 15 e-mail recipients, he got only one reply.

The reply came from that lady: "Thank you for the reminder", she wrote "I can`t wait to begin. The motivation that you gave me in our talk is still present and I`m very much excited about what`s ahead. See you on Monday. Thank you!"

My client didn`t convince the lady to attend his seminar. He only applied the learnt pattern and led the lady, now his client, to change her belief about her capabilities or better yet, about herself as somebody who believed it was impossible to handle all that knowledge. This strategy exists to dismantle beliefs and already at this point you made a good start in achieving a personal change, action and motivation in a certain area. But you still haven`t implanted a new belief. What you could do now is go with autosuggestion or you could try something even stronger.

Quick new powerful belief programming strategy

This consists of saying three statements that are undoubtedly truthful in our mind, and the fourth one is connected to our new desired belief.

For example: "I learned how to speak. I learned how to walk. I learned how to ride a bike. I will learn how to dance."

In that way you created a flow of irrefutable truths and put in something that will become the truth in our mind`s representation.

Most probably you`ve already heard about this strategy from sales calls representatives:

Sales representative: Hello
Me: Hello
Sales representative: Have I reached mister Sasha?
Me: Yes, you did.

Sales representative: So, you`re mister Sasha?
Me: Yes, I am.
Sales representative: Do you know a mister George Smith?
Me: Yes, I do.
Sales representative: Mister George Smith warmly recommends you as a person who is interested in the same things as....

In tele sales, when they induce a yes set, there is a 3 to 4 time's higher possibility that the answer to the next meeting, arrangement or question, will be yes. Let`s get back to our challenges, though. In order for it to be more successful, we can turn the strategy into a cause and effect statement.

"If I learned how to talk, if I learned how to walk, if I learned how to ride a bike, I will learn how to dance."

To strongly imprint the desired belief into your mind, it`s important to repeat the exact statement more than once. I usually run this strategy by myself when I detect a limiting belief.

Frequently I do it before bedtime and it looks like this:

"If I could learn how to speak, if I could learn how to walk, if I could learn how to ride a bike, I'll learn how to fly a plane. If I could learn how to write, if I could learn how to count, if I could learn how to drive a car, I'll learn how to fly a plane. If I could learn for the most difficult exam, if I could learn how to hold excellent presentation, if I could learn how to be more successful year after year and if I could earn more and more money, then I will learn how to fly a plane."

With this flow I always refer myself to a personal experience and the only thing that`s important for the first three statements is for them to be truthful. By doing that you neatly packed a new desired state to the place in your mind where all the other previously insurmountable and now joyful experiences hide. Right?

Task solution:

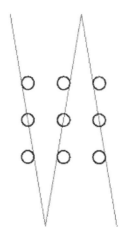

If you immediately turned to this page, I suspect you didn`t manage to solve the task. The reason for failure lies not in intelligence but in the belief we adopted when we were just children, doodling in our coloring book. During this activity, our motoric system still wasn`t developed enough and we would often cross the predetermined lines. When that happened, our teacher or parent used to say, "Color inside the lines. Don`t go outside the lines." Because of that experience, the first strategy of solving this task is staying inside the lines, at least for most of us. It doesn`t occur to us that we could leave the lines.

With these topics I complete the part about value, beliefs and identity influence, their mutual correlation and impact on our behavior. In the next chapters, you will understand how we receive, process and act under the influence of information coming from our environment. You will also understand to what extent we actually posses a free choice. It is not my intention to disregard the importance of genotype on how we currently see ourselves, people around us and the world as a whole. I will still transfer the bigger part of the influence to all of the environmental inputs that determined our belief, value, behavior, capability system and eventually our Identity.

WHY WE OFTEN DON`T UNDERSTAND OURSELVES OR OTHERS

Analogue and digital information

You must have heard of the terms analogue and digital. Any given information can be either analogue or digital. In many ways they support understanding and Misunderstanding. Today`s computers work exclusively with digital information, while we humans receive and process information both in an analogue and digital way. Digital information is characterized by limited number of values while analogue information have unlimited number of values.

What does this information look like?

Let`s take the light bulb example. Most of us have a switch with which we turn the lights on and off. When we press the switch in one direction, the light is on and when we press it in another direction it`s off. The digital information in this case is zero or one:

1=light on
0=light off

If we install a light-dimming regulator on the switch, then we have ourselves a possibility of an analogue adjustment. First we turn the light on digitally, pressing the one and then we adjust the light intensity. That means digital information in this example has only two states (light either exists or doesn't exist) and analogue information has an unlimited number of states because by moving the regulator just a little bit, we get different information. The major feature of digital information is rigidness while one of analogue information is flexibility, because of its number of states. What`s also important to note here is that an analogue information isn`t as precise as a digital one.
No matter how much we move the regulator while the light is on, the digital form is satisfied, the light exists. When we return the switch to the zero position, there is no light and therefore the regulator doesn`t have a function.

Another example is the TV signal. Analogue signals were originally used to broadcast picture, as opposed to today when we use the digital one. With the analogue signal, depending on the antenna location and position, we would get a better, slightly better, not so good or awful picture. Luckily, today`s TV sets receive a digital signal which means if a signal exists (1) we enjoy a perfect picture and if not or if it`s bad, we simply don`t receive a visual input (0).

This is similar to the light bulb example. There`s no possibility that the light is slightly lit or a bit down. Using a digital system, it`s either, or. What happens when we turn just one of the zeros into a one and just one into a zero? Automatically the meaning also changes. During a movie, if a signal is tampered with, the screen will show little squares or the TV will let us know there`s no signal because it received invalid data – invalid zeros and ones. In general, the digital information has to be very accurate to be able to give a clear input/output. On the contrary, the analogue information doesn`t have to be that accurate because with it the TV receives something, it may be a blurry but still recognizable picture, a dashed picture or in the best case, a perfect picture just like a digital signal one.

The ways in which we receive, process, organize and interpret information

While transmitting the information during communication, we use analogue and digital information. We receive information from the outside world through our five senses: vision, hearing, touch, smell and taste. They arouse certain sensations in us and trigger the same experience, as we often misguidedly assume. You would be surprised how misguidedly!

Let me explain. I`ll use a simplified four category division of this information:
1. Visual information input (marked V)
2. Auditory information input (marked A)
3. Kinesthetic information input (marked K)
4. Digital information input – using words (marked D)

The first three information categories refer to analogue information and the fourth is digital. In everyday communication we use arms, legs, our head, eyes, voice, and words in order to convey certain information or experience to the recipient.

We can divide our communication channels to:
1. Verbal: words, content
2. Paraverbal: the quality of the voice without content: rhythm, intonation, volume, and tempo
3. Nonverbal: gesticulation, mimics, and body posture.

Taking into consideration the digital and analogue nature of information, we can assign communication channels a type of information. I mentioned that digital information has to be very accurate for the message to be clear and by changing just one symbol, we get a different output. With analogue information, it doesn't have to be as accurate because it carries a range of states. Having this in mind, what do you think about which communication channel would send a digital message and which one would send an analogue one and why?

Same piece of information, different set of meaning

Analogue information is transmitted through the nonverbal and paraverbal channel, meaning voice and body posture, while digital information is transmitted through the verbal channel.
Let's take this for an example:
The English language has 26 symbols and thanks to their numerous combinations we form words, for which we then create meaning. Let's take a three symbol word and see what happens if we just change one of the symbols:

SAT
PAT
FAT
BAT
CAT
RAT
HAT
MAT

The verbal or content information is the only one that belongs to a digital category because by changing just one symbol, we lose the meaning of the original information. And we go back to the digital accuracy importance rule.

Body posture, gesticulation and voice qualities belong under the analogue category information because everybody pronounces a sentence differently. On my introduction seminars I always ask a question: Seeing that we communicate with content that is digital information, how big a percentage do you think we're conveying in that way? In other words, from 100 percent of the sent information, how many would you attribute to content (digital), how many to voice quality and how many for gesticulation?

Digital clarity

In order for us to be understood in the process of communication, we must communicate with content, right? Does that mean that content deserves all the credit for message clarity? Participants usually say yes. They are convinced that content carries between 70 and 95 percent of meaning.

After that I choose two participants and tell one of them to explain the word "spiral" using only words without any kind of gesticulation. Almost always participant's hands twitch in front of them and I warn them again not to use gesticulation and to try again. It's almost impossible to describe a spiral for everybody to understand exactly what you mean without using your body as a tool. If you're suspicious, try for yourself.

The answer to the previously asked percentage question:
- 7 % words – verbal communication– digital channel
- 38 % voice – paraverbal communication – analogue channel
- 55 % gesticulation – nonverbal communication – analogue channel

In order to transfer as accurate information as possible, we have to use all the channels available, even though 93 percent of a 100 goes to the analogue channels and only 7 percent to the digital one. If you're still doubtful, try to ask a person in the street to give you point A to point B directions without using gesticulation. Or try to explain for yourself to somebody else how to get from here to the railway station, and you`ll see what I mean.

How many times were we misunderstood or didn`t understand at all a message in the way were meant to? Didn`t it become an everyday thing? One more message meaning influence is made through the channel it`s been received. For example, a spoken word will trigger different meaning than a visual symbol, touch, smell, etc. The same word spoken out with a different tonality accompanied with different nonverbal expression will convey a totally different meaning.

Martha just came back from a hair stylist. She comes back and you notice her:
1. "Martha, your hair style is great. Who did it?" (Using gesticulation you acknowledge that you`re really interested)
2. "Martha, your hair style is great. Who did it?" (Through a smirk in a provocation attempt)

In both cases we have completely the same accurate digital information, but the way we say it is different. And the way Martha receives these two messages is incomparable. Experts also confirm that the majority of meaning is conveyed through analogy.

When I was a college sophomore, I was in a class called Developmental Psychology. During one lecture we received a questionnaire, due filled out till next lecture. The questionnaire consisted of very specific inquiries like date of birth, number of pounds you weigh, when you learned how to walk, did you crawl, etc. On the next lecture the task was for all students to classify this information in a common chart so that everything could be in one place.

When it was my turn, the chart was already half full so I could clearly see what my colleagues filled in before me. The most interesting column for our current topic was the one where we should have stated if we crawled. The first 14 students answered with yes or no to that question and I noticed the 15th filled in: a little bit. That wasn`t the answer they were looking for because it was unspecific. If that student crawled a little this means he crawls and that`s a yes. What they wanted was an accurate digital either or information and the answer this student gave was analogue because it went outside the predetermined framework. The reason behind it is individual interpretation of words. This example of a specific digital information show how even answers to seemingly precise questions can be subjected to an analogue interpretation.

There`s one other important reason for understanding the distinction between analogue and digital information in human communication. We use digital language (content) but our interlocutor`s interpretation is always analogue, in other words, adjusted to his or her understanding of what a group of symbols means precisely. The majority of misunderstandings come just from that different analogue processing of the outside information, like the one in the following example.

Mum: "You said you were going to tidy up your room."
Child: "Mum, but I did tidy it up."
Mum: "You're lying, I was just now in your room and it`s messy."
Entering the room together
Child: "What`s messy here? It`s nice and tidy."
Mum: "You call that tidy?!"

The value here is mutual: a tidied up room
Criteria: analogue different

Each person recognize their own set of criteria based on which they interpret one and the same digital information that enters from the outside world and just that individual interpretation becomes a source of our misunderstandings.

MODEL OF THE WORLD

We build our own reality

"There are no two human beings that possess the same experience. Our model of the world is a result of our experience and it`s created to lead us through the world. Every one of us, based on our own experience creates a different model of the world, meaning that every human being lives in a different reality..."
A Korzybski, Science and Sanity

A map is not the territory, and a word is the term it denotes. Every one of us has a right to our own model of the world that will fit in our experience. We`re all creators of our world and we build our own individual reality.

Narrow comprehension - negative reaction

Imagine you`re at sea, on a pleasant vacation. You`ve found a beautiful hidden beach, from where you have a clear view of the sun until the moment it sets. The sea has completely calmed down in the cove that evening and you soak in the emotions that your senses are filled with. There is the smell of pine trees, sand and sea (kinesthetic). There is a beautiful display of colors that only the sun can create playing with light and reflection (visual). Only the sound of crickets and a few sea gulls interrupt the silence (auditive). Lying on your air mattress, you enjoy the sentiment, allowing the barely noticeable waves to softly cradle you and carry you from the shore - softly and slowly. In half an hour it took you barely 50 meters and you`re not bothered with it. Ah, what serenity. Suddenly from your right side, somewhere above you head, the peacefulness is disturbed by an abrupt splash. But it seemed far away. You don`t think much about it and continue to relax. The next moment, the splash happens on your left side, much closer and louder this time! You open your eyes and look in that direction. From the rippled sea, out comes a fin!

What do you think happens next? How do you react?

When I ask the same question during a seminar, I get different reactions: "I freeze, scream, jump off the mattress, start swimming desperately, etc." After the participants exhaust all the answers that cross their minds I curiously say, "I wasn't aware that all of you are afraid of dolphins? People usually like dolphins so I'm a bit dumbstruck that everybody here reacts in a funny way." At this point they start to laugh.

How do you know that a fin = shark = danger?

Interpreting the world based on own truth

Have any of us had a personal, real life experience with a shark or at least his fin? Most likely not, but we've watched the movie *Jaws*. In this case, the visual information of a fin emerging from the sea affects our sense of sight in a way that we tend to assume what is connected to the fin underneath the surface without actually seeing it. This is then analogue information, because the fin alone is imprecise information, which we unconsciously decided to interpret according to our closest association. In that way we formed a complete picture in our mind, whether or not we saw it completely.

Therefore, we can assume that experience doesn't have to be true and personally lived in order to evoke a certain reaction.

Although we want to believe we're objective, on examples like this, we see to what extent the information our senses receive are objective and to what extent they are under the influence of past experience and beliefs we implemented.
Imagine that a bushman child found itself in a situation like that, a child that never watched TV, read newspapers, books...and certainly didn't watch *Jaws*. If it found itself in the same situation, what do you think would happen? How would a child to whom a fin doesn't mean anything react?

Remember your own childhood and assume that child's behavior. That child would react with a curiosity and swim towards the fin, curious to find out what it is. The measure of precaution would depend on his age and attained experience.

Wrong presuppositions - undesirable outcomes

One of the fundamental NLP presuppositions is Alfred Korzibsky`s principle: A map is not the territory. According to that principle, we as human beings never have the opportunity to behold reality. The only reality we`re capable of beholding is the one inside of us.
The more experience we gather in life, the bigger our map becomes. That can both enrich and sabotage us. Let me show you what I mean in this example from Korzibsky.

"One day, Korzybski was giving a lecture to a group of students, and he interrupted the lesson suddenly in order to retrieve a packet of biscuits, wrapped in white paper, from his briefcase. He muttered that he just had to eat something, and he asked the students on the seats in the front row if they would also like a biscuit. A few students took a biscuit. "Nice biscuit, don't you think," said Korzybski, while he took a second one. The students were chewing vigorously. Then he tore the white paper from the biscuits, in order to reveal the original packaging. On it was a big picture of a dog's head and the words "Dog Cookies." The students looked at the package, and were shocked. Two of them wanted to vomit, put their hands in front of their mouths, and ran out of the lecture hall to the toilet. "You see," Korzybski remarked, "I have just demonstrated that people don't just eat food, but also words, and that the taste of the former is often outdone by the taste of the latter.""
(Essenties van NLP)

To sum it up, Korzibsky offered students biscuits. The biscuits were visually attractive. When the students put the biscuits in their mouths, they didn`t exhibit a negative reaction that might have happened if the biscuits weren`t tasty. After they ate the biscuits, they additionally confirmed they liked them. A simple story if it weren`t for another input in a form of a word that completely changes the situation. That new input turns something that was once tasty (sensory) into something disgusting. The senses convinced the students that the biscuits were tasteful and the new word gave a whole new meaning to the message, consequently changing the reaction. If they hadn't seen the dog logo, they would have been convinced the biscuits were delicious. And who knows, maybe they would ask the professor after the lecture where they could buy some more.

The process looked like this:
Biscuits = look good = I could try them
Biscuits = tasty = after they have been tried
Biscuits = for dogs = vomit and disgust

Sensory proof that something is tasty obviously isn`t enough because a word and a picture associated students to a content in their minds that belatedly created a meaning of disgust.

Personal belief and value influence our perception

We come to know the reality through our senses, more precisely through the filters of our senses. And our senses alone are limited. Considering we can`t experience reality, we`re forced to build and fill our personal maps that will represent reality for us. The structure of the maps will depend on the information we receive through our senses and the way that information links to our previous memory and other existing experiences. Specifically, those personal maps of the world are responsible for how we perceive certain situations and what meaning we appoint them. That generally leads us to the conclusion that all our outside stimulus reaction doesn`t depend on real reality but on the reality as we perceive it in our map.

Imagine, as you`re reading this book, that you see a snake slithering right towards you. Would you jump out of the chair? Would you scream? Or would you stay seated so as not to disturb it? Now, I want you to imagine how a herpetologist, a snake expert, would react. He would immediately know what to do. In an instant he would recognize whether the snake was poisonous or not, and how to deal with the situation. No matter what, the herpetologist would surely react with curiosity, wouldn`t he? What is the difference then, between most of us and the herpetologist? The difference lies in the richness of the map, the individual model of the world. That model of the world interprets the information in one map as: "Look how interesting this is!" and in the other: "Run, this is dangerous!"

Why do we behave the way we do? The world is so complicated and filled with different information that we are forced to simplify it in order to be able to comprehend it. And the maps that are being formed in that way are always selective because they leave out and merge information. We pay attention and focus on those aspects of the world that interest us and are important to us, while we ignore or delete others.

"In a forest walk, the impressions of an artist, a botanist and a lumberjack would be very different because they each have focus on different things and with that they create a different experience in that forest.

We use senses to get to know and to study the world. The world represents an unlimited variety of sensory experience and we are capable of comprehending just a small part of it. And that part that we do comprehend is censored by our unique cultural, language, value and belief experience. Everyone lives in their own unique reality, built on sensory impressions and individual life experience and everyone acts according to their own standing point. The way we simplify the world in order to understand it resembles the map drawing. Maps are selective: they leave out and merge information at the same time being invaluable when exploring an area. What kind of map you will create depends on the things you perceive and the place you want to arrive. The map isn't the place it describes. We perccive those aspects of the world that interest us, and ignore all the rest. The world is rich and the number of its various interpretations hasn't been exhausted yet.

They say a man turned to Picasso and asked him why he didn't paint people the way they really looked like in real life. Picasso was puzzled: "I really don't know what you mean."
The man then showed a picture of his wife: "Look," he said, "my wife, for example looks like this."
Picasso looked him and said with disbelief: "She's very small, isn't she? And flat also."

If you've ever walked down a pine forest, maybe you remember certain sensations. If you didn't have that opportunity, you most probably reconstructed experience from similar situations and used TV or other media material. Your experience was then a blend of memory and imagination. A great part of our thinking is usually a mixture of memorized and constructed sensations. The same neurological pathways are used for the internal display of experiences as for the experience itself. The same neurons create electrochemical charges measurable with special machines. The thought has a direct physical effect, the mind and the body form a single system. For a moment think about eating your favorite fruit. The fruit isn't real, but the saliva is." (Introducing NLP: Psychological Skills for Understanding and Influencing People, O'Connor and Seymour)

People possess a set of individual experiences that mold that person's reality and that reality is unique for that particular person, just like a fingerprint. Those models of the world or maps we form during our lifetime are based on our personal experience. The ways in which we perceive the world we live in are made up of an intricate net of habits, rules, values and beliefs. These are the differences that make us distinctive, that make us incomparable to any other person, more precisely from any other model of the world.

The meaning of an experience refers to a relationship our internal experience and outside occurrence have. This means that our internal experience of the outside occurrence will most probably be linked to a previous set of experiences connected to that particular occurrence more than with that particular occurrence. Stated in NLP language: different maps of the world will produce different internal meaning for completely the same information from our mutual territory.

Having a lot of money for some people means success, while for others it may mean a burden or a risk. Meaning of a state or situation is a natural consequence of the interpretation of our experience. The meaning we form and the way we form it mostly depends on the flexibility and richness of our internal representations of the world. A limited map of the world will most probably produce a limited understanding.

For example, going to school during wartime depended on the danger level. If immediate danger was expected or announced, school was not an option. Children being children, we would wish for an announcement of an immediate danger because in our then limited maps, this meant no school and no obligations. This is why we happily embraced the "savior" siren that would bring more holidays.

The meaning we get from a certain event or a stimulus largely depends on the context. The same message received in different contexts can create a completely different reaction. In other words it can hold a completely different meaning. For example, we will react differently if we hear a gunshot during a war or in the Olympic game stadium, we will react differently if we witness a knife murder in a dark city alley or in a theatre. Context perception is as important as our ability to create meaning.

Our personal intention presuppositions, that lie behind someone's behavior also create framework that affect our message interpretation. Once I commented on a social network posted picture with "hehe" and not long after that I received a message: "Why so mean Sasha? " I was surprised because "hehe" and "haha" hold completely the same meaning in my map, which wasn't the case in that person's map.

Cause and effect connection beliefs, between our perception of an event and our beliefs, refer to a greatly determine the meaning that each of us give to a certain event.

"If she doesn't call, it means she doesn't care about me!" The way I would show somebody I don't care (if I were the person behind the quote) is that I wouldn't return the call and that may not mean anything to the map of the person in question. That person might think that I don't want to be boring - that I want him or her to rest from me for a day. Surely that is one of the possible interpretations?

The influence beliefs have on our perception and understanding is best illustrated with this example.
A year ago I decided to buy a bike. I limited my budget to $500. Upon entering the first bike shop, I noticed a bike I would like to own. Considering 10 years have passed from the moment I last rode a bike, I couldn't say my bike knowledge was on a high level. For me, a bike is a bike. The price tag on that particular bike said $349. The price was acceptable. I called for a shopping assistant and told him:"

"Sir, I would like to buy this bike, "pointing with my hand on the exact bike I was talking about. The next moment the assistant was sighing and stuttered: "Sir, this is, in my humble opinion the best bike in the shop and the best in this rank on the market." He continues to talk about the bike with enthusiasm and evident excitement while I was thinking to myself what is all of this commotion about. It was just a $350 bike, why would he possibly talk so much about it and compliment it....I already said I would buy it...when suddenly I realized I should probably take one more look at the price tag....and it said $3449 I missed a digit. It all became clear - his effort and reaction. As a cycling beginner, I was not ready to invest that sum of money. Now it became awkward.

The point of this example is that up to that moment, in my map, in my mental frame, a bike that would cost $3500 didn`t exist. At least not in a shop where "normal" people buy bikes. The mental frames of our perception, in other words the frame through which we look at a certain situation, message or event, creates an internal frame through which we will filter a certain event and then we will pin a meaning to it. And the mental frame completely depends on our previous experience or education. My previous experience was that a bike could cost $1000 or maximum $2000, but no more than that. That kind of belief defined a frame through which my sensory perception simply didn`t perceive another digit. The meaning of a new stimulus is always a product of already existing beliefs and experiences. That experience defines all our understanding or misunderstanding in the following moments.
Every map, depending on the preferences of the person who created it, has a role to erase, distort and generalize certain aspects of a territory. This means that we will each perceive a territory differently.

Often a situation happens in which we stumble upon misunderstanding. Misunderstandings or conflicts are always a result of differently organized maps that represent the same territory.

Expand your personal model of the world

"Do not judge the Southerners because of their attitude and behavior because they are the people we would have been under the same circumstances."
Abraham Lincoln

Without any doubt, our surroundings created our maps, more precisely our experiences in that particular surrounding. As Lincoln put it, we can`t judge a person who owns a different map than ours. It isn`t a different map by accident. We mustn`t judge if we don`t understand. We can paraphrase the presumption; Map is not the Territory into: Respect the Map of Others; it is like that for a Reason. From that perspective it becomes clear that there`s no one true or right map of the world. Our map represents our individual viewpoint. Our map of reality can be poor/limited in one context and rich/wide in another, but absolute comprehension is still handicapped. The wider our map gets, the understanding of a certain territory is, leaving the map options to choose from a variety of behaviors.

Bandler and Grinder, the NLP founding fathers, explain how the creation of such a map looks like in one of their first books: "Imagine a child who sits for the first time in a rocking chair, gets carried away during the play and turns over together with the chair. The child can create a belief that rocking chairs are unstable and dangerous, that he will never sit on them without fear of caution. If a child matches that rocking chair with all the rocking chairs in the world, in his model of the world, than all the chairs come under the rule: "Don`t rock on the chair." But if a child creates a wider model of the world in which he differs regular chairs from rocking ones, it doesn`t create such a generalization and with that he has more behavior choices."
(*The Structure of Magic, Vol. 1: A Book About Language and Therapy*)

For another richness and poverty map example, let`s take this hypothetical situation. You`re walking along the road with your partner and suddenly three muggers jump in front of you and start threatening you with a knife, demanding that you give them your valuables. You will probably behave according to the situation that your map is programmed for in stressful situations. If you`ve never been in a fight, you will probably start to tremble, wanting the situation to disappear as fast as it can because of the possible consequences. You will probably give away your valuables and your future will depend on the muggers` goodwill. On the other hand, if you and your partner were by any chance martial arts experts, this would mean you have a much bigger behavior span. That means that your maps are wider than those in the first example, because next to the giving up option you also have a protection option. You could attack, you could defend, you can hit and run or you can disable the muggers and call the police. The chosen option depends on other information located in the map and gathered at that moment, but one thing is certain: a rich map allows you choices and a poor map limits you, in this particular case rendering you helpless.

All of the examples lead us to the utmost reality comprehension value, in other words better territory knowledge. The way we meet each new territory is called mapping. The value of mapping refers to improved understanding, planning and communication about a phenomena whether or not we ever found ourselves in a situation we`ve mapped. The mapping of a certain territory allows us to predict and expect future events. The wider your map gets, the more considerate you get, the more resources you acquire, the more options you have. In this respect being aware of a wide map value on a daily basis is very useful, and that`s exactly why we`re going to talk about it more in the following pages.

THE WAY WE CREATE OUR PRIMARY EXPERIENCE

Why do we delete, distort and generalize?

Neurolinguistic programming named three mechanisms through which we filter encountered information and give it our own subjective meaning. These mechanisms are: distortion, deletion and generalization.

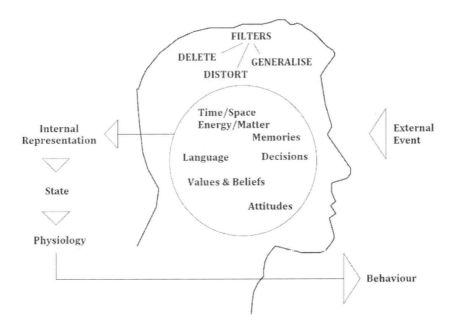

It`s important to understand these filters in order to understand the way we process information from the outside world. The filters are a key element in forming our maps, in other words our models of the world, of reality.

George Miller, an American psychologist, in his article "The Magical Number Seven" showed that the human brain can`t receive more than seven bits of information per second (give or take two, depending on a person). This makes conscience pretty confined. Consciously we can focus on certain content in a certain moment and understand only that content, nothing else. Just now you`re focused on this sentence you`re reading and you`re not thinking about what you had for lunch yesterday, at least not up to the moment I mentioned lunch.

Consciously, our mind can process from five to a maximum of nine pieces of information, while unconsciously it can receive four billion. In order to be attentive of the present moment, all of the other seemingly irrelevant information has to be deleted so we could focus on the most important ones for us. More precisely, they have to be deleted, distorted or generalized.

In order to give you the best view of these very important mechanism, along with my experience I used excerpts from the NLP Encyclopedia.
"Our sensory organs are also filters that have limited information gathering capacity. We take in only a part of outside world information and that information are determined by our neurological and genetic limitations.

Take for instance a bee looking at this page. It would experience the page differently than you would, mostly because the whole bee sensory organization differs from human sensory organization.

Only because the molecules of the chair we`re sitting on are invisible to our eyes it doesn`t mean they don`t exist or move. We just don`t possess a precise enough tool to recognize them. Our filters are crucial factors determining which outside world information we`re going to take in. NLP considers filters as reality lenses. Those lenses can be sensory, linguistically, social or cultural.
Camera records a particular event by receiving light signals and filtering them in a clear image, but our filters are much more complicated than that. The reason behind it is that people not only look, but notice, and noticing means giving outside stimuli meaning. It means nothing to a camera whether the bus on the street is yellow or not, but to us it signal the bus is transporting children."

"Perception is the first and most important step in adjusting outside world raw information to our reality. Only when seen information gets colored by our unique set of experience does it signify anything to us. In other words, a fin above the water doesn`t mean anything as long as we don`t create a mental picture of the missing part of information. Our perception is also a decisive filter constructed under the influence of nurture and other social factors from the environment we function in. Cultural filters we studied from birth have strong impact on focusing our attention. Every one of us posses a personal history that`s been molded through a fragment of the world we were a part of. Those interactions create and define our maps, our models of the world using experience, and most of that experience alternatively develops unique interests, habits, feelings, sentiments and set of behaviors."

The way we filter information from the outside world

"Filters influence out attention span because through filters we define values: what we consider important and what we consider unimportant, that part occurring unconsciously. The nature of our filters can be described in a metaphor: If we go through life hammer in hand, we`ll notice a big number of nails. This means that the way we`ve organized our filters affects the things we`re going to notice with our five senses in the surroundings. We will receive many information, but depending on the way the filters are intertwined, folded and arranged, we will focus and notice only five to nine pieces of information per moment, while all the other information will also be received, just not consciously accessible"

"We all possess filters and they impact our reality, perception, opinion and behavior. The key to change is understanding the filters and filters, as it was already stated, are a result of a taught experience and if we become aware of the fact this experience originated, how our map is filtered and organized: we can change. This book`s main purpose is to impact your filters and widen your map about behavior understanding and possibility of change. The only way to do it is filter reorganization."

Our filter`s pros and cons

Deletion filter

"Deleting is a process with which we selectively direct attention to certain dimensions of experience and neglect other. With the help of deleting we reduce the world to those dimensions we are capable of handle at a particular moment. That reduction can sometimes be useful, and other times a source of pain for us and people around us."

Situation one: You visit friends you haven`t seen for a long time. You greet them, enter the living room, sit on the couch and start to catch up.

Situation two: You`re in the middle of home makeover and you visit friends you haven`t seen for a long time. You greet them, enter the living room, and sit on the couch (the same as in situation one). Suddenly you start asking questions about it: where they bought it, how much it cost, how comfortable it is...and look at those lovely drapes, I have to buy drapes...

The surrounding in situation one and two is identical, but you`re going to notice the things that are important to you in that moment, that are in accordance with your current wishes, ideas and values. In the first situation, you almost don`t experience the couch, you delete it, and in the second situation you notice nothing but the couch because it poses a value to you, and delete everything else.

Now, as you`re reading this book, you don`t think about the rhythm of your breathing or your blinking speed. You don`t think about your hair-style or what you had for lunch. You also don`t think about all those sounds that can be heard in your surroundings, do you?
At least you didn`t think about it up to this moment, and now you`ve started because I`ve pointed it out for you. Before this moment, the pointed out information was left on your filters. Now that they`re conscious, they`ve become a center of your focus. To sum it up, the deletion filter serves to focus just to those things important to us at a particular moment. It selects according to our needs. However, the fact we don't perceive consciously an information doesn`t mean it doesn`t effect us.

To illustrate what I mean, let me share a personal example of mine. One morning I jumped in my car and set out for a seminar. I was driving along the main road for about 20 minutes and upon arriving at my destination, I called up my assistant to tell him to buy Jaffa cakes (biscuits with orange filling and chocolate topping) on his way over. My assistant said, "Why should I buy Jaffa cakes, we`ve never bought them before?" I replied that he just buys them full stop - if not for anybody else, for me. I`m craving Jaffa cakes today. My assistant bought and brought Jaffa`s. Half an hour later, participants started arriving and they begin to ask me the same question my assistant asked me, "Sasha, how come you bought Jaffa cakes, this is the first time right?" I simply said I felt like it. New day, new Jaffa`s, old questions. Didn't I know why I bought Jaffa cakes? Well I didn`t, I just wanted a bit of change, I was craving them. "The next time you`re going to drive the main road, "states the smiling participants, "notice the billboards." And really, on my way home from the seminar I counted 14 Jaffa cake billboards. These billboards haven`t imprinted on my conscious mind, they didn`t find themselves in the five to nine information. But this example illustrates that all information has an affect on behavior, whether they`re filtered out or not.

Generalization filter

"Generalization is a process in which elements or pieces of personal models of the world are detached from the original experience and represent the whole information category, and our experience is just one of the examples in that category. Our capability to generalize is essential to learning and mapping process. In order for us to better understand and interpret the world around us, it`s necessary to simplify it, or to put it in other words: to map it."

If for example we learn that a car is something consisting of four wheels and a driver, we`ll automatically generalize that everything on four wheels is a car. A child looks at a truck and says, "Mum, look, a car!" Mum is trying to explain it`s not a car, but the child is completely puzzled and wonders how this isn`t a car. Mum educates, "Cars are small, trucks are big," pointing to the truck. So the mother points her finger to the truck, the child looks in that direction and connects the word truck to the picture it sees.

In the next situation, the same child sees a dredge and say,: "Mum, look, a truck!" Now the Mum tries to explain it`s not a truck, but the child insists it`s bigger than a car and has four wheels, therefore it must be a truck. Mum educates again, "Yes, but this one is yellow, has two big and two small wheels. Dredges look like that." The child learns: "How did you say this truck is called?" "I said it`s called a dredge," Mum replies patiently, "and it`s not a truck it`s a dredge. Repeat after me: dredge". "Dredge," says the child. "That`s my boy."

The learning process is such that we have to work our way from a smaller group of concepts to the greater meaning. One of the functions of the generalization filter is just that: strengthening our gradual map in spreading. However, it can also limit us.

Let`s take for example a generalization experience:
You arrive for the first time at a foreign country for a vacation. The first thing that happens is the taxi driver tricks you and drives around so he can charge you more. After that you arrive to a hotel and at the reception desk they charge you $3 on your bill. You try to forget it, set out to your room and decide to freshen up and go out for a drink. After you have had a couple, without getting a receipt, the waiter claims that you`ve had more than you know you had, and you, again not wanting to ruin your vacation for the first day, pay even for the things you didn`t drink. If something similar happens, an inevitable generalization will form in your map.
The generalization will most probably be: "The citizens of this country are thieves, crooks, and fraudsters, etc." During vacation conversations with your friends, you`ll say, "Avoid that country as a traveling destination if you don`t want to get robbed."

Let`s take into consideration that your belief arose from just three or four situations that happened and that that country has hundreds of thousand or millions of citizens. You agree that surely not all of them are thieves. Maybe you`ve just had bad luck meeting the wrong people and having an experience like that. It`s impossible that all citizens are like that, isn`t it?

The information exiting your maps, whether or not you met all of them is that the country is a nation of crooks and thieves. In your map you are completely right because it`s your opinion, but all in all, your experience is limited and based on that fistful of limited information; you created a generalization and labeled the whole country.

Also the famous sentence: "You're always late," signifies a generalization and it's wrong, no matter how often the other person is late. He or she is most probably not late every single time. Maybe that person is late only while meeting us and arrives on time at every other occasion. As we don't have that experience, so saying the generalizing statement of always being late makes it true only in our map, not the whole territory. The statement, "You're always late" means that that person didn't arrive on time anywhere a single time, which is almost impossible.

If we form a generalization towards somebody, like, "You're always late" or "Everything she says is stupid", even if that person comes on time or says something clever, you will filter it out because it won't conform to the previously generated belief you generalized about that specific person.

Distortion filter

"Distortion is a process that allows us changes inside our sensory experience. Fantasies, for example, prepare us well for future events. All great work of arts, novels, revolutionary scientific discoveries...have included momentary realities. Distortion can in that sense be extremely useful, but it can also be limiting if the outside world information wasn't interpreted correctly."

The way to influence our filters to notice and experience more

A man had a belief he wasn't worthy of attention. He complained to Bandler and Grinder that his wife never gives him the attention, or more precisely, input that would signify attention towards him. Visiting him in his home, Bandler and Grinder saw that his wife was in fact giving him attention in different ways.

"However, the man had a strong belief about his own value/worthlessness, that the input coming from his wife wasn't in accordance with what he believed in so he literally didn't hear his wife. "That's not attention, that's the way my wife behaves when she wants something". A person that was rejected once forms a belief that he or she isn't worthy of attention. Considering that the husband's model of the world possesses that experience, the distortion also affects the generalization filter and he HAS TO either delete the attention giving behavior either give it another meaning" (Pribram, 1967)

There are good examples how distortions originate happen during lectures. When I explain the distortion filter, I stand before the participants, cross my arms, stretch my lips into a smile and pose a question, "What does this mean?" The answers vary but the most common are those connected to resistance, negative attitude or sometimes because of the smile on my face comes a comment that I'm satisfied. How is this possible?

People that say that I have a negative attitude are just those people who probably read a nonverbal communication guide book and for that reason distorted the information to fit their map. Their gained filter from the book was crossed arms = negative attitude. That filter was so strong, on the other hand, that it affected the deletion filter, not letting them notice a smile on my face. When I manage to make them notice the smile they inevitably say, "Oh now, that's a completely different story!".

WORDS AND THEIR MEANING

"A few words can change the course of someone`s life for the better"
Robert Dilts

A map is not a territory!
A menu is not a meal!
A word is not a concept it represents!

The key difference in communication between human beings and animals is the use of speech. All human accomplishments, whether positive or negative, involved the use of speech. We use speech in two ways. Firstly, to represent our experience (reasoning, thoughts, and fantasies, etc.), and the other is when we use our speech as a system of representation; we create a model of our experience. When we use speech for communication we present that model to others. We use speech to present our experience to others, and that makes it the model of our world. Despite words being digital information and thus more accurate than non-verbal information, in daily communication they adapt to our existing maps. The word "clean" is digital to all of us, but the way each of us interprets it analogically is very different, as we have seen in the example of the mother and son and the cleaned room criteria. If I tell you I own a car... you know I own a car. "Car" is just a word like any other which specifies a certain category, and within that category each of us will process the information and turn it into a very specific image, which will greatly differ from mine and any other image. When reading that sentence, someone will imagine a Mercedes, someone a Toyota, someone a Jeep... and the only thing that we agree upon is that I own a car. When you hear someone say that they have a wonderful pet – based on your own assumptions you create an image of a cat, dog or a rabbit, and that image in your mind will be an image you've already seen. If you have a dog, "a pet" will automatically remind you of a dog, or more accurately, your dog. That is because you have to connect with an association or information closest to you. Images in our minds differ greatly, but at the same time words can be the same, no matter how digital and accurate, and everyone sees them differently within their models.

"Wrong words at the wrong time can be hurtful and damaging"
Robert Dilts

Consider this sentence from Bandler and Grinder`s, *Structure of Magic*:

"A seven-year-old girl named Lara fell over a cushion in the living room and bruised her right arm hitting a wooden chair.

Now consider this one: A child had an accident.

Both sentences have the same meaning, but the first one gives more accurate information. The active subject of a sentence can be replaced with a passive one.

For example: "A house was built," instead of "John built a house." Not naming the builder doesn't mean that the house was built itself. There is still a builder. This kind of omission points to a worldview where we are helpless observers, in which events happen by themselves and nobody is responsible. Most of the problems in interpersonal relations come from understanding someone's message wrong. Sometimes someone will get angry with us, and we will not understand why. The reason lies in the analog channel."

Sentences like:
- I'm arriving soon.
- Darling, I've cleaned the house.
- I'll do it by the end of the day.

These sound pretty clear, don't they? But the word "soon" can be 5 minutes in my world model, and two hours in someone else's.
"To clean the house" might be to take out the trash for someone and for someone else that there isn't a milligram of dust.
"By the end of the day" can be until 5 PM, which is the end of my workday and for someone else until 11:59 pm.
Despite words being digital information, which are more accurate than non-verbal information, they adapt to our existing maps in everyday communication.

Words as the main source of misunderstanding

But we still believe that we understand each other, and when conflict arises, we get mad at others for not fulfilling their promises. The most common reason for anger is that we didn't understand the meaning certain words have for our partners, clients, coworkers and friends. A solution to this problem can only occur with further search for the meaning of the message the other person gets, because otherwise misunderstandings can occur. Words by themselves have no meaning, which is clear when we hear a foreign language we do not understand. We give words meaning with ideas anchored to objects and experiences during our lives. We don't all see the same objects and we don't all have the same experiences. That is an often cause of misunderstandings in communication, but on the other hand, different maps and meanings contribute to the fullness and diversity of life. It will surely be *easier* to agree upon what an apple means or looks like, because we've all seen it, smelled and tasted it. Although, with such specific words there are differences in color and size, aren't there? If there are discrepancies in our minds with the word "apple", what about abstract words like "respect", "love", "politics"? These words could cause us to argue long into the night.

The word "success" to someone may mean to earn their first million, to someone else it could mean to educate and properly raise their kids, and to yet another person it may mean to find their purpose in life. Having a lot of money could mean success for some people, while for others it can mean a burden, risk, or even fear. All of these are different interpretations, which hide behind a same word because of analog, individual understanding. Words are a basic tool for presenting and understanding, and very often if there is no proper word there is no proper way for us to understand a certain experience. For example, some indigenous peoples don't understand the word "lie" and they don't understand the concept because that kind of behavior doesn't exist in their cultures.

People are able to recognize 7,500,000 different distinctions in the visible color spectrum, but the natives, i.e. the native speakers of the Maidu tribe are only aware of three different color categories. Those three categories cover eight colors in the English language. That means that a Maidu speaker has less perceptive distinctions in the area of visual observation. The speaker of English will write about two objects, which have different colors: "One book is yellow, and the other is orange." The Maidu speaker will say: "Two tulak books."

Richard Bandler in one of his classes provided a similar example. It was about a tribe on Tahiti whose language didn't contain the word for self-confidence (self-esteem). Every member of that tribe is jolly, happy and smiling from ear to ear. Everyone is self-confident even though they don't know that word. Why? If we know the word self-confidence then we also know that we must meet certain criteria or conditions for self-confidence. But, the very existence of the words such as self-confidence, courage, success, pleasure, etc. has certain negative sides, and those negative sides lie in the fact that each of those words has an opposite. So by knowing or understanding the word courage we must understand the word fear, because a lack of courage is fear. Lack of success is failure. Knowing the word self-confidence means that we're aware of a state in which there is a lack of confidence. Can we change our truth, which limits us and start believing in some other truths?
If we know that everything is actually a lie, or putting it nicer, our own personal limited model of the world, we can create new convictions and meanings, which will be more useful to us.
Based on all the examples we can ask how much our life would be different if we didn't know words like "self-confidence", "failure", "impossible", and even "ugly".

The sentence: "Arrive on time," may sound very specific but it isn't because it's filtered by each individual.
In every group of students with whom I worked during my first few years, I had problems with people arriving on time. "Arrive at 9:00AM" resulted in students arriving from 8:45 to 9:15. After a few days even the students who had been arriving on time began to arrive late because they had seen that we hadn't started before 9:15. When we say to someone, "See you at 9:00," that information sounds accurate, but is vague enough to be manipulated – it is impossible to arrive exactly at 9:00:00, right?
When someone would arrive at 9:02 I'd say, "You're late." He'd say, "No I'm not, because you haven't started yet."
I solved this problem by very accurately defining, i.e. digitally defining what "on time" actually meant and also I created a punishment for being late.

The pattern I used was:

"Tomorrow I'm expecting you UNTIL (instead of) 08:49:59 because we start at 08:59:59 at the latest, and if you're one second late you'll have to sing the national anthem in front of the whole group."

With this move I digitally specified the information and synchronized the maps of every student.

Since then there are fewer problems with being late, and if someone is late, our day starts with the anthem. The result of arriving on time came from my use of more accurate communication. When students had taken advantage of that, I didn't want to admit it, but it was solely my responsibility because I didn't convey the information properly.

Until we clarify, i.e. digitalize the non-specific words such as soon, quickly, on time, during the day, etc. we will encounter misunderstandings because a map is not a territory. Synchronizing maps is the basic task of successful communication and mutual understanding.

Also, instead of putting the focus on synchronizing our maps with our coworkers and family members, we have an even more important task. That task is to realize what those words mean for us in our maps. Without knowing our map, the words that we use to describe our maps, we will have a hard time understanding our personal goals and needs.

When we say, "I want to be successful," that means nothing until we define which digital criteria needs to be met so I can freely state, "I did it." If your answer is for example: "To earn $1,000,000", that means if you own $999,999 you aren't there yet. If you don't define what being successful means in your own map, you can make $1,000,000 and still believe you should be successful, or in other words, that you're not successful yet.

The questions we can ask ourselves in order to better define our maps are:

What does being successful mean for me?
What does being happy mean for me?
What does having good relationships mean for me?
What does looking good mean for me?
What does losing weight mean for me?

Remember, words have no meaning until we give them one.

The aim of these four parts (analog and digital information, walking on someone else's territory and words) are aimed at making you understand the importance of understanding and defining your own models of the world.

A map is not a territory, and a word is not the concept it represents. Every human being has the right to their own model of the world, which will fit their experiences. We are all makers of our own world and reality is our individual construct.

CREATE A STRONGER VERSION OF YOUR MODEL

People who control their environment are the people who get what they want

Give me a dozen healthy infants, well-formed, and my own specified world to bring them up in and I'll guarantee to take any one at random and train him to become any type of specialist I might select – doctor, lawyer, artist, merchant-chief and, yes, even beggar-man and thief, regardless of his talents, penchants, tendencies, abilities, vocations, and race of his ancestors.
John Watson, American psychologist who established the psychological school of behaviorism.

Every behavior is learnt and adjusted to the environment lived in

Watson wanted to say that, through good preparation of the environment, which possesses certain conditions, we could influence the behaviors, which will develop in this environment. By orienting behavior, working on the values, beliefs and abilities of the child, it's possible to condition the development of their intended identity. Through the right learning strategies it's possible to orient the raising and education in the wanted direction to a great extent.

When we talk about learning strategies, it's also important to mention two pioneers in the field of behaviorism, Pavlov and Skinner. Pavlov gets the credit for his work on reflexes, while Skinner is credited for his work on learning, or behavioral modification.

During his research on the physiology of digestion in dogs, Pavlov noticed that, rather than simply salivating in the presence of food, the dogs began to salivate in the presence of the lab technician who normally fed them. Pavlov called this anticipatory salivation psychic secretion. From this observation he predicted that, if a particular stimulus in the dog's surroundings was present when the dog was given food, then this stimulus would become associated with food and cause salivation on its own. In his initial experiment, Pavlov used a bell to call the dogs to their food and, after a few repetitions, the dogs started to salivate in response to the bell. Pavlov called the bell the conditioned (or conditional) stimulus (CS) because its effect depended on its association with food. He called the food the unconditioned stimulus (US) because its effect did not depend on previous experience. Likewise, the response to the CS was the conditioned response (CR) and that to the US was the unconditioned response (UR). The timing between the presentation of the CS and US is integral to facilitating the conditioned response. Pavlov found that the shorter the interval between the bell's ring and the appearance of the food, the more quickly the dog learned the conditioned response and the stronger it was.

Why do we reject certain behaviors and accept others?

An example of a conditioned reflex:

In layman's terms, a "normal" reflex is the one that exists in us, the one we got biologically, like the reflex of a baby when you track your finger over her foot. A conditioned reflex is a reflex we had learned at some point in the past. For instance, if we put our hand to the hot stove only once, or stuck our finger in an electric outlet, we experienced pain and our neurology connected that pain with that specific behavior. If the pain was strong, we decided that it was our first and last experience of that kind. After that, if someone brings a lighter to our hand, we will react in that instant and remove our hand from the lighter. If half an hour later the same person turns on the lighter behind our backs, we'll react even before seeing the fire because we connected the visual stimulant (fire towards palm) with the audio stimulant, and now just the audio stimulant triggers the reflex.

The existence of a previous experience is a necessary condition for developing a reflex. This experience is the one where the reflex is created, and in the future it's triggered in the same or similar way. It is important to mention that we do not necessarily need to have a personal experience in order to create a reflex, by which I'm referring to the example with a fin in the water from the first part of the book.

Good examples of a conditioned reflex are the red and green traffic lights. When the traffic light in front of us turns red, we don't think whether we should stop or not, but we reflexively press the brake pedal. Even in situations when we don't see other cars on the crossroads, when the light turns red the reflex triggers automatically. Red and green lights had no meaning until we learned to understand them, what meanings were associated with them and what the consequences would be if we did not respect them. But the rules could have been set up differently: red could have meant start, and green stop. Then our reflex would also be different.

Operant conditioning is a term that was coined by B.F Skinner in 1937[1]. Operant conditioning is distinguished from classical conditioning (or respondent conditioning) in that operant conditioning deals with the modification of "voluntary behavior" or operant behavior. Operant behavior operates on the environment and is maintained by its consequences, while classical conditioning deals with the conditioning of reflexive (reflex) behaviors, which are elicited by antecedent conditions. Behaviors conditioned via a classical conditioning procedure are not maintained by consequences.

Skinner coined the term operant conditioning; it means roughly changing of behavior by the use of reinforcement, which is given after the desired response. Skinner identified three types of responses or operant that can follow behavior:

NEUTRAL OPERANTS: responses from the environment that neither increase nor decrease the probability of a behavior being repeated.
REINFORCERS: Responses from the environment that increase the probability of a behavior being repeated. Reinforcers can be either positive or negative.
PUNISHERS: Response from the environment that decrease the likelihood of a behavior being repeated. Punishment weakens behavior.

Behavior that does not lead to an outcome is a result of wrong presuppositions and generalizations

To illustrate the three types of operants, we will use an experiment called: "Little Albert" experiment (1920):

The aim of Watson and Rayner was to condition phobias into an emotionally stable child. They chose Albert from a hospital for this study at the age of almost nine months. Albert's mother was a wet nurse at the Harriet Lane Home for Invalid Children. Albert was the son of an employee of the Phipps Clinic at Johns Hopkins University in Baltimore, where Watson and Rayner were conducting their experiments.

As the preliminary to the experiment, Little Albert was given a battery of baseline emotional tests: the infant was exposed, briefly and for the first time, to a white rabbit, a rat, a dog, a monkey, masks with and without hair, cotton wool, burning newspapers, etc. During the baseline, Little Albert showed no fear toward any of these items. Albert was then placed on a mattress on a table in the middle of a room. A white laboratory rat was placed near Albert and he was allowed to play with it. At this point, the child showed no fear of the rat. He began to reach out to the rat as it roamed around him. In later trials, Watson and Rayner made a loud sound behind Albert's back by striking a suspended steel bar with a hammer when the baby touched the rat. Little Albert responded to the noise by crying and showing fear. After several such pairings of the two stimuli, Albert was again presented with only the rat. Now, however, he became very distressed as the rat appeared in the room. He cried, turned away from the rat, and tried to move away. Apparently, the baby boy had associated the white rat (original neutral stimulus, now conditioned stimulus) with the loud noise (unconditioned stimulus) and was producing the fearful or emotional response of crying (originally the unconditioned response to the noise, now the conditioned response to the rat).

This experiment led to the following progression of results:

Introduction of a loud sound (unconditioned stimulus) resulted in fear (unconditioned response), a natural response.

Introduction of a rat (neutral stimulus) paired with the loud sound (unconditioned stimulus) resulted in fear (unconditioned response). Successive introductions of a rat (conditioned stimulus) resulted in fear (conditioned response). Here, learning is demonstrated.

The experiment showed that Little Albert seemed to generalize his response to furry objects so that when Watson sent a non-white rabbit into the room seventeen days after the original experiment, Albert also became distressed. He showed similar reactions when presented with a furry dog, a sealskin coat, and even when Watson appeared in front of him wearing a Santa Claus mask with white cotton balls as his beard.

Besides the basic biologically conditioned reflexes and behaviors, everything else was learned, i.e. conditioned. The good news in all that is that by understanding that we're conditioned; we can turn things to our advantage and take conscious control over new conditions... unconditional unwanted patterns and condition new and desirable behavioral patterns.

For an everyday example of operant conditioning, let's take a student who studied day and night for a month for a difficult exam. He took the exam and passed with an A. The student received feedback from the environment that such behavior gives an excellent result. Through this experience he creates a pattern: with this level of studying, I'm going to be a straight-A student. After this, the student will take each exam as seriously as when he took this one because he knows exactly what prize awaits him and for exactly how much effort.

Another student will invest three times less time, take the exam and fail. By this punishment he will get this feedback: I have to try harder than this in order to pass the exam.

In the chapter on values you read about positive and negative motivation, and now we can project this onto those two students. The more successful student will have positive motivation because he received reinforcement for his efforts, while the other student will have negative motivation in other situations as well: I have to study harder in order to pass the exam (to avoid punishment).

Let's take another situation into consideration, one that is most likely the most negative. Imagine a student who studied for a minimal amount of time for a difficult exam, got lucky with the questions and got an A. How will this student be conditioned? This is a case of negative reinforcement because the prize was not in accordance with the effort put into studying. This student will try to use the same or similar approach for his next exam. If this pattern is not soon interrupted with a punishment, his approach will not change. It will not change because there is no need for it to change, considering that it provides the wanted results... for as long as it lasts.

The rule is as follows: having a positive reinforcement increases the probability of repeating the behavior, which led to the prize, and negative reinforcement reduces it. In order for a behavior to be repeated, there must be a wanted stimulant, a wanted prize, which motivates certain behavior and there must be a belief that certain behavior will lead to a certain result.

The problem arises when we generalize our strategies. Something works, and we become convinced that it works every time and within all frames.

I will take the example with a child who is learning to walk. The child is trying, getting up from the floor, falling, and this repeats countless times. But what happens when one of the parents sees the child fall and hit his head on the floor? Does the child start crying when he falls and hits his head for the first time? You may think he does, but I am asking for the very first experience when it happens. When a baby falls and hits her head, the parent runs towards the child, lifts it up, and starts to kiss and cuddle her. Is this not so? What happens next is that the child starts crying. Many witnessed children who throw themselves on the floor to attract their parents' attention; they start crying and are successful at it. Some are more or less successful; this depends on the parents and their reactions to the child's behavior. But let's say, for example that the child is successful in attracting attention with crying. What happens when the child is a bit older, goes to a shopping mall with his parents and sees a toy that he likes and the parent says NO? Of course, the child uses the strategy that he knows will work, because it has worked X times before. If the parent tries to communicate with the child that there are better toys at home and the child continues to cry, the parent has the following choice:

Option A: To buy the toy for the child in order to make him stop crying.
Option B: To spank the child and let him know who has the final say in the outcome (as I was lucky to experience)
With option A, the child was encouraged – Crying produces results.
Option B sets clear boundaries – Crying may, but doesn't necessarily have to lead to the wanted result.

People who got the prize for choosing the option A and proved that this kind of behavior produces results will try to generalize crying in every possible situation, and crying will become their main means of getting what they want. When they grow up crying will most likely stop, but the strategy will be very similar. These people will, in their 30s, 40s and later, try to use the pattern with their families, friends, and fellow workers: Why are you acting like that, you don't love me at all! I'd give anything for you and I'm always there for you and I can't believe you're being like this. You don't care for me as much as I care about you… and similar forms with the same goal. Can we blame them? Of course we can't. The map is not a territory and we would be the same if we had received the same stimulants from our parents.

Skinner gives an exceptional example of generalizing of this strategy.

Skinner had a group of students who had done a lot of research with rats and mazes. And somebody asked them one day "What is the real difference between a rat and a human being?" Now, behaviorists, not being terribly observant, decided that they needed to experiment to find out. They built a huge maze that was scaled up for a human. They took a control group of rats and taught them to run a small maze for cheese. And they took the humans and taught them to run the large maze for five-dollar bills. They didn't notice any really significant difference. There were small variations in the data and at the 95% probability level they discovered some significant difference in the number of trials to criterion or something. The humans were able to learn to run the maze somewhat better, a little bit quicker, than the rats. On the second day, the cheese and the five-dollar bill were removed from the maze, and the same participants were asked to repeat the maze. All of the humans repeated the maze, but only seventy percent of rats repeated their maze. On the third day, only thirty percent of rats repeated the maze. But most all of the humans kept repeating the maze. After a week, none of the rats would repeat the maze, but a significant percentage of the humans kept running through the maze (to find no five-dollar bill). After a month, there were still several humans who kept returning to the lab to run through the maze.

The conclusion, like in the previous example, with a relatively small number of stimulants, people are, unlike animals, prepared to generalize a strategy even without reinforcements. When the stimulant is gone, animals do not get reinforcement and completely stop, but people mostly do not, because they act out of conviction. This truth has its plus and minus side. People are willing to go the distance, believing that they will achieve what they set out to do, which happens on occasion. But on the other hand, using a strategy that obviously does not provide any result is silly isn't it?

The way to avoid behavior generalization

Many children have a very early negative experience with hospitals and doctors. A child gets sick, the parents take him to a hospital and the doctor gives him an injection (pain – punishment). When parents take the child to a hospital exclusively when it is necessary, the child will be conditioned in his mind: hospital=pain, i.e. doctor=pain.

The reason for such a response is the exclusivity of the experience. If the child would experience pain in 3 out of 10 trips to the hospital, the reaction would only occur for the real pain, but in this way it can also appear visually – by connecting the pain with the doctor's white uniform. If we want a positive reaction, it is necessary to create a pleasant experience in a certain number of trips, and that is to remove the negative one.

A good example of such conditioning was given by Caesar Milan in his book. When I was a teenager I had a dog. Since we had a big backyard, we never took him for walks. We would leash him only when we would take him to the vet, who was several blocks away.

The first time we took him to the vet he was relatively calm, but when he was stabbed with a needle he reacted and jumped off the table and we chased him all over the office. We leashed him and took him home. The next time, after X months, we leashed him and started going towards the vet office. When we attempted to turn in his street, there was resistance – his reflex triggered prematurely. We carried him to the vet office, and the whole time he acted like he was being stabbed. The third time when he saw me with a leash in my hands he started to run from me. I couldn't catch him.

Caesar Milan (The Dog Whisperer) outlined a very simple strategy in his book by which dog owners could condition their dogs to avoid problems similar to mine. He states that the dog should be taken to the vet 2-3 times, only to be in the same room with other animals, and while it is there, reward it with dog cookies. My good friend had read Caesar's book before he bought a dog and did the vet conditioning. He says that the result of previous rewards in extraordinary – the dog has no negative reactions, even when on the veterinarian's table.

Create stimuli that generates a desired behavior

If after everything stated here we try to connect the path by neurological levels, from the environment to identity and the behaviorist Watson's introductory quote, we can come to the conclusion that things/activities which we love are the result of positive experience, i.e. conditioning with positive experiences. Things and activities we do not like are simply the result of bad or uncomfortable or even painful experiences, and we decided to avoid such activities.
There is no content that is difficult by itself, arduous and uninteresting, and vice versa. We gave those contents such a meaning in our maps. But if there is a new reinforcement experience, things could easily change. For this I will give an example from my own experience.

 I was in the fifth grade. We got a number of new teachers, which was quite stressful by default, and the most stressful part was the Art class. Even before this class I couldn't say that I liked Art, things got worse. The Art teacher was the scariest teacher on the face of the Earth! She would change her moods in a second. From a calm and peaceful person who talks about her pets she would leap out of her chair in a second and start insulting and even hitting the child who would, according to her criteria, mess about. I was sick from going to school on the days when we had Art, and I was not the only one. This time I will generalize, and say that we were ALL sick of going to school when we had Art. One day I came to school with a new hat. Since none of the other teachers warned me to take it off, I wore it during classes. Before Art class I took it off and put it in my bag. After the bell marking the beginning of the class, the teacher walked in as happy and smiling as never before. She gave us a task and sat in the front row, her back facing me. In a sweet voice she told us of her pets, how she feeds them, how she plays with them, how she talks with them. After about ten minutes I decided that the teacher was in such a good mood today that nothing should bother her, so I decided to take the hat out of my bag and put in on my head. After a few minutes, the teacher faced towards the class and saw the hat. She leaped out of her chair, ran to me and hit me in the back of my head so hard that I hit my head on the table and the picture in front of me. But that was just the beginning. She screamed in my face, 'You're a yokel, a yokel! Who's raising you? Your parents are yokels for raising you this way. Look at your drawing you yokel, it's worthless.' She took my drawing and tore it up. Incidents like this one happened frequently but no one dared to report her because we were afraid that if we did, that the situation or her behavior would become even worse.

That is behavior conditioning. After that experience, not only did I not wear my hat in Art class, I didn't wear it to school at all.
I participated in Art class just to have a passing grade. I simply hated Art class, and I would avoid it whenever I had the chance. I didn't even have my own paper folder; I used to ask other students for paper and art utensils. This lasted for two and a half years, until that particular teacher retired. At the beginning of the next half term we got a new teacher. On her first class she gave us a task to draw a flower bud with a pencil, and later to paint it with watercolors. Even on this class I had no art set, so I was sitting next to my friend Natalie, watching what she was drawing and looking around the class. As soon as Natalie did the sketch with the pencil and started to add red paint to the petals, there was a knock on the door. A student

entered and said that the Music teacher sent him and asked whether the Art teacher would release some of the students (for about twenty minutes) who sang in the choir. They were supposed to agree about a concert. The teacher said yes, several students went out, among them was my friend Natalie. As soon as they left the room I had an idea, a malicious idea. I decided to smudge her drawing, not outside the lines, but for it to be nowhere near what Natalie had in mind when she had started painting. Natalie had a short temper. That's why messing with her painting had a special appeal. I sat on her chair, took the brush, wet it, and looked at the colors. I'll take a bit of this (blue), a bit of this (red), a bit of this (yellow), and by combining these colors on the brush I painted over her red that didn't have the time to dry. For every petal I used a new combination of colors. For the first time in at least two and a half years, I truly enjoyed Art.

At the next instant I heard a voice behind my back, to the left, 'Boy, what is your name?'

I turned around and saw the teacher. 'Oh no', I thought, 'the new teacher's first day... I'm dead.'

I replied, 'Sasha, my name is Sasha.'

'Give me your drawing, Sasha.' Now I'm really dead. My hand trembled as I handed her the drawing, and knowing that I couldn't get out of this one, I expected the punishment.

The teacher said in a soft, warm voice, 'Sasha, this is wonderful.'

'Miss, are you joking?'

'No, Sasha. This is wonderful. When you finish, bring it to me and you will get an A.'

It still didn't dawn on me that she had been serious. I asked her a few more times if she was joking. In the end I decided to confess that the painting was not mine, but the color choice was mine, and that I can draw one just like it for an A. I felt that I could be honest. There were no consequences. I took a paper, painted the picture, handed it to the teacher and got an A – my first A ever in Art class. After such reinforcement, the rest of the story is predictable. By the end of the 7th grade, most of my drawings were on the boards. Not only that, but I decided to invest additional work into some pictures at home. Art became a relaxation class.

Despite the fact that Art did not have any value to me, and that I was convinced that I couldn't draw or paint... that it simply wasn't for me and could in no way be a part of my identity, with a positive reinforcement and conditioning which continued through other works and excellent grades, there was an incredible change.

Who knows, maybe I would have also liked Math or Physics if I had a teacher with such attitude and communication skills. Think about it, doesn't the way in which we perceive certain content depend on the medium? If the medium (the person who passes on the information) is someone who inspires fear, could we truly enjoy a content or activity?
If you think about some activities that you dislike, perhaps you could remember specific experiences as to why.

In line with this example, I discovered an interesting story on conditioning or learning. In his book *Steps to an Ecology of Mind*, Gregory Bateson told an interesting story about the time when he was studying dolphin communication patterns at the Hawaii Institute of Marine Biology. He observed trainers while they were teaching dolphins various tricks that were then shown to a paying audience. On the first day, when dolphins would do anything unusual, such as jumping out of the water, the trainer would blow his whistle and throw them a fish. The dolphin understood very quickly that such behavior was awarded with fish: he would repeat the trick as often as possible and expect a prize. The next day the dolphin jumped out of the water expecting a prize, but he got none. He would repeat the jump several times, but to no avail. Then, irritated, he did something else – he started to spin. The trainer then blew his whistle and threw a fish to the dolphin. Therefore the dolphin started to repeat his new trick and was rewarded with fish. He didn't get fish for the yesterday's trick, only for something new. This went on for about two weeks. The dolphin would approach and do tricks he had learned on previous days, but in vain. Only when he would perform a new trick would he get a prize. That was most likely very frustrating for the dolphin. But, on the fifteenth day it seemed that he learned the rules. He swam around frantically and made an impressive performance by including eight completely new and unusual tricks, four of which had never before been seen to be performed by dolphins. The dolphin raised his level of learning. Not only did he understand how to create new behavior patterns, but also the rules on how and when to use them. Another thing: during these two weeks, Bateson observed the trainer giving the dolphin fish out of context, for no particular reason. When he asked him why, the trainer replied enthusiastically: "I have to keep good relations with him. If we don't have them, he won't try to learn anything."

I strongly believe that everything is possible when two conditions are fulfilled: a good personal attitude and a good choice of teachers.

Inputs that generate transformation

There is a famous saying: When in Rome, do as the Romans do. That saying implies the possibility of a simple change of behavior patterns for all non-Romans who come to Rome. When you're there, change your behavior to be more like them (contextual behavior modeling). See what they do and do it too. When you come to Amsterdam, you must experience what it offers, and we all know what those activities are. People who have never tried narcotics are ready to get out of their frames in Amsterdam, i.e. they're ready to adapt to the frames of the environment. This leads to the fact that the frame in which we are largely affects the behaviors that will manifest within it, even if we don't understand the purpose of our behavior.

As the first example of how the frame and behavior of an individual within that frame provide inputs according to which we consider something to be normal and allowed, I will take the case of Sylvia Likens.

Sylvia Marie Likens was an American murder victim from Indiana. She was tortured to death by Gertrude Baniszewski, Gertrude's children, and other young people from their neighborhood. Her parents, who were carnies, had left Likens and her sister Jenny in the care of the Baniszewski family three months before her death, in exchange for $20 a week. Baniszewski, two of her children, Paula and John, and two neighborhood youths, Coy Hubbard and Richard Hobbs, were charged and convicted of the crime. Her torture and murder were described by the prosecutor in Baniszewski's trial as "the most terrible crime ever committed in the state of Indiana."
Baniszewski began taking her anger out on the Likens girls, beating them with paddles, after payments from their parents failed to arrive on time. Baniszewski focused her abuse on Sylvia, accusing her of stealing candy that she had bought from a grocery store, and

humiliating her when she admitted that she once had a boyfriend. Paula Baniszewski, who actually was pregnant at the time, kicked Likens in the genitals and accused her of being pregnant, although medical examination proved that Sylvia was not and could not have been.

Mrs. Baniszewski encouraged Hubbard and other neighborhood children to torment Likens, including, among other things, putting cigarettes out on her skin and forcing her to remove her clothes and insert a glass Coca-Cola bottle into her vagina on at least two occasions.
When Likens urinated in her bed, she was locked in the cellar and forbidden to use the toilet. Later, she was forced to consume her own feces and urine.

Not long after she was imprisoned in the basement and the initial torture by Gertrude's children began, the children from the neighborhood got involved in the torture too.
The interesting thing is that the children from the neighborhood, who had harassed Sylvia, as you can see in the movie American Crime, when asked why they had done it, had no specific reason. Because everyone had done it, and they continued to do it because none of them had any negative consequences, there was no punisher.

Another well-known example of indirect behavior learning:
"Stephenson (1967) trained adult male and female rhesus monkeys to avoid manipulating an object and then placed individual naïve animals in a cage with a trained individual of the same age and sex and the object in question.

The experiment was divided into several parts:
At the beginning of the experiment, five monkeys were locked in a cage. There was a ladder in the center, and a banana was hung from the ceiling above the ladders. As soon as the first monkey saw the banana he would race towards the ladder. When the monkey would start to climb the ladders, the researchers would spray the monkey with ice-cold water. But they would also spray the other monkeys, not just the one who tried to climb the ladder.
When another monkey tried to climb the ladder, the researchers repeated the procedure and sprayed all the monkeys.

Can you recognize the conditioning pattern?

Trying to climb the ladder = cold water for everyone = pain (punisher).

After all the monkeys adopted the pattern of keeping away from the ladder, the researchers replaced one of the monkeys with a new inexperienced one, without the conditioning experience. The new monkey (without the conditioned experience in his "map") would race towards the banana as soon as he had spotted it. But, the other four monkeys (with the existing "folder" of previous experience) would attack the new monkey and thus stopped him from climbing the ladder. By stopping the new monkey, they avoided being sprayed. The new monkey is being conditioned: If I try to move towards the ladder, I'll be attacked… without knowing the reason of the previous attack.

The researchers gradually replaced the conditioned monkeys (the ones who experienced the spraying with water) one by one with new monkeys, and every time one of the new monkeys would try to approach the ladder, it would be attacked by the rest of the group.
At the end of the experiment, all the monkeys from the first group were replaced with new, i.e. "water-unconditioned" monkeys. As none of them had been sprayed with water, they had no clue why, but still they attacked the fifth monkey.

I have another interesting example that was presented by a participant in my seminar. A few decades ago a behavior pattern emerged, and nobody knew why. Children under the age of 10 all over the American continent would kill cats by hitting them on the head with a hammer. Nobody could figure out how such a cruel pattern could appear so fast with young children. Maybe you are familiar with the example. They saw the pattern in cartoons. The mouse would bonk the cat on the head with a hammer and stars would start circling over the cat's head. The children understood that hitting the cat with a hammer makes stars over his head appear, so they would hit cats hoping that the stars would appear.

On the basis of these examples, we can conclude that there are certain patterns in our maps, in our behavior, for which we don't have a particular reason – we'd just seen someone else do it (a parent, a friend, a boss, someone in the movies or cartoons) and decided to behave according to that pattern, because that behavior is "expected" within a certain frame.

Our behavior depends on input we receive from the environment. This input affects us whether we're aware of it or not. An input can be visual, auditory, kinesthetic, olfactory and gustative.
For example, I don't know if you're aware of the fact that a person who is walking by a bakery without the intention of entering automatically slows down (because of the olfactory input – the smell of bread/bagels).
Have you ever entered a store, taken a product from a shelf, walked a couple of feet, spotted the same product by a different manufacturer and decided to replace the previously taken product with this new one?

Of course you have, we all do that. We simply decided to change our decision, based on the criteria that we were aware of, more or less. That had to happen because you'd had an experience, which triggered a new decision. Here I'm referring to my earlier personal example: Jaffa cakes. I didn't know why I wanted to eat orange cookies until the participants pointed out X billboards which I had passed on my way to the seminar.

The scariest example of unconscious programming via new inputs that I have experienced personally, happened in Orlando in 2007 where I was attending a few seminars. After the first lecture on the first day there was a coffee break. I headed out to get a coffee with milk. I took a cup and poured myself a coffee. I reached for the milk that was in a transparent fireproof bowl, and just before I started to pour milk in my cup I noticed the color of this "American milk." It was not similar to the milk I'm used to in Europe. Visually it looked like someone had mixed 70% milk and 30% water. The color just didn't match my criteria so I decided to drink only black coffee.

A few days later, among friends whom I'd met on the seminar the rumor had it that I usually like coffee with milk, but that I'm not even considering trying "American milk."
There were jokes at my expense: 'Come on Sasha, take some milk, what's the worst that could happen? Sasha would you like a coffee with milk today... I'll pour it for you if you want...'

Of course, it didn't even occur to me to pour that milk in my coffee. One afternoon, about ten days after the seminar had started we had our usual 15-minute break. It so happened that I had been sitting in the front row, and there was a crowd at the exit so I guessed that it would take me about five minutes to get a coffee. I decided to get outside the hotel and have a cigarette with my friends until the crowd disperses. There were about ten of us in a circle. We talked and made jokes. After five minutes I put out my cigarette, told my friends: 'I'll be right back, I'm just going to get a cup of coffee,' and went towards the hotel entrance. I made a few steps and heard a member of my group calling after me, Murat from Turkey… I couldn't make out what he had said. I stopped, turned around and asked him to repeat what he had said because I couldn't hear him. He answered: 'Nothing, nothing, just get your coffee; we'll talk when you come back'. 'OK', I said, and went to get my coffee. I started the standard procedure. I took a cup, poured the coffee, took some sugar, and suddenly I saw the milk. I told myself, 'You're so stiff; you've been avoiding this milk for the last ten days. What's the worst that could happen if you took some milk? After all, the coffee is free and if it's bad, spill it and make a new one. Take the milk and try, how can you be sure that it's bad if you didn't try it?' And so, I gave up and decided to pour milk in my coffee.

I was returning to my friends holding my cup and mixing the sugar with my spoon when Murat saw me and suddenly grabbed the hand in which I was holding the cup. He looked in the cup and started laughing like crazy, leaving me without an answer as to why. Other friends also joined Murat – looking into my cup and laughing like crazy. No one can stop laughing enough to explain why they are laughing. After they finished laughing, Murat looked at me, with eyes filled with tears after a big laugh, and asked, 'Sasha, how come you took a coffee with milk?' I said, 'because I wanted to get out of my frame, I wanted to try and see if the milk was good or not. It was a last minute decision.' 'Are you sure that is the truth? Are you sure that was your rational choice, Sasha?', Murat wanted to know. 'Yes, of course, why wouldn't it be? I really wanted to try the milk this time.', I replied. Murat replied: 'OK, I understand that you wanted it, but the reason was not your rational decision.' 'What do you mean? Explain, please.' 'Sasha, do you remember when you went to get your coffee and I said something and you didn't understand and you asked me to repeat?' 'Yes, I remember… what about it… I didn't understand you, I don't know what you said.' 'You not hearing me played no part, as far as I can see, because you took what I'd told you to take.' 'Murat, wait. What did you tell me? Take a coffee with milk, and that's why I did, or what?' 'No, of course I didn't say to take coffee with milk – with your resistance to the milk, you would never accept such a direct suggestion. I said: Coffee is brown!' I was shocked. How was it possible for me, who work on these patterns, who live for these patterns? How could I get programmed so easily?

If you don't understand the suggestion, I'll further clarify it now.

Murat said: 'Coffee is brown.'

Is represents equality. In other words, for coffee to be coffee, it must be brown (only in my head if the suggestion sticks). Thus, black coffee is not coffee (in my head). Since I fell for this suggestion, it was almost impossible for me to return with black coffee.

In my seminars, I end this story with the comment: So much for our free will.

So, what am I trying to say?

What I'm trying to say is that every good/bad input leads to a reaction, which will be triggered by a stimulant in the future. The input could be the aforementioned visual, auditory, kinesthetic, olfactory, gustative, or a set of words which we say to a certain person or which come to us.

Stop for a moment and think about a couple of questions:

If you occasionally enjoy alcoholic drinks, think and say whether your very first experience with a glass of alcohol was pleasant or unpleasant. Specifically, the flavor – was your first reaction when you tried it 'Mmmm, this is good?'

If you drink coke, was your first experience with it result in the reaction 'Mmmm, this is so good...'

If you're a smoker, was the same positive reaction triggered when you lighted your first cigarette?

If you wear jeans, was your body's first reaction 'Jeans are so comfortable'?

Then what happened to make some of these activities or contents pleasant and we truly enjoy them? The simple answer is: We were programmed, or conditioned to enjoy these activities and contents.

Coke is cool! Cigarettes are cool (Marlboro Man)! Jeans are cool and sexy!
The suggestions are the same like in my example with 'Coffee is brown'. When we, consciously or unconsciously, decided to believe that it is true, that our maps say it's true, we started to enjoy all those things that at first our bodies classified as tasteless and uncomfortable and even disgusting.
Pizza is cool!

My whole family enjoyed pizza. OK, almost the whole family, everyone except for my brother Luka. Nobody could understand why Luka didn't like pizza. Pizza tastes good; everyone likes pizza, how come he doesn't (map is not a territory was an unknown assumption back then)? For years we would order pizza and Luka wouldn't even smell it, let alone try it. One day when Luka was 5 or 6 he ran into the house and yelled, 'Mom, Dad, I want a pizza!' 'Luka, how come? You don't like pizza,' Mom replied. 'I want to eat a pizza, please Mom order me a pizza.' Since then Luka is, like most people, a pizza lover. Can you guess what caused this behavior? You can't think that this came about without any stimulant, or environmental input?

Luka saw the Teenage Mutant Ninja Turtles cartoon. We all know what the Ninja Turtles do, don't we? The Ninja Turtles are well-known pizza enthusiasts and when they order pizzas, their whole body (shell and limbs) shows the enthusiasm that they then transfer to the children who love them. If you think back to the part about authority on the chapter on beliefs, you know that authority is the person for whom we believe that he or she knows better than us (a parent, a teacher, a trainer), and in many cases the authority is a person we admire. If we admire someone, we are ready to take up their values, beliefs, and even part of identity in order to be as similar as possible to our idols, our role models.

The good thing about this is that by better understanding the way in which these forms condition us, we can better control their power over us. We cannot control them absolutely, but we can do our best to shield and protect ourselves from a great number of those inputs.

Also, a great value lies in the fact that by knowing and understanding inputs we can change the people we care about.

If we agree that the change depends on the interactions of what is within us and what we receive via our senses, the question arises... how to use this?

One day in my class there was a young, ambitious dentist. She told me about her experience and asked for a solution. She said, "I have a five-year-old niece, and we cannot motivate her to brush her teeth. Can this be changed? Can she be programmed to brush her teeth, for her resistance to be removed?"

I personally believe that pieces of advice don't usually make people smarter, which I learned on NLP, and instead of advice I will try to give an answer through metaphors or analogies. I started by saying, "Do you agree that few people really enjoy mopping floors, window washing, vacuuming, etc.? My question for you is, why is that? Why don't people enjoy these activities while on the other hand they enjoy a good movie or a good book? Could that have anything to do with inputs we received by looking and listening to our elders and our parents while doing some of those activities? Try to think, what was your mother's facial expression when during the weekend instead of resting she had to kneel on the floor and clean up? What noises did she make? You were little and maybe you approached your mother and asked her to play with you. And your mother said "Come on (leave me alone) I can't, I have to clean." in that specific voice. In that moment you received multiple inputs: a visual input, what she was doing; an auditory input and the sentence I cannot, I have to X; and in the end you received the emotion. What was that emotion?

While on the other hand, when one of the parents said, "Let's watch a movie tonight," what was the reaction? What is the difference in the way when something is said in the first case as opposed to the other case? What is the emotion that is transferred to you in that conversation?
Could you imagine what would happen if you had asked your mother to play with you, and she said, with a smile on her face, "Not now, not now, Mommy is enjoying her cleaning... I clean because I like it, and you also like a nice and clean home!" Do you get the idea?

That's how I finished my story.

The dentist e-mailed me several days after the seminar: My niece brushes her teeth twice a day!

I asked her to describe how she'd done it, step by step.

In her next e-mail she described the whole process:

I arrived at my sister's with the intention to try what you'd said in your seminar, but I wanted to do it my way. First, not to be too obvious, I played with her for about twenty minutes in the living room. After we played, and when she was in a good mood, I said, "You stay here now, and auntie is going to do something only adults do. Please don't follow me. You won't? Promise that you won't." My niece laughed and didn't want to promise. When I got up I said once again that she couldn't follow me. My niece gave a "wicked" little laugh. I knew I had her. I went to the bathroom, humming to myself. I took a toothbrush, put toothpaste on and started brushing my teeth while still humming the tune. My niece was standing in the doorway giggling, and I was showing her non-verbally, by nodding and waving my hands that she can't come in, and continued to hum. The next minute she ran into the bathroom and took her toothbrush. I decided to react: "No, just don't put toothpaste on; toothpaste is just for big girls." My niece laughed and tried to take the toothpaste, but I decided to play some more: "No, no, you can't..."

The result: the niece brushes her teeth twice a day.

The point is: by changing the input, we change the meaning of experience. By changing the experience someone has about something and within a certain frame, we affect the change in behavior.

The experience that inspired me originally comes from my days when I worked as an underground garage cleaner.

My mother used to work 10-14 hours a day in order to feed me and my two brothers, and to put us through school. A few weeks after I enrolled in my third year of college, we had a conversation in which she said, 'Sasha, I'm very tired; it's hard for me to work for the three of you. Could you please try to make things easier, financially? Could you work a few days a week and try to co-finance yourself?' I said that of course I could – my goal was to make it easier for her. I had an arranged job in the parking service. I thought that I would work a maximum of two days a week and that my job would entail selling parking tickets, writing tickets, etc. I came to the interview and got the job. My superior didn't explain what I was to do, but he asked another worker to show me. He called me, took a broom and bucket and showed me what pieces of trash should immediately be collected from the floor. When I realized what the job was about I had a feeling I was in a nightmare. Not only did I hate cleaning, I loathed it, and now I had to do it. Okay, I thought, I'll grind my teeth, clean up for today and that's it. My supervisor asked me to call him at the end of the day, when I was finished. It was one of the longest days of my life. I called him around 5 PM and said, "Mr. Mio, I'm finished." To this he replied enthusiastically, 'Well done Sasha, great Sasha, you're finished already. I'm glad you're with us, Sasha. When does it suit you to come in tomorrow, 5 or 6 AM?" "6 AM', I answered automatically." "OK Sasha, see you tomorrow, go and have some rest. And tomorrow pick up those larger pieces of trash like today, and when you finish with that, call me." I realized too late that this was not a one-day job, but I had no choice – I had to help my mother, and Mr. Mio was an interesting person. The second day I was at work at 6 AM, cleaned all the larger pieces by noon and called Mr. Mio: "Mr. Mio, I'm done, I picked up all the trash from the floors." And again, the reaction was the same. "Well done, Sasha, great! Tell me, do you have a class at college today?" I said, "Not today, no." 'Sasha, I have something to ask you, but only if you have the time..." I instantly replied, "I have time, Mr. Mio, what is it?" He said, "Could you please check the descents between the floors, dust gathers there every few days, so if you could sweep a couple of doorsteps and check if anything gathered. If there isn't, you're done for the day. And call me when you finish, be it in 15 minutes or an hour or two." How do you say no to such a man? I cleaned all the descents, which took over two hours. I called Mr. Mio and said, "Mr. Mio, there was dust, but it's clean now." "Well done Sasha, you're done for the day. Thank you, you're a great worker. Make sure to call me tomorrow after work." "Yes Mr. Mio." On the third day I picked up all the larger pieces of trash relatively quickly and it occurred to me to check the descents again, even if it was only one day away. And a good thing that I did – there was dust again. After I finished I called Mr. Mio and said, "Mr. Mio, I cleaned all the trash and checked the descents for dust, and cleaned those, too." His reaction: "Well done, Sasha, great self-initiative, you did something I didn't expect." "Thank you Mr. Mio." Mr. Mio said: "Sasha, tell me... since you finished so quickly, and if you have some time, could you check the hydrant boxes... you know the ones where the fire hoses are... every week there's dust on them, so check if there's any now. You take a wet cloth and wipe the box."

During the next two weeks Mr. Mio would give me another task each day, in a non-invasive way. Every day I checked everything he suggested on the previous days. From the person who hated cleaning, in two weeks I became a person who lived for the moment in the day when I get to call Mr. Mio and tell him that this garage was as clean as a children's hospital. I enjoyed taking care of the garage and other tasks Mr. Mio assigned me when my cleaning speed increased. He was an exceptional leader, master of communication and a nice person. Why did I follow him? It was because he was a role model. He was coherent, he was just and motivating, and he provided proper input at the right time. A few weeks later I asked him, "Mr. Mio, how come you didn't tell me that there's so much work here, but you only told me to clean the larger pieces of trash? How could you let the garages be so dirty while I worked my first and second week?" He wisely replied, "Sasha, we needed a good worker, and if I showed you all that there is to do here, I wouldn't see you on the second day."

Another one of my role models is the famous hypnotherapist Milton H. Erickson. The importance of this experience is in isolating the visual input. You see how that works. I can personally testify on the effectiveness of this approach because I had the same problem for five years. I tried it all, from diet change, creams, etc. and nothing helped. Not until I joined the army and had other things and activities in mind.

Skin conditions by Milton H. Erickson:
"A woman doctor from the East called me up and said, "My son's a student at Harvard and he has an extremely bad case of acne. Can you treat that with hypnosis?"
I said, "Yes, why bother bringing him to me? How are you going to spend Christmas vacation?"
She said, "Usually we take a vacation from medical practice and go to Sun Valley and ski."
I said, "Well, this Christmas vacation, why you don't take your son with you? Find a cabin and remove all mirrors in it. You can eat your meals in that cabin, and be sure that you keep your hand mirror in

the safety pocket of your purse." They spent the time skiing and the son couldn't see a mirror. His acne cleared up in two weeks' time."

How did such a small change cause the acne to disappear?
Simply, there was a change of focus. Everyone who's ever had problems with acne knows how much acne can affect one's mood. When I had those problems I used to spend hours in front of a mirror. I would look at my face and feel shame and disgust. Those conditions caused by looking in the mirror started a behavior – squeezing acne. After squeezing, the face often looks worse than before. This visual information triggers an ever worse state of mind, and our thoughts are linked to the condition of our face. In every interaction with other people, those who don't have that problem, we check if they may be looking at our squeezed-out face. Every different look is interpreted as if the person we are talking to is thinking about acne. Life becomes filled with acne, which is impossible to get rid of. The problem is impossible to solve because we are always thinking about it; we are always in front of the mirror and squeezing. By changing the focus, i.e., removing the mirror, we didn't get rid of the acne, but we just changed the state and thus sabotaged the loop. No mirror equals no bad feeling – no squeezing. When the squeezing stops, the problem goes away.

To conclude, the easiest way to solve a problem is by controlling the input we receive from the environment. We simply decide either to eliminate or to ignore it. The content of the input by which you solve a problem is yours to decide.

The key: Influence yourself with the right inputs

As you've seen in the previous examples with new input, we can conclude that the most of our personal changes come from what we saw, heard and felt. We often ask ourselves why children from the same parents and genetic heritage, who were raised in the same way and lived within the same framework, are different.

I emphasize, I do not completely neglect temper, but I give greater value to input, i.e. experience that forms our internal maps.

How is it possible that a father and son have completely different models of the world?

I often find myself in situations in which successful self-made businessmen ask me, 'Why doesn't my son have the same ambition as me? Not the same, but at least a bit of the ambition I possess? I tried to transfer my values to him; I tried to set an example about the attitude which leads to success, and in his case that is completely missing.' After I hear such an experience, I ask them, 'Isn't it true that you were raised in harder circumstances than him?' 'Yes, it's true.' 'Well, that alone gives you greater motivation, greater values and ambition to get away from that condition, the condition in which you didn't want to be. He hasn't lived in those conditions and his map tells him that he's happy having what you made and that he doesn't need any more. Isn't that an option? Another thing, could you remember, when you were a child, what motivated you to be so ambitious? I assume it wasn't your parents, because they weren't wealthy?' The answer I tend to get to that question is, 'Movies, it was movies. I was inspired by movies.' '

Could you think about my explanation? I'm not saying it's 100% accurate. Your son isn't nearly as unhappy with his childhood as you were – that's the first factor, or motivational trigger. You had a strong negative motivation. The second factor: to this motivation you added the inspiring rags to riches movies, which made you believe that you too can do it. Even if your son saw the same movies, because of the lack of that state of dissatisfaction (motivation) that you had possessed in your internal map, those inputs would not stick with him in the way they had stuck to you.

In order to decide to change anything, at least two conditions must be met. The first one is condition. This condition can create either a negative motivation if we are unhappy with our condition or a positive motivation if we saw, heard or felt that there is a wanted state that we want to achieve. If there is no state, there is no value to move from the point at which we currently find ourselves. But, that is not enough.

To know what we want or don't want represents a value; in order to even think about achieving that goal, that value, we must have conviction. In the example with my businessman friend, the conviction came from rags to riches stories/movies, and it is as follows: If he could do it, so can I. Such conviction further strengthens the motivation and leads us one step further... towards searching for a strategy that will lead us to our goal in the fastest, or easiest, or most painless way possible. If there is no strategy, we again find ourselves in problems and our motivation weakens, and vice versa. When these conditions are met, we must choose the right environment that will trigger the necessary behaviors for achieving the condition we're going for. Remember from the previous chapters that the environment is the one that defines the most important condition for change, because if the environment doesn't support our wanted state by inputs and opportunities, we have only two choices: either change the wanted state or change the environment.

"No problem can be solved from the same level of consciousness that created it."
Albert Einstein

Every book you've ever read is an input, every movie you see is an input, every conversation you ever had or are having is an input, and everything is an input. The only question is whether the inputs you allow yourself or which you choose on a daily/monthly basis lead you to the state in which you want to be.

My everyday strategy for accessing inputs is this: What benefits do I get by watching this show or movie, by reading newspapers, by reading this book, talking about a certain subject, etc.? Is this content helping me to become my better self? How will this content affect my perception, and how can this content contribute to my action? If I watch daily news, how does that contribute to me? How does information on the recession contribute to me? How does information about the bad things that happen daily to people around the world contribute to me? That is something that goes on whether I wanted to or not, and I have absolutely no influence on those events. Knowing that bad things happen can only provoke my sympathy, but my sympathy upon receiving this information doesn't solve any of those problems.

Two years ago I moved into an apartment in which there was no TV. For as long as I can remember, I have been a TV addict. I would walk into the apartment and automatically pick up the remote and turn on the TV – whether there was anything good on it or not, the TV was on. I used to fall asleep in front of the TV, as well. Picture this situation: I've been asleep for hours with the TV on, and I'm woken by an explosion and gunfire from the movie *Saving Private Ryan*. How does that affect my mind, my internal map and how does that affect my state the next day? It must have some influence.

So there was no TV in that apartment, and since I hadn't known how long I would be staying, I had no intention of buying one. For the first few weeks I missed my conditioned behavior of watching TV, but I solved it by watching movies and documentaries on my computer. I would watch exclusively what I selected, the content which could benefit me. After a few months I came over for lunch at my girlfriend's house (she is now my wife). After lunch, I sat on the couch and automatically turned the TV on. There was a series on, and a few seconds later the commercials started. It took me less than a minute of watching TV to realize that I was watching junk for my mind. Low-quality content and commercials that exists only to program my mind for spending. I turned off the TV. It took almost a year for a former TV addict to lose his previous value and conditioned form of taking the remote control... I didn't have the chance. I married my girlfriend and together we went searching for a new apartment. There was a huge plasma TV in the apartment we were interested in. My reaction to the landlord was, 'We'll take it, but please remove the TV from the apartment.' The landlord agreed and asked us whether that could wait for a few weeks because he was just leaving on a business trip. We agreed. A few weeks later he called us to ask whether it suited us for him to pick up the TV the next day. It was already too late, I replied, 'NO.'. My old pattern had returned and I was spending a lot of afternoons hooked to the TV and except for good shows on Discovery and NG, I was mostly feeding my mind with junk. Luckily, 9 months later the landlord cancelled our lease because he wanted to move back in. We changed the location and again there was no TV in our new apartment. We compensated for the TV by buying a projector (without TV subscription) and agreed to turn the projector on once a day and watch only what we choose. So, I'm not saying that you shouldn't have a pattern of turning the TV on and leaving it on without having benefits. I would very much like to own a TV if I could trust myself enough not to watch shows which don't benefit me, news which doesn't benefit me, and commercials which don't make me smarter but make me dumber. I found my strategy for controlling inputs from the outside world, and it's a strategy that I know my identity can support. If you have your own better strategy for controlling negative and/or useless inputs on a daily basis... go for it. TV isn't bad by itself, it's only bad when we cannot control what we watch and when we cannot resist what we watch and get no value out of it.

How to choose the right inputs

Before choosing any activity, ask yourself: What's in it for me?
What exactly do I get out of it? How does the time invested in watching, reading and listening to this content contribute to becoming my better self?

Can this content make me more motivated? Can this content make me smarter? Can this content make me more capable? Does this content contribute to making me a better parent? Does this content enable me to make more money? Or whatever it is you value...

If the answer is NO, then there is no value for you and your future. In other words, those inputs would be useless for you. What doesn't contribute doesn't necessarily have to be harmful, but in my map useless is also harmful because it's a time-waster.

I have a few friends for whom I could say they are whiners. They always complain. 'There is no work, did you see the news? And the situation will get worse. It's hard.' As soon as I hear this, I tell them directly, 'Please stop complaining. Don't poison me. I have my own world in which I don't accept those ideas and it is useless to even discuss that. Such topics and information are not the object of my interest.' It may sound rude, but if I don't benefit from a conversation I would rather be rude than poisoned. I try to change the topic towards happier things, but some of my friends seem deaf to those things.

What does such communication bring us? How does it affect us? If we accept the assumption that the situation is hard, and that it will become even harder, this assumption ceases to be an assumption and transforms into our personal belief. If there is a belief that something is hard and that it's outside my abilities, we will block our behavior and won't move from that spot. Remember that values and convictions are either generators for new behaviors or they're 'blockers'. Convictions on impossibility ground us in place. Considering that some of them have such beliefs, even when a solution is offered, they wave their heads and see impossibilities instead of possibilities.
 Remember, the reason for this is that our convictions are strong filters that greatly influence our perception of what we see and what we ignore (delete).

Inputs that can make you go bankrupt

A few months before I opened my second company I would walk through town and see a lot of businesses that were doing well. When my company started to fail, I would simply filter out, i.e. delete those businesses which were doing fine. I would walk through town and only see closed bars and companies. My everyday communication with my friends came down to: 'Did you hear who else shut their business? Did you know he went bankrupt, too?' In my head I erased the existence of successful businesses and was blind to seeing them because I didn't want to be the only one to whom this was happening. My communication then served no other purpose except justifying that everyone was having a hard time, and that the failure did not depend on me, but on the situation. That is partially true, but how does that help me get out? How does that help me change myself, change my approach and finally succeed? It doesn't! And the inevitable happened. Who was to blame? Was it because of my inexperienced workers or the situation in the world? No, I was to blame because I had been unprepared and had pre-programmed my doom. Inspired by rags to riches literature I created a conviction, a conviction that became a self-fulfilling prophecy. This conviction was: Every great entrepreneur has to fail at least once.

That claim implies that I couldn't be a great entrepreneur before I failed once. My value was to be a great entrepreneur, and to become one, I had to fail once. I'm not saying that the crisis had nothing to do with my failure with my second company, but I'm saying that with my conviction I buried myself in advance. OK I'll fail once then with my next company I'll be a great entrepreneur.

Later I met a man who had also bankrupted a couple of months before we talked, and he tried to transfer his conviction to me: 'Every great entrepreneur has to fail 3 times. Terrible, isn't it?' After hearing that I realized that I had been very lucky with my conviction. If we want a quality change and if want to avoid bad things happening and good things to happen more, we have to start filling out our folders with proper inputs.

After quoting Jim Rohn: You are the average of five people you spend the most time with, or Cervantes: Tell me who are your friends and I will tell you who are you, I think that the inputs coming from people around you would top my list. What are those inputs like? Are they encouraging or restrictive and do they sabotage you?

I'm not suggesting you should make an instant cut or simply remove your whining friends from your life, but you should reduce those gatherings and if possible, become direct when they start to complain and say, 'Could we please change the subject? What good things are going on in your life?'

From which friends, or those who aren't friends yet, does my invested time yield the best benefits? Who can improve me with a positive attitude, interesting knowledge or understanding? Who among the people around me can give me top quality encouraging inputs?

The biggest, and to me the funniest compliment I ever personally received was from my best man a few years ago, 'Man, after a drink with you I feel like I can build a house with my bare hands.'

Who are the people around you who can motivate you to build a house? Choose them and start building. Your house is your internal map and every ingredient makes that house firmer, nicer and safer.

What are the other contents with which I can fill my internal folder?

In search of a useful, more improved model of the world inputs

Ask yourself these questions:
Which books can I read to fill my internal map in order to be a better, more capable and happier person?
What kind of movies can help me to raise the bar for my values and convictions?
Which activities can I be a part of in order to develop behaviors that will make me a more capable and valuable person?

In other words: What do I have to see, hear and feel in order to fill out my map, my life, with new and better resources and conditions? Whether it is going to the theater, a seminar, cinema, class, or something else, make sure you're aware that it is valuable and why it is valuable for you.
Time is the greatest value because it cannot be compensated. That's why if you go to a class, theater or a cinema and you see that you're not receiving useful inputs and not realizing your value, simply leave that environment. Those few dollars you paid for the ticket are worth less than wasting time and receiving unwanted inputs in your map.

If you always do what you've always done, you'll always get what you've always gotten. If you want something new, do something new...so choose the right inputs.
-NLP presuppositions

Make your life more CONSCIOUS

Why are you on autopilot?

In this moment in time, while you're reading this book, you are most likely in autopilot mode. The reason why - because you usually read books on similar topics. The pattern of reading about this topic is a part of your existing map, isn't it? There is a small chance that I'm wrong. If I'm not wrong, congratulations for getting out of your frame.

Whether you take the same route to work every day, order food from the same restaurant, you only order the food that you know is good because you tried it. Maybe you're not in the first category, maybe you eat at a different place every time or maybe you eat different food every time. But one thing is certain: in both cases you're on autopilot mode.

If you're in the first category, the result of your behavior is an experience in the distant past when you decided to play it safe. You decided to stick with what you know, with what is tested. If you're in the second category, by my personal criteria you achieve far greater value because you created a richer map of visual, auditory and kinesthetic experiences. But, both forms are exclusive, which makes your map and the behaviors which come from it very predictable or in other words, automatic. In both cases you are strongly conditioned to behave within a known pattern, and that is something we have to fight.

Smith put it scaringly bluntly in his book The Flinch: "Straight-A student. Straight to college. Straight to work. Straight up the corporate ladder. Straight to the suburbs...Damn, you've been scared straight. Is this you? Corridors lead you from bed, to breakfast, to your car, to work, and then home. You have a cubicle you come to every day. You go to the same lunch place. You watch the same shows. You like the same food."

The fight against autopilot patterns

"They could replace you with a small, predictable robot. And one day soon, they probably will."
Julien Smith

Most people I know personally are the same people they were 15 or 20 years ago, only today they have loans and more commitments in every sense of the word. They are stuck without knowing it. What keeps them within the same frame? It is the decision that the frame in which they live is "safe" and the other one is risky. The very habit of the map's frame is the problem, and that is why, especially people from the first category, those who play it safe, are victims of environmental conditions. The environment and its inputs completely define and determine their behavior by deliberately and covertly imposing the values of how things should look like for them to be truly happy. The worst part is that they don't do anything about it, most likely because they either don't know they can do it or maybe they convinced themselves enough that the things they own and will own make them happier than the loans they pay and will pay make them sadder.

I personally was enormously fortunate that, based on experience, I realized where such behavior could take me and where it will surely take me unless I change my pattern. Of course, I was not that smart to wise up and get the point, but I've had an experience that shook my map. Shaking of the map is, as you have learned, a necessary preliminary work to every change. I owned two businesses and had employees 8-9 years younger than myself. I lived for being successful. By success I understood being a great businessman, and I returned all the money I'd made back into the business. On the other hand there were my employees who'd just finished high school and some of them took out loans and bought cars when they had gotten their first paychecks. All of my employees drove better cars than me. I simply couldn't afford it. When I went bankrupt and had only $200 left, I was thinking about every dollar I was going to spend, 'If I buy product A or product B, what is the actual difference, if it is the same product?' And I would end up buying the cheaper product. I realized that in most cases, concerning food, specifically, there is no great difference in quality or even taste. If I had never ended up in a situation like that, a situation of dire emergency, I would probably still be buying brand-name products and would never try the cheaper ones. I never would have realized that in most cases it is basically the same product. I would have simply decided to trust the brand and wouldn't take chances. I know people who are disgusted to buy store brand products, and the worst part is that their disgust doesn't come from experience, but from conviction. They never tried it, and they are disgusted.

The hardcore pattern destruction

Habits (or wants) are routines of behavior that are repeated regularly and tend to occur subconsciously. In the American Journal of Psychology it is defined in this way: "A habit, from the standpoint of psychology, is a more or less fixed way of thinking, willing, or feeling acquired through previous repetition of a mental experience." Old habits are hard to break and new habits are hard to form because the behavioral patterns we repeat are imprinted in our neural pathways.

The key to change, i.e. expanding the map is hard and consists of changing hundreds of such patterns which determine our behavior and make it 99% predicable. I'm not saying all habits are bad, I'm just saying that they don't necessarily have to control our lives. How often have you caught yourself in the pattern of automatically placing products in your shopping cart, without thinking twice? We want to avoid that! I don't forbid myself to take the same product I've been buying so far. I'm only saying that I'm trying to create conscious decisions as much as I can. I want to revive my mind in those situations in which I'm sleeping, i.e. walking a known path.

Habits as a personal addiction

I like to call habits our personal addictions. I call them addictions because they are so conditioned and incorporated into our everyday lives that by failing to repeat one of these actions, our body feels the pain. They have a psychological and a physiological component. If you brush your teeth every day before you leave the house, what happens when one day you decide to skip it? Not repeating that action becomes your main preoccupation of your conscious mind. 'Does my breath stink? What if other people notice? How can I solve that problem? Where can I buy a pack of gum?' And when you buy gum, your need for non-smelly mouth is now satisfied and your "pain" and conscious burden stops and you can finally relax and give in to your daily automatics knowing that "I am in control!"

Consciously controlled habits

One of my business role models was and still is a man who was an exceptional leader. His name is Milan. His position in the company with hundreds of employees wasn't important as he was respected by all, and a role model to everyone. All of his employees had good salaries and enjoyed their work and contribution. It takes great communication skills for such a result.

One time he told me a story. In his company he set high moral and humanitarian standards. One day he told his employees that, according to their own possibilities and wages, they have the opportunity to help someone who needs it. He suggested that every month employees collect $30 per person. Of course, that gesture was not mandatory, and no one is expected to do it as a must, but with his communication and leadership skills everyone supported the idea.

At the end of the first month, the secretary knocked on Milan's door, came into his office and said: 'Milan, here's the money we collected for that family amongst ourselves and now I'm bringing it to you.' Milan looked at her and said: 'I think there was a misunderstanding. I have no intention of taking that money and giving it to a family, and the fact that you collected the money does not mean that you solved the problem. You didn't actually invest anything in the goal. You opened your wallets, took out the $30 and now you feel good. You did this more for yourselves than you thought about how this $30 from each of you will help this family. Someone might have been glad to give this $30, and many did so because it was expected of them or because they were embarrassed not to give.' The secretary asked what to do with the money.
Milan said: 'Here's what: give the money back to everyone and tell them this – We won't be collecting the money, and if your decision to

help is sincere, do it like this: invest a conscious effort. Take your $30, get in the car, drive to a store and think. You have a single dad and two underage children. What do they really need? When you think about what they need, buy $30 worth of things.
Only then have you done a good deed,' Milan said.

What did Milan actually want to do for his employees? Milan wanted to provide an experience for them. To give $30 is only the experience of giving money away. He wanted them to have an actual real experience and to invest a conscious effort to truly see that as helping.

This pattern became a habit among the employees, but only with that amount of money; everything else was conscious decision making based on the story about a family who was being helped certain month.

Our habits provide us with a sense of safety and control over our lives. We created our comfort zones; we want to be better, to get more out of life. But, not many people are ready to leave these safe patterns. We assume that leaving the patterns could be painful; the truth is that this very idea, i.e. mental image within our mind that something is painful or can be painful creates that pain without real experience. The reason for this is that the human mind doesn't significantly differentiate between a real experience and a mental image.
For example, if you're watching a horror film, you know that is only a film, but the combination of visual and auditory inputs/stimulants creates a representation without endangering your life. Imagine a situation where you're holding a lemon. You take a knife and cut the lemon in half. Take one slice of lemon and squeeze it into your mouth. There is a reaction in this moment, and the reaction is only based on what you've read, i.e. a fake experience. The reaction is the result of a previous experience and assumed reaction to this experience.

Experiences stored in our maps, whether direct or indirect, have conditioned us to avoid potentially unpleasant situations, and to repeat the pleasant ones. That's how the firm framework of our maps was made: the assumption that a future experience, a situation will cause pain.

Escaping pain zones

The Flinch is the moment when every doubt you've ever had comes back and hits you, hard. It's when your whole body feels tense. It's an instinct that tells you to run. It's a moment of tension that happens in the body and the brain, and it stops everything cold. When coming across something they know will make them flinch, most people have been trained to refuse the challenge and turn back. It's a reaction that brings up old memories and haunts you. It tightens your chest and makes you want to run. Flinch can invoke a fear of a certain kind of person, a kind of racism or xenophobia, or a fear of new technology or outside influences.   It whispers in your ear so you'll dismiss a good idea that requires a lot of change. The flinch doesn't want you to change. Its agenda is to keep you in status quo.

Behind every flinch is a fear or an anxiety—sometimes rational, sometimes not. Without the fear, there is no flinch. But wiping out the fear isn't what's important—facing it is.

The first exercise for understanding how the Flinch operates on you: When you're at home and have five minutes, go to your bathroom, walk up to your shower and turn on the cold water. Wait a second; then test it to make sure it's as cold as possible.

Do you see what's coming?

If you do, you should tense up immediately. You should feel it in your chest. You might start laughing to release the tension—and you haven't even stepped inside. You're predicting a flinch that hasn't happened yet. You're already anxious about it—about something that hasn't happened and won't kill you—anxious about something that barely hurts at all.

Ok, do it. Now is the time to step in the shower. As the cold water hits you, you might shout or squirm. But the discomfort lasts only a second. You quickly get used to it. You get comfortable with cold, instead of trying to avoid it. You put yourself in the path of the shower to speed up the adjustment process.

Remember your reaction. You can use this method for everything. A moment before, the flinch seems so uncomfortable that you might talk yourself out of this. You convince yourself that it's pointless, but it isn't; it's training. You need to build a habit of seeing the flinch and going forward, not rationalizing your fear and stepping away. Start doing the opposite of your habits. It builds up your tolerance to the flinch and its power.

The same night I finished reading *"The Flinch"* I decided to do this task, i.e. is to check the truth behind the Flinch idea. I entered the bathroom, opened the tap and set it to cold. I removed my clothes and before I entered, I created the idea of entering a cold shower in a minute. There was a painful reaction and I was ready to give up for a second - exactly as Julien described it. But, I plucked up my courage and decided to go all the way. I got in the shower, and frankly, I think it was one of the three most painful experiences I'd ever had. After about ten seconds I heard that little voice in my head that everyone knows: 'Okay Sasha, you tried it, it's done, turn the tap to warm.' I was about to turn it when I realized, yes, I tried it, but I am again consciously aiming to avoid pain, to avoid the Flinch. And I repeated the procedure with the goal of seeing how much can my inner dialogue "work me over" to make me stop. I felt incredible pain, and when it became intolerable, I shut the water to recover. I repeated this procedure three more times. When I was done, I opened the shower door, took my towel and started to dry. I noticed something very interesting in my body's reaction to this new input. When I shower in hot water and take a towel, I usually quickly rub my body with the towel in an attempt to warm myself as fast as possible. This time, I moved slowly and calmly, there was no rush as usual, I felt really pleasant. When I left the bathroom I had a strange feeling in my head, like everything was silenced, and that I was peaceful and tranquil, as if nothing bad could ever happen after this, nothing that would shake me significantly. Try it for yourself, I highly recommend it.

Inspired by this experience, I started thinking about exactly how many experiences we define as painful that is actually painful, and how many are conditioned. In my next class a few days later I asked the students the following question, 'How many of you wash your faces in the morning with warm water?' About half of them raised their hands, the others washed in cold water. Both groups were in an exclusive pattern.

The following question was, 'Who finds washing your face in cold water painful?' The result: only those who washed in warm water. The conclusion: even pain and pleasure are the result of repeated patterns, i.e. habit. By this analogy, what is opposite of habit, whatever the habit was, results in a certain level of pain.

For the next few days I decided to follow my inner dialogue and try to catch myself in any automatic patterns, whether they were patterns of behavior or thinking. My wife would say, 'Sasha, could you please vacuum the apartment?' I would say: 'Yes, in half an hour!' And that's where I would stop myself. Whoa, my automatics… 'No, I'm sorry, I'll do it now.' For every automatic pattern I noticed, I would automatically act differently. After those initial few days I realized it was not so hard and decided to make it a habit. At first I thought that thinking about and following all these personal patterns would occupy my conscious mind too much, but I learned to track my kinesthetic, feelings and inner dialogue. Today, as soon as I feel resistance towards something, like answering a phone call from a person to whom I don't feel like talking, or a phone call which I assume will end negatively, under the assumption I see it, so not always, I instantly decide to do the opposite. You have to try this strategy because it feels so good. It is an amazing feeling when you create the ability to control and defy your automated map, and not the other way around. Of course, this depends on how much good pressure you can take.

The Von Restorf effect

People often ask me how come I have such a good memory. I reply that I wouldn't say that I had a good memory, but I believe that having a good memory is no problem if you decide every day to do different things, or same things in a different way. The reason for my memory is not in being a genius, but a wealth of different experiences. If you stop for a moment and think, when old people, our grandparents tell us about "interesting" details from their lives, from which period are those stories? These come mostly from their youth, right? Growing up is filled with new and intensive experiences, and considering that the mind remembers the content combined with emotions, their stories come from that exact life period. The rest of their lives up until they are 70-80 is not nearly as interesting because it could be summed up like this: We got married, built a house, then your mother was born, then your uncle was born, etc. more or less… then we got grandchildren… Besides these key events, the rest was on autopilot.

Try a test.
Imagine you have a shopping list. You have 5 seconds to remember it. After 10 seconds close your eyes and try to name the things on the list.

- eggs
- bread
- butter
- potatoes
- 2 jars of peanut butter
- tomato
- lettuce
- juice
- pickles
- apples
- oranges
- kiwi

How many items did you manage to name? This is not a test of memory, but a test of how your mind leads to remembering.

There is a phenomenon called The Von Restorff effect. The effect is named after psychiatrist and children's pediatrician Hedwig von Restorff 1906–1962). This is also called the isolation effect and predicts that an item that "stands out like a sore thumb" (called distinctive encoding) is more likely to be remembered than other items. There is a bias in favor of remembering the unusual.

Exercises that will create new neuron pathways

The mind tends to remember more easily the content at the beginning (first 2-3) content at the end and something in the middle which jumps out of the frame either by form or by content (2 jars of peanut butter).

The reason why I believe that I have a good memory is because, unlike the people who praise my memory, most of my days contain something unusual. My Von Restorff effect is on a daily basis, while usually with people who have a day job and frequently engage in similar activities, it only happens on a weekly or a monthly basis. It is a shame that I didn't have such an effect during my education.

Here's a simple memory recipe: every day do something that you wouldn't usually do and that will be remembered. Just leave your map's framework.

When I was working in the garages, my friend Nick showed me the book called *Keep Your Brain Alive*, which inspired me immensely and which I read over and over. (*83 Neurobic Exercises to Help Prevent Memory Loss and Increase Mental Fitness* written by Lawrence C. Katz, Ph.D. & Manning Rubin)

Neurobics is based on solid scientific ground; it is an exciting synthesis of substantial findings about the brain that provides a concrete strategy for keeping the brain fit and flexible, as you grow older. The goal of Neurobics is to create actions that create new and different patterns of neuron activity in the brain.

There are numerous myths about the aging brain that neuroscientists are disproving daily. With the help of exciting new technologies, the traditional view of the way the brain ages is being rapidly revised. Evidence clearly shows that the brain doesn't have to go into a steep decline, as we get older.

New brain cells can be generated in adults

In fact, in 1998, a team of American and Swedish scientists demonstrated for the first time that new brain cells are generated in adult humans.

Also contrary to popular belief, the mental decline most people experience is not due to the steady death of nerve cells. Instead, it usually results from the thinning out of the number and complexity of dendrites, the branches on nerve cells that directly receive and process information from other nerve cells that forms the basis of memory. Dendrites receive information across connections called synapses. If connections aren't regularly switched on, the dendrites can atrophy. This reduces the brain's ability to put new information into memory as well as to retrieve old information. Growing dendrites was long thought to be possible only in the brains of children. But more recent work has shown that old neurons can grow dendrites to compensate for losses.

The exercise program calls for presenting the brain with non-routine or unexpected experiences using various combinations of your physical senses—vision, smell, touch, taste, and hearing—as well as your emotional "sense." It stimulates patterns of neural activity that create more connections between different brain areas and causes nerve cells to produce natural brain nutrients, called neurotrophins, that can dramatically increase the size and complexity of nerve cell dendrites.5 Neurotrophins also make surrounding cells stronger and more resistant to the effects of aging.

Neurobic exercises use the five senses in novel ways to enhance the brain's natural drive to form associations between different types of information. Associations (putting a name together with a face, or a smell with a food, for example) are the building blocks of memory and the basis of how we learn.

What consequences does this predictability (habits and routines) have on the brain? Because routine behaviors are almost subconscious, they are carried out using a minimum of brain energy—and provide little brain exercise. If you drive or walk to work via the same route every day, you use the same brain pathways. The neural links between brain areas required to perform that trip become strong. But other links to areas that were initially activated when the route was novel—such as a new smell, sight, or sound when you rounded a certain corner—get weaker as the trip becomes routine. So you become very efficient at getting from point A to point B, but at a cost to the brain.

Neurobic exercises are designed to fit into what you do on an ordinary day—getting up, commuting, working, shopping, eating, or relaxing.

Keep your brain alive and defy automatic behavior - starting now!

So, let me tell you exercises I did to break my routines and make my brain more alive. The first exercise I tried was brushing my teeth with my non-dominant hand. The result: rough, uncontrolled movements. I nearly injured myself with my toothbrush. One automatic action that was a routine for decades became a real challenge. The dominant hand unconsciously tried to grab the toothbrush during each brushing. After a week of brushing with the non-dominant hand, movements become more synchronized, and brushing became safer. New neurological links were made.

The point of neurobic isn't necessarily to give up on your daily activities, but to try to stop automatic actions within your daily activities.

My first activity during my morning cleaning of the garage was to clean the oil stains from the floor (oil leaked from the cars). I tried to do this with my non-dominant hand as well, after succeeding in the toothbrush task. This time I managed to synchronize the movements faster. Of course, in this case there were no fine motor skills, but believe me, it's hard to quickly change the pattern. It is not nearly as simple as it may seem. Third, I took it upon myself to come up with new and quicker routes from point A to point B, no matter the vehicle I was using. This resulted in a slew of mistakes and wasted time, but the final result is that now I know the city better than my wife who was born in it. As Niels Bohr said: 'An expert is a person who made the maximum number of errors in a very narrow field...' and I'm holding on to this principle.

When the idea for the book *Be Your Better Self* was born, I created a few focus groups that worked on given patterns on a weekly basis. One of the tasks was to influence our filters, i.e. to spot what we visually or auditory unconsciously delete and don't let into our conscious mind on a usual route from A to B. The results were incredible. One of the participants spotted a bakery that had been there for over five years, and she had been taking that same route at least 3 times a week, literally passing several feet from it.

If you're interested in more neurobic exercises, make sure to get the book *Keep Your Brain Alive,* and for starters, try to determine which daily routines, i.e. automatic patterns you can try to do differently today. Also, think about which Flinch you will face in the shortest possible time. The easiest strategy: You will recognize the Flinch by internal resistance to an action. As soon as that resistance appears, decide to do the opposite. Do exactly what that feeling forbids you.

The Map improvement System

If you`re really determined to go on a personal development quest and have failed so far, the time is now to receive a very simple system or strategy on how to succeed in your quest without excuses. Previously I talked about options, so to start off with I would like to clarify a bit what kind of options we consider good and what kind of options we consider bad.

When we want to achieve a certain goal, we need strategies. We need a range of choices with the help of which we`ll find the most appropriate one that will help us achieve that goal. The bigger the range of choices we have, the easier the goal will be achieved.

Be aware of your options

Negative options are those that turn us away from the goal and those are the ones we need to reduce or in the best-case scenario, we need only one of those. One goal and one option and the option is: goal achieved, full stop.
A simple example: Imagine you`re travelling from New York to Miami. Starting point NY, goal Miami. In order for you to reach Miami you have several means of transportation: plane, car, bus, motorcycle maybe, bike and by foot. The only thing that counts is reaching Miami because this is your goal.

Having more options in terms of goals would mean that you`re on your way somewhere on a bike, let`s say, and after a few days of traveling you suddenly decide that Jacksonville is kind of nice. So you decide you`re going to stay in Jacksonville. At one moment Raymond realized that he gave himself too big a task and he decided to stay in Jacksonville. Why did Raymond decide to stay there? Because he had that option as an exit strategy in his head, no matter if this strategy was born along the way or it was implanted before.

In other words if you`re resolute then there`s no other option or event standing in your way that could distance you from your target. Something might happen that will slow you down and for that situation we're going to prepare with extra options inside the strategy without touching the targeted goal. People often enthusiastically take up a project, they tell everybody around themselves about the endeavor, about their new activity, their new love. Then somehow, it doesn't take long to hear the following words, "It's actually not for me, I found something even better." When you think about it, there's always something better. The important thing is to know the difference between better and easier, the distinction many people don't make. They don't think about positive long-term consequences and personal satisfaction at the end of the road where they've beaten a bunch of fears (Flinches) and where they had to burst out the frames of their maps. It's difficult for Raymond back at the gas station, up to the moment when he's out of options and when he has to go back to college, but at least he's not dead.

"Man's mind, once stretched by a new idea, never regains its original dimensions."
Oliver Wendell Holmes

Two strategies exist to get you where you want to be

If you want to change, you have two options:

1. **Complete association into the wanted state or content (Analogue strategy)**
   A good example would be going to a summer camp that extensively focuses on a certain skill or an intensive seminar that lasts for days in a row. Any place where content is handled quick, exhaustive and where you are completely absorbed in what you do. I'm personally a big fan of this approach because it gives me the opportunity to think about nothing else but the topic of my interest for a designed period of time. Complete association eliminates daily disturbing factors. For example, you work for the whole day at the end of which you have to go to a foreign language course. An unsolved problem at work occurred that you now have to carry in your head with you on the course.

2. **Daily drill or discipline perseverance (Digital strategy)**
   An example of a daily drill would be going to the gym every day, or on a group exercise, a martial art class or creating a regular book reading pattern. This is a model that is susceptible to personal manipulation due to predictable always occurring side problems that eventually lead to a change. By change I mean value adjustment where a person will skip a fitness training/language course/reading wanting to solve a problem that is also situated high on the value list. The excuse of changing the schedule will always be an excuse like lack of time and physical or mental fatigue.

Usually people don`t have trouble with the first option. Results ensue if you cooperate. The biggest challenge poses handling the second option, where we are allowed to use quitting excuses to avoid finishing what we`ve started. The goal of this chapter is to resolve this problem - excuse and self- sabotage elimination.

Analogue and Digital strategies:
In order to remind you, there is a distinction between the two and it lies in their precision or imprecision.
Analogue information: "I`m arriving at your place soon!" This piece of information is prone to be interpreted differently based of a respective map.
Digital information: "I`m arriving at your place in 5 minutes!" This piece information leaves little manipulation space, in other words hides no alternative meanings. It is precise.

A) **Analogue Input Strategy**
   You`ll use Analogue Input Strategy when you want to instantly enrich your map or identity with new valuable characteristics.

Two years ago I felt I was getting pretty out of shape. Due to a lack of exercise that lasted many years, my body turned into something I didn`t like. I didn't even own a sweat suit. Friends thought of me as sport lazy, I wouldn`t even over exaggerate if I would say they thought I was incompetent. Some of them used to joke that they couldn`t imagine me running, while others added I wouldn`t even know how. On top of that I realized I was confining my self too much into my own map and I started playing it safe. Additionally I had a problem with personal consistency. I would promise to do something and then change my mind a few days after that. Too many options - too many bad options. For me to resolve all three problems with one blow I opted for the Analogue Input Strategy. As I mentioned above, by this I mean I was completely associated in my state and committed to one goal alone. Without options or alternatives. I posed myself a question: How could I work on representation of me as an adventurer, sportsman and a consistent person making just one move? I knew if I wanted to achieve all that, I would have to make a breakthrough. It hit me one Sunday night. I was so enthusiastic that I couldn't sleep. My Monday was free and I decided to wake up at 8am, buy a bike, T-shirt, some sweat pants and cycle to my hometown situated 50 miles from where I was.

It's important to mention here that my last biking experience occurred in 2005 and this was 2011. My decision was final. But as it had been years since I had been involved in any sports activity, I simply didn't know where to find bike shops in the city. The quest lasted for a couple of hours. I almost found myself postponing the bike adventure because I couldn't find a bike that would suit my needs and my budget at the same time. The moment I just thought about postponing, I remembered my girlfriend who stood in disbelief when I told her what I was planning to do. She said, "Don't go calling me after 10 miles when you change your mind and want to give up on the whole thing!" I couldn't let her be right and encouraged myself to persist in the bike search. The thing I inevitably had to do in order to start sooner was raise my budget, because, I gathered, the more I wait, the more my mind is going to play tricks on me. I started cycling at 12:30 pm. I was wearing shorts, a T-shirt and a back-pack. No other accessories. After the first 12 miles, I felt my palms were going numb on the sides. How was it possible I didn't remember to buy gloves?! From leaning on the bike wheel my hands went completely numb. My girlfriend's words were ringing in my head the whole time, she knows me better that anyone. On the 25th mile, I climbed off the bike and went in a store to get a sandwich and some water. I couldn't even hold the sandwich properly with my hand because of the numbness. And what's more, I found myself in trouble when trying to climb back on the bike, it hurt! So what I did, I switched from one butt cheek to the other to relieve the pressure. Sitting in the middle was out of the question. And I was only half way through! After crossing one quarter of the way more, I arrived to the place my grandmother lived. I decide to stop by and take a short break so that my butt and hands could loosen up a bit.

When she saw me riding a bike she couldn't believe her eyes. A few minutes later it started to rain cats and dogs. Since I was visibly exhausted and taking into account new weather conditions, my grandmother tried to convince me to sleep over saying it was highly irresponsible and stupid to continue my way, worn out in the heavy rain. To tell you the truth, her suggestion sounded one hundred percent logical to me. I decided to wait and see if the rain would simmer down. Unfortunately that didn't happen. The weather was getting worse by the minute and my dear grandma insisted that I stay. Nobody would blame me if I stayed, I thought. I have a legitimate reason and the mere journey I covered so far makes a huge difference between who I was yesterday and who I am today. The moment that thought found it's way into my mind, another appeared, "Saša, if you don't get up, right this moment, sound out you grandma, go out, climb on your bike and go, you'll stay here and quit the whole thing. This is what's going to happen." I listened to the voice and I did it.

One more fragment of the way was lying in front of me. Hilly, unfinished road constructions, mud, rain, and wind were waiting for me, too. As soon as I finally arrived in my home town, I immediately phoned a couple of my friends and panted, "I'm here, are you up for some drinks?" Two of them arrived and seeing me with the bike all muddy, worn out (and proud) they had the same reaction as my grandmother did. Imagine their poor maps, people who couldn't even picture me in a sweat suit or running, now see me on a bike with 50 miles of road behind me. Time passed by and while recuperating from that instant analogue experience I heard people talk about it. Some of them even called me an adventurer. The outcome was achieved. That is the power of analogue experience. Quickly and efficiently I updated my map with a new experience, and my identity with "adventurer"-at least in the eyes of others. After that experience I enhanced my identity through other sports and activities. I'm a big fan of the expression, "You gotta fake it until you make it." When we manage to convince key people from our environment that we're capable of doing something, we'll gain the extra boost we need.

Muhammed Ali said it best: "I am the greatest...I said that even before I knew I was!"

Start with yourself and start with a question: What kind of instant analogue activities can you do in order to change the personal perception of you and others, under the condition that it happens in the direction of what`s important for you.

B) Digital Strategy Input

A client of mine, who struggled with a weight loss problem for years, asked me for a solution. I answered her with a question of my own, "What`s stopping you from working out?" She proclaimed that she works out indeed, from time to time, when she has the time. I was curious: "What do you mean? How much time do you need per work out?" She said she needed three hours. A half an hour to get ready and arrive to the gym, the same amount of time to get back. And two hours for a thorough work out. A thorough work out can be done in my map for 45 minutes, I say. "You can`t possibly do a thorough workout in that amount of time. You need at least two hours (her map, her belief). Everything under that is like you didn`t do anything," she complains. I conclude, "In other words, if you have two hours and 45 minutes and you decide to go and work out, that wouldn`t make sense?" "That`s right," she said.

In this example you can see an example of an interpretation problem. What a thorough workout means for that person, what criteria must be met to be considered a work out and how to get her to work out? In her map, the client interprets that the most important criteria for a thorough work out is time. Since she often can`t afford herself that much time, she found a valid excuse. She found an exit option that distances her from the wanted goal. The action trigger has been set to 180 minutes and when the time span doesn`t match the optimally predicted one, the action trigger disappears.

People always dwell a lot on how long a thing needs to be worked on in order to produce the best results. They are well prepared to quarrel about it – there are hundreds of opinions about the same thing that has the same goal. The goal is to do something, not to wait for the ideal conditions for it. I would like to point out at this stage, the importance of the process versus content. First, let me clarify what I mean whey I say process: I specifically mean going to the gym and lifting just one weight is more important than not going to the gym at all. I never experienced anybody saying to me that they arrived to the gym and they didn't feel like performing the work out. The problem lies in the action of going to the gym. The going is the trigger. When the person is already there, he or she will find a value and perform the work out. It surely happened to you, you most probably weren't in the mood for an activity at a certain point and despite that feeling went on and did it. In the end you felt pretty satisfied with your decision, didn't you? The key to personal progress, the motivational shift lies in the understanding of the process over content value. In other words the key is in moving the trigger location from, in this case, the time criteria to the "just do the first step" criteria.

Let me clarify with an example by what I mean by a process trigger.

There was a seminar participant that studied at the Faculty of Economics and Business. She was a junior and always complained how she couldn't find the motivation to study. To my question of what was stopping her, she replied that the content was so boring that she just can't talk herself into action. Wanting to detect the root of the problem I intentionally bombarded her with questions to get her into a state of frustration. She would give me the most accurate answer from that state. When she entered into frustration, she looked straight at me and said, "Listen, it's not a problem for me to study once I start. Starting poses the biggest problem for me. Getting that book into my hands and opening it up." That statement was as accurate as it gets. I proposed the following: I told her I was busy this week and that I couldn't help her and that in the mean time, I want her to do a little assignment that will only take a second. Was she ready to hear the assignment? She replied, "Ready!" I continued, "I ask you to find and fold nicely in a visible and accessible place all the exam literature you need. Can you do that?" She said of course. I added that she had to pick up a book once a day, turn the page to where she last stopped studying and immediately close it. "Also," I pleaded, "don't attempt to study the following week, don't even think about it, so that you are able to complete the designated assignment."

She wondered why this was important and how it would help her in passing the exams. I reassured her to leave it alone for the moment and that we would get onto the exam passing issue just as long as she completes the assignment.

"So all I have to do is take a book in my hands once a day, open it and close it?" She wanted to make sure she got it right.

"Yes, that`s all you have to do." I patiently confirmed. In a week I called her to check in and see if she had managed to keep to our agreement or not. She said she didn`t. She said she didn`t manage not to study. For a first couple of days she would open and close the book, just as we agreed, and then she started studying.

"Wonderful," I said, "You did it all by yourself, you don`t need my help."

Why had she started to study? Because the sentence with which she described her problem was: "it`s not a problem for me to study once I start. Starting poses the biggest problem for me. Getting that book into my hands and opening it up." She stated it very clearly while defining the problem. My goal was just to fondle that first trigger. When the trigger was off, it automatically led to the next step: "it`s not a problem for me to study once I start."

The model I am going to explain in more detail on the following pages was created in my most disorganized phase, in which I regularly neglected all the things I had learnt so far. To be more precise, that was the phase just before the moment I lost it all. It was beginning of 2009. And as I wrote in the Introduction, I couldn't sleep, was always on the verge of crying, the moment I fall asleep the trembling of my body awakes me. When I do sleep, my feet constantly moved. I stopped shaving, I stopped dressing up nicely, and I stopped combing my hair. All of my self-confidence, motivation and zest was gone. What`s more, I transferred all the first company money to the second company so it was all gone. It took me two years to come from a garbage man to a two company owner. And only three months after I have achieved it I wished it had never happened and that I still worked as a garbage man. Will I ever come out of this, and if I do, how long will it take me? Those were my ritual daily questions for a bad morning, for a bad day and for a bad sleep.

One night, after I read *Think and Grow Rich* by Napoleon Hill, I decide to read another famous money self help book. Money was the biggest issue for me then, so it seemed like the natural choice to make. The book was called *The Richest Man in Babylon* by George S. Clason and while reading it I came across a metaphor. This metaphor altogether changed my viewpoint on personal change.

This is a story about Arkad. He claimed to be the richest man in Babylon.

"Once upon a time in ancient Babylon there lived a very rich man. His name was Arkad. His spending habits caused him to be famous widely. He was a generous man. He proved very generous to his family and lavishing towards is own pleasures. Nevertheless, his fortune would become bigger and bigger, no matter how fast he would spend it. A few of his childhood friends came up to him and asked him: "You Arkad, are much happier that we are. You became the richest man in Babylon and the rest of us are struggling to survive. Yet, a long time ago, we were equal. We went to the same schoolteacher; we played the same children games. Not in these games or in the school classes were you better than us. In the years that followed you were not more honorable a citizen than the rest of us. You didn't work more dedicated than us. How come this fickle fate decided to single you of all people out? How come it let you enjoy all the good things in life and decided to leave out all the rest of us, who are just as valuable as you?"

His friends asked him to explain the way he came into possession of all the riches. So, he kindly recounted his personal Rags to Riches story.

When he finished, one of his friends concluded: "You really were lucky, Arkad!"

Arkad replied: Lucky? You think I was lucky? The only thing I was lucky about was wanting to progress. Would you call a fisherman happy? A fisherman who had been studying the habits of fish for years so that he could throw his nets in a better way? Chance is a cruel goddess who doesn't waste her time on those who aren't ready."

"You had great will power to persevere even when you lost all of you savings from the first year. That makes you really special," said another of his friends.

"Will power," Arkad retorts, "What a nonsense! Do you think will power is the thing that gives strength to a man for him to lift up a burden that even a camel cannot carry or to drag a load that even an ox cannot move? Will power is just a determined intention to complete a self-imposed task. If I were to pose myself a task, however small it might be, I would make sure it gets done. Otherwise, how will I trust myself concerning big things? If were to ask myself to drop a pebble into the river every time I would cross the bridge going to town, I would do so. When I would pass the bridge on the seventh day and forget to throw a pebble I wouldn't say, "Tomorrow I`ll throw two pebbles, it`s the same thing." Instead, I would return and throw the pebble. Nor I would say on the 20th day, "Arkad, this is ridiculous. What is the point of you throwing pebbles every day? Throw a fistful and complete the task." No, I would not do or say such a thing. When I set a goal, a task to myself, I complete it. Therefore I am very cautious not to pose myself too difficult or impractical tasks, for which I am not completely certain I can trust myself completing them.""

After I read the story, I realized I don't have pebbles of my own. Even if I had them, I would probably solve that problem by throwing in a fistful. This opened up for me a whole new perspective.

I defined my own pebbles, my own daily tasks. I wanted something for the body, something for the mind. The first pattern I chose was physical exercise. I determined exactly what I needed to do in order to benefit my body. Today we all know very well that body and mind are interconnected and that if we feel happy in the mind, the body will react in a visible way. The simplest example is a situation where we`re slouching and than suddenly stand up straight. What emotions follow the body posture?
Another example is trying to stretch your lips 15 times in a row into a smile. It becomes funny, right?
The reason behind it is even when we fake a smile we impact the motoric part of our brain cortex which alternatively triggers neurotransmitters that are being released when we authentically smile. Remember that in the previous chapter we were mentioning our brain not recognizing much of a difference between a real and fake/imaginary experience.

Here are my pebbles:

In the exercise pattern I added three separate patterns: pushups, squats and crunches
Drinking pattern: I determined the maximum limit of coffee intake, since I drank a lot of it
Consistency development pattern: turn up on time every time, since I was almost always late everywhere

News pattern: every day, learn a new word from the dictionary
Personal development pattern (visual input): Read a motivational book or watch a motivational movie
Personal development pattern (audio input): Listen to an audiobook before I go to sleep
Organisational development pattern: I decided to plan the following day in detail, at the end of the previous one

I overdid it with the number of patterns in the beginning and if I didn't have a big dose of motivation, I wouldn't have made it. I should have gone with two to three patterns per week, just so as I didn't overload my conscious mind. Today I would recommend everybody start off with one pattern per week so that the mind can be conditioned gradually and that you don't overwhelm it. After the first week, I suggest adding one or two more patterns onto the same strategy.
This was and easy and simple way to amass my daily fuel.

The principle was easy. Digital. Did you throw the pebble or not? There's no manipulation space, like I'll throw two tomorrow. You can find yourself extremely motivated one day and say to yourself that you're going to perform 100 push ups per day. You can state that under the influence of the state you find yourself in, but do you think this pattern will be sustainable through the whole 100 days? No, because you can't predict what state you're going to be in the day after tomorrow. It can happen that you're too tired or demotivated to do even a half of it or even one fifth. In other words, if you define a goal: I will do 100 push-ups for the next 100 days, you've condemned yourself to 100 percent failure in advance. I'm not saying it's impossible, I'm saying it's improbable. For the mind's sake it's better to one push up per day for one hundred days that one hundred push-ups in a day. Considering this was all about digital input, meaning state 1 equals success, state 0 equals failure, my task was simply to conform with that digital norm. The times when I was motivated, I would do 50 push ups, the times I was feeling sorry for myself I would do just one. But most of the time I did more that one and that first one was just a trigger. To further trace the development of my new patterns or daily inputs towards my better self, I created a chart.

Day	1	2	3	4	5	6	7	8	9	10	11	12	13	14	15	16	17	18	19
PU	✓	✓	✓	✓	✓	✓	✓	✓	✓	✓	✓	✓	✓	✓	✓	✓	✓	✓	✓
SQ	✓	✓	✓	✓	✓	✓	✓	✓	✓	✓	✓	✓	✔	✔	✔	✔	✔	✔	✔
CR	✔	✔	✔	✔	✔	✔	✔	✔	✔	✔	✔	✔	✔	✔	✔	✔	✔	✔	✔
CFE	✔	✔	✔	✔	■	✔	✔	✔	■	✔	✔	✔	✔	✔	✔	✔	✔	✔	✔
AOT	✔	✔	✔	✔	✔	✔	■	✔	■	■	✔	✔	✔	✔	✔	■	✔	✔	✔
NEW	✔	✔	✔	✔	✔	✔	✔	✔	✔	■	✔	✔	✔	✔	✔	✔	✔	✔	✔
VI	✔	✔	✔	✔	✔	✔	✔	✔	✔	✔	✔	✔	✔	✔	✔	✔	✔	✔	✔
Ai	✔	✔	✔	✔	✔	✔	✔	✔	✔	■	✔	✔	✔	✔	✔	✔	✔	✔	✔
PLAN	✔	✔	✔	■	■	✔	✔	✔	■	■	✔	✔	✔	✔	✔	✔	✔	✔	✔
KYW	✔	✔	✔	■	■	✔	■	✔	■	■	✔	✔	✔	✔	✔	■	■	✔	✔

Legend:
1. PU = push up
2. SQ = Squat
3. CR=crunches
4. CFE- less than 3 cups of coffee per day
5. AOT = arriving on time when meeting with someone
6. NEW = new dictionary word
7. VI = Read a motivational book or watch a motivational movie (visual input)
8. AI = listen to an audiobook (auditive input)
9. PLAN= detailed next day plan
10. KYW = keep your word

Let me repeat, every day my assignment was to do only one piece of a particular pattern and if I found myself motivated, I could perform as many pieces as I like, but nothing is transferable to the next day. I can make 500 push ups exclusively for my own benefit, but it won`t be visible in the chart. Two marked fields in the cart have greater value than a note of 500 push ups in one and an unmarked other field. The field is marked with ticks and blacking it up. If yes then tick, if no they black. At the end of the day if I`m too tired to read a book, all I have to do is open a book and read a title or a sentence. And if I`m awake and motivated I can read 5 books.

They count the same. The goal of the digital input is to be successful and not overwhelm myself with non-realistic long-term goals. The outcome is to complete all patterns on a daily basis - even those I`m least motivated to do. The one`s I`m least motivated to do I can complete performing just one piece, which would take me approximately less than a minute. For example, in the morning I didn't manage to do my work out and in the evening I'm too tired to do it. I collect my strength and do the following: one push up, one squat, one crunch, open dictionary-pick word-read meaning-close dictionary, turn on audiobook-listen to first sentence-turn off audiobook. This is obviously the worst-case scenario strategy but I don't think it's cheating. Cheating is throwing a fistful of pebbles the next day. With this strategy you contributed to your visual, auditory and kinesthetic conditioning. I emphasise again that this is a worst-case scenario and that you should avoid it ever happening. Have in mind that the goal is daily inputs and self-conditioning, not necessarily quality. There is absolutely no excuse for this model.

People will say that this kind of quick pattern run doesn't make any sense, but they're wrong. Those who say it won't go to the gym if the haven't got 3 hours to spare and they won't study because it's a problem opening up a book.

Remember, neither quality nor quantity is intended here. The goal is just to scratch the triggers that affect the wanted behavior. Or better yet, think of how Lincoln put it: "Once I start, I'm too lazy to stop."

Let me give you another example. My daily exercise pattern exists from the day I learnt that digital inputs work, so that has been four years. In that four years, it happen surely a 100 times that I haven't been motivated and I just decided to do that one push up or two. Based on this permanent experience, on the level of Identity, I have become a person that works out daily. People who think they understand patterns correctly will claim that for example one push up or a minute of exercise doesn't do any good. That's just their belief. One good doctor friend of mine repeatedly points out that a minute of exercise isn't good enough. That you need XX minutes of training.

But that good friend of mine struggles with intensive interval trainings. Starting, neglecting, getting frustrated and starting again. He finds himself in a circular loop while this model offers you stability. Furthermore, digital inputs don't challenge intensive workouts, on the contrary. The leading benefit of this model is that it doesn't support routine breaking. Next to the nine above mentioned patterns there are two more. One of them I`ll mention in the next chapter, the other one I`ll tell you about now. It`s name is KYW, and the meaning behind it is keeping your word that you`ll comply with all the above patterns. That`s the only pattern that`s crossed with the rest of them. Specifically it means that at the end of the day, you don`t perform just one of the predesigned patterns, you automatically have to blacken the KYW box.

This is a platform for new inputs and new habits. The process of installation is digital not analogue, meaning if you wash your teeth before going to work in the morning and you didn`t wake up on time, it`s highly improbable you won`t wash your teeth - you`re going to put that toothbrush inside your mouth at least for three seconds, right? Even if only to conform with the pattern you've made for yourself. Am I correct? So, don't be concerned on the precise effect those three seconds have on your designated patterns.

Your first step is to select a range of patterns you would like to apply. The only condition is that these patterns contribute to your overall wellbeing. The chart has to be put in a visible place. Because if it`s not part of a routine, if it`s not implemented and conditioned, the mind will forget to run it. Take a little tip from me, kick in one or two patterns immediately after waking up in the morning, because with this kind of conditioning, you`ll trigger the rest of the patterns. If you perform them only at the end of the day, no matter how simple they may seem, you won`t make it. This comes from experience, working with no less than seven focus groups. It`s crucial to trigger the pattern in the morning, simply because mornings mold daily frames. Take for example diet changing patterns. If your first meal in the day is healthy, that meal will considerably raise the odds of continuing with the healthy streak during the whole day. But if you stumble already on the first step and eat an unhealthy meal, you lower the odds of eating healthy for the rest of the day.

This is very important. In literature you`ll often find a piece of information that states the mind needs 21 days to create a habit. That`s a generalization and an untruth. Possibly at a certain percentage yes, but remember that map is not a territory and what applies to one person, doesn`t necessarily apply to the next. If you`re working on creating a new habit for yourself through the Digital Input Strategy, you must repeat the pattern as many times as it takes you to feel pain from not doing it. Like in the case of teeth washing. In one`s map this can happen in 12 days in another`s in 400. My map says it`s 100. Unlike routine habits you don`t have use from, here you have a strategy of how to create habits from targeted activities in the easiest way, in that way adding one contribution more to becoming your better self.

"There is nothing training cannot do. Nothing is above its reach. It can turn bad morals to good; it can destroy bad principles and recreate good ones; it can lift men to angelship."

Mark Twain

Modeling successful patterns

Maybe you've already chosen the forms on which you want to build your behaviors. Maybe you haven't. Maybe you need more strategies. The most important strategy of successful communicators is called modeling.

We can agree that everyone wants to be successful in some way. You probably have your role models whom you look up to. It can be your childhood hero, a famous person, your manager or a local leader whom you want to emulate. Such people give you motivation to be like them because of what they have accomplished. Most of my success mentors have been those people who have accomplished things through difficult situations, yet emerged to conquer the unfavorable circumstances to emerge as winners.

Achieving results comes from knowing the strategy

How do you follow the footsteps of the great and successful people you so admire? The only sure way is to do what they did. If you want to accomplish what someone else has accomplished, the thing you need to do is to model what they do. That is to say that you model their behaviors, actions and habits. You have to speak the way they speak, act the way the act and adopt their habits. That is the fastest way to become like them. This is not that you become someone else, no. iI says that you become like someone else. There is a difference between the two.

People like to dismiss the notion of modeling, but they fail to realize that we model other people every day. The only difference is that we do it unconsciously, without realizing it. If you live with someone for a long time, you soon begin to behave like him/her. So modeling happens every day, therefore, why should you model a successful person consciously? You should not allow yourself to become a victim of circumstances but you should become a driver of your life and lead your life to the direction you dream of reaching, instead of allowing circumstances beyond you to dictate how you live. Modeling other people's (the successful and the great individuals) behaviors is the shortest and most accurate way of success. You cannot invent success. That is like saying that you cannot invent hard work. Therefore, anything that you think constitutes success has already been achieved by someone. Your work is only to adopt and model them. That is why we call them role model-you model their role.

The importance of narrowing a model

The basic principle of modeling is to see and hear the behavior of your model in a certain frame, try to repeat the same and see the result integrated in our model. If within a certain frame I do not posses my own strategy on how to achieve a certain goal, I will not waste time finding one, because a personal strategy is made through the trial-and-error process. Instead of that, before we want to achieve something, assuming you have something in mind, we will ask ourselves, 'Who of the people I know achieves that result without problems? Who achieves this on their own, with almost no conscious effort?' In other words, who in this environment possesses the automatic (unconscious) strategy of completing that goal or task? The next step is to precisely follow their patterns. After that comes implementation. Implementation is done like this: You have to speak the way they speak, act the way the act and adopt their habits.

How long will this take?

The person doesn't necessarily have to be a role model, but the only important condition for them is to do a certain activity, which you find important, or is better than you. That person generally doesn't have to suit you at all, because you're not modeling the identity, just their behavior, i.e. strategy.

Maria, a participant in my seminar, presented a simple example on how to apply modeling. Her company had a two-day team building. The activities were kayaking, indoors soccer, pulling rope and archery. When it was time for the archery, a group of about 30 stood behind the instructor. The instructor was explaining how to hold a bow and fire an arrow, looking towards the group and towards the target. Maria was the only one who stood parallel to the instructor, while the others stood and listened. All the things the instructor was explaining and demonstrating while holding the bow and arrow, Maria did without a bow, imitating him (modeling). There were a few laughs from her coworkers, because they didn't realize what she was doing. But, as you can guess, it became clear when they tried shooting the target. By copying the movements and behavior of the instructor, she put in the behavioral patterns of the person who was better than her in that context, and just by applying them; she achieved a much better score than her coworkers. Modeling is the fastest learning strategy.

Just see what works, or believe it could work and adopt the pattern, and try it out. If it doesn't work... you made an error somewhere along the way or you missed a step.

Imagine a situation: your child wants to play tennis. You take them to a tennis court, rent the racquets and started to play. None of you have the experience of practicing with a professional trainer in your maps. You can think that tennis is easy; you only have to get the ball across the net. Since you weren't trained, you will use the resources you have available. You will hold the racquet as you think it should be held, and you will hit the ball like you assume it should be hit. After a few tennis experiences, you develop, i.e. condition those forms through the process of your own experience. Your child is now extra interested in tennis and you decide to enroll them in tennis school. The result: the trainer has to invest X more time to un-condition the wrong technical patterns. Patterns created in a wrong way constrict and significantly slow down the learning process.

The biggest mistake you can make is either to start on your own or to pick the wrong model. My friend who is a tennis trainer says that there are a lot of patterns that even professional tennis players have wrongly conditioned, such as the way of holding the racquet. The reason for this is that during the making of these patterns they learned these things in a wrong way, and today they cannot change them and this inability to change keeps them from reaching the top. Wrongly learned patterns make a strong framework. You can be so headstrong that you go through walls, but if your learned strategies are not on the top level, i.e. don't come from the best possible models, you will reach a wall, which is impossible to knock down or jump over.

In the process of learning NLP, I was highly motivated to become an exceptional coach. I knew that the prerequisite of becoming an excellent coach was to become an excellent presenter. I wanted to have the best strategies to pass knowledge onto others. In order to achieve that, I defined my models. Who are the best presenters in the world? Which exceptional presenters do I know? So, I defined a few of them. I will keep to Richard Bandler, the co-creator of NLP, and Tony Robbins. If I wanted to be an excellent presenter, I had to adopt their patterns within that framework. So, what did I do in order to adopt their patterns? First, I went to the store and bought earphones with the longest cable available. The cable was over 2 meters long. Next, I decided to follow a daily digital pattern. I would find a lecture on YouTube, either Richard's or Tony's, plug in the headphones and put them on. The lecture started and I watched exactly what they were doing and tried to repeat the same, as accurately as possible. The first pattern I focused on was moving on the stage. The second one was hand gestures. When I had adopted the first one, I would move on to the second one. After gestures, I focused on facial expressions and voice quality. As far as voice is concerned, I would try to mirror as many of their elements as I could, from volume, rhythm, to changes in modulation. I worked on it for 60 days and I can say that I was very happy with the result. Along with the technical part I adopted by observing, I got another bonus: a change of state, i.e. a better attitude during presentation. I haven't mentioned this before, but presentations were a nightmare in my first two years of college. I couldn't imagine myself standing in front of all those people and talking, even if I knew all of them. And now, through education, i.e. modeling, I learned to truly enjoy presenting.

A few years ago, a friend of mine shared a YouTube clip on a social network. The title was FlyBoard. I clicked out of curiosity to see what it was about. The clip was remarkable and I instantly became interested. Considering that the FlyBoard is a completely new product, I'll explain what it is all about if you haven't had experience with it. The FlyBoard is an adrenaline toy for adults with whom you can imitate movement and jumps of a dolphin in the water, and much more than that. There's a hose that is about 82 feet long and is connected to a jet ski. That hose leads to your board with pedals. The

FlyBoarder floats on water with the leg board attached, and when the driver of the jet ski accelerates, the pressure fills the hose with water and it moves towards the board to which you're tied to.

This hose splits in two on the board right beneath the heels, and points the pressure vertically to your body. It enables you to rise as far as 33 feet above water. When I saw that clip almost two years ago, I told myself, 'You have to try this! You have to try this as soon as possible! You have to try this, no matter the cost!' But, there was no chance, because the FlyBoard wasn't mass-produced at the time. In 2012 I was on a holiday at sea with my wife. One morning, we went for a coffee at an Internet café. I had my laptop with me and I surfed the Internet. I don't know how, as this is not something that I usually do, but I found myself on one of the Groupon pages, and noticed a FlyBoard offer on a beach only 10 miles from where we were staying. When I saw that offer in a café full of people, I jumped out of my chair like there was nobody there, and yelled: 'YESSSS!' I wasn't aware of the people around me, as I was fully absorbed in the moment and only aware that I'd have the opportunity to achieve what I had promised myself. My wife bought me a coupon, and I made a reservation for the session three days after that. For those three days I did some... you guessed it, modeling.

I saw every single video on YouTube in order to try installing patterns in my attitude, trick patterns and everything else which could make me a top FlyBoarder on my first try. I arrived to my appointed session, but it was crowded so I started talking with one of the fly boarders or FlyBoard instructors in order to receive more inputs that could improve my strategy and experience. The instructor started talking about how people got scared and that it takes them 15-20 minutes to stand in the water and rise a few meters above it. I asked him very precise questions in order to solve those problems and complete the visual information from YouTube. When I had gathered the necessary information, I sat with my wife for a drink and waited my turn. While there, I was mentally creating a strategy for my first rise from the water and the jump. My turn came. The instructor gave me a vest and tied me to the FlyBoard. He explained how I should behave during exit and return and that he'll try to raise me gently until I balanced out. But, something unexpected happened. When we moved away from the beach he signaled me to take another, more appropriate position (turn on my chest) and yelled that he's about to accelerate and I should straighten my legs and try to rise above the water.

He accelerated and I ended up a 5 feet above water and decided to jump like a dolphin. I leaned forward and jumped. I was approximately 10 feet under water when I heard that the jet-ski engine was off. Since my hands and legs were tied to the FlyBoard so that I couldn't swim to the surface, I was out of air and the vest was slowly lifting me upward. I drank some seawater and rose to the surface. The instructor had a surprised and worried look on his face. 'Are you all right,' he asked. 'Yeah, just let me get all this water out. Why did you stop the jet-ski?' He replied: 'What you just did... nobody did that the whole summer, rose from their first try and made the dolphin. Good job. Let's go again.'

What happened next was a real show, I tried every trick I had seen on YouTube; everything worked out exactly as I had modeled in my head. The ride was supposed to last 15 minutes, but the instructor was so enthusiastic and simply didn't want my ride to end. When we finished my session, he asked me, 'How long are you on vacation for?' I said: 'Another week.' 'OK', he said, 'From now on, you're a demo rider for the FlyBoard on this beach.' Brilliant; I was so thrilled with the experience that I would have surely come back at least twice and paid full price, and now I'm a demo rider. My job, i.e. the promo rider's job consisted of 2-3 rides in the afternoon in order to attract new clients. Seven days and about 20 rides later, I was asked to represent my country on the FlyBoard world championship in Qatar.

What's the difference in the whole story between what happened to me on that beach (becoming a demo rider) and what happened to others who took 15 minutes to rise above the water and not experience this as they should have – this was supposed to be adrenaline filled, fun and exciting, rather than stressful and burdening. A vast majority of people who decided to try the FlyBoard didn't have enough inputs. I know that because I observed them for seven days. Their inputs consisted of watching only the previous or several previous riders before their turn. The performance of those who saw more riders and our demo ride was better. Those who saw only the person before them mostly managed to rise out of the water several times at the end of the ride. So, the secret is in modeling a map, which is better than our own.

A well-known proverb says: Success is a science of being totally prepared. Or, in our language, preparation consists of modeling the people who are successful in a certain framework. By taking up their patterns, we achieve the same results.

Modeling just one pattern

There are no rules in modeling: we can model behaviors, roles; even isolated forms. I emphasize that everyone in our environment has at least one pattern for achieving a certain goal that is better than our own. When you notice a person achieving something quicker and in a more elegant way than you, ask yourself: 'What exactly is he doing and in what can I do in order to achieve such a result or response?' After you collect the necessary information, apply it.

In the previous chapter, I promised to list another pattern that was a part of my digital input strategy. I will once again refer to the experience with my second company. Every Monday, I would receive calls from the suppliers who'd threaten about what will happen if I didn't pay what they asked. Monday was the most stressful day of the week because of those calls. I had negative physiological reactions on Sunday evenings – I felt the Flinch. My strategy was honesty: I would explain the situation I was in every Monday the same, and said that it was in my interest to pay them, but I can't be 100% sure that I would be able to collect the wanted amount in the allotted time. After saying that, they would switch to a state of aggression, and I would switch to a state of begging, pleading, etc. only in order to finish the conversation as soon as possible, only to end the pain coming from that conversation as soon as possible.

One Sunday night I turned the TV on one of the James Bond films. In a scene near the end, James Bond had been captured by the villains and tied to a chain above a pool with sharks. The chain began to descend and Bond came closer to the surface – "sliding" into almost certain death. While watching that scene I focused on Bond's face, i.e. the emotional response caused by that situation. I noticed Bond's facial expression, which didn't give away the state of fear about what was coming next. Instead of scared, he had a serious expression, darting his eyes left and right as if searching for a solution, as if there was one. In that moment I thought: 'Wait a minute, if James Bond can have that state in the moment when death is moments away... how can I whine so much in front of people who threaten me?' I made a decision. I will create a new pattern and name it James Bond (JB).

Don`t think, just MODEL

That pattern will represent my behavior in difficult and stressful situations. When such a situation occurs, I will take up James Bond's body language, mimic his face and tone of voice. And we'll see what happens. When I received a call from a supplier, I took the necessary actions, prepared, and answered the phone with a new attitude and a new voice which you must be familiar with: 'Good day, this is Sasha, how can I help you today?' The content of the communication was the same, but my condition was different. The situation is what it is, unchangeable, but if that were the case, why would it cost me my condition? Instead of being stressed out for hours after the call, this time in spite of the unfavorable situation, I felt great. **Condition is the only thing we can change in unfavorable situations**. I have absolutely no use for stress. When you don't have a solution in sight, don't punish yourself further in your head, that's of no use. It's good to think about a solution, but stress is mostly unnecessary, especially the one which can last for hours or days after an uncomfortable experience. Don't you agree?

Maxwell Maltz:
"How can I be happy," asked the businessman. "I have just lost $200 000 on the stock market. I am ruined and disgraced." – "You can be happier," Maxwell said ..."by not adding your opinions to the facts. It is a fact that you lost $200 000 on the stock market, it is your opinion that you are ruined and disgraced. "

As you've seen from the James Bond example, the person you're modeling can be anyone, whether a person from your office, a family member, a friend or a movie character. The only important thing is for you to recognize the pattern as useful, apply it and see what happens – see the difference. And congratulate yourself on changing your state, changing it to the better.

So what are you waiting for? Look, listen, recognize and apply… as simple as that.

Finale

Personal perseverance struggle

I used to be a really unorganized and inconsistent person. I would get good results, and achieve my goals, but my achievements didn't match all that I had said I would do. I would talk a lot and do very little within a deadline. I would find X number of excuses for why I didn't do something. The most common excuses would be: 'I didn't do it, but look at what I did do, isn't it even better?' When I enrolled in my third year of college I said: 'I want to be among the first from my generation to graduate, and within a maximum of two years.' When the fourth year started, I started my first business and started ignoring my college obligations. I completed my four years of study on time. And so passed a year since I finished my classes and I hadn't passed a single exam. People would ask me: 'didn't you say you would be among the first graduate students in your generation? Half of them had already graduated, that means you failed.' I would say: 'Yes, but that was before I started my company. Isn't this path better than being without a company, money but with a college degree?' A good excuse, isn't it? But it's still just an excuse. Who says that one is better than the other? And what gave me the right to give up on the goal that I defined for myself? Of course there may be currently better and more pleasant things to do, and previously made goals become distant and unattractive when compared to something we are currently doing, what helped us to rationalize the delay and even give up on what we had started.

CDS perseverance tears down all excuses

One day I decided to add a digital pattern of personal consistency (PC). The goal of that pattern was to install a trigger in my everyday communication during the verbalization of any tasks I planned to do in the future. The meaning of the PC pattern was this: I'll realize everything I say with the assumption of doing it in the future.

At the beginning of the consistency training, I started with small everyday activities. I didn't want to give myself too large of a task that I wasn't 99% sure I could finish. I was guided by Arkad's model: Don't give yourself tasks that can overload you, because you will give them up. I also used another model: I have to practice on small stuff in order to trust myself when the big things come.

You know those situations when someone calls you and asks whether you have the time for lunch or drinks and you say, 'I can't today; I'll talk to you tomorrow.' Tomorrow comes and you forget to call. And you think to yourself, 'OK, there are no consequences for this behavior, and anyway we'll see each other or talk next week.' That was the starting point of my consistency training.

The beginning was the hardest. I would black out my pattern several times a week, and mostly on stupid things. My wife would ask me to buy something on my way back from work. I would say 'Yes', and forget about it. By doing this I would black out the field of personal consistency and keeping my word in my patterns. Or, 'Sasha, could you vacuum the apartment today?' 'Yes, I'll do it this evening.' – and then I'd forget to do it.

After the initial failures because of total idiocies I realized how much most of us are conditioned to not fulfill what we promised. The reason for this is that we mostly don't receive punishers that would modify that pattern. If you have a pattern of being always late for meetings, missing deadlines, etc. the reason for this is that you have never been really "burned". But generally speaking, burns come, just not in the form of burns. Rather, those wonderful things that happen to people with a high level of personal consistency do not come to us.

In the first weeks of failures I decided to keep track of my communication in order to finally realize the new and wanted pattern. I was extremely cautious over what I promised. When someone asked me for something that I wasn't 99% sure I could deliver, I would say, 'Look, I'll try, but I can't promise.' It was very simple – if I hadn't promised and I complete the task, great, but if I had promised and I fail, I would cross out the PC pattern. If those were the only two options, I'd rather select the safer one. I used to say 'Consider it done,' but now I'd say, 'I'll give my best to do it, but I can't promise 100% that it will be done in X time.'

Be careful what you agree to

Only when I was 99% sure that nothing except sickness could prevent me from doing the task, I wouldn't say that I will finish it, but I'd make a promise. The sentence is: 'I promise to do this by 14:00 tomorrow.' When I say 14:00 I mean the time frame from now to 13:59:99. If I missed the deadline, which would mean finishing after 13:59:99, I would cross out the pattern. I would eliminate every excuse I could give myself. To finish at 14:00:01 = a failure of my personal consistency. It may sound stupid, and you may wonder: what is the difference between 13:59:99 and 14:00:01? For the person you promised to, nothing, but for you it is huge:

Task completed by 13:59:99 = digital 1 (one) = I have my personal consistency.
Task completed after 13:59:99 = digital 0 (zero) = I did the task, but I have no personal consistency.

The beauty of digital patterns is that you can never fool yourself and that is the most important outcome of training patterns and communicating with yourself and others.

Stay loyal to your integrity

Just like Richard Feynman said, "The first principle is that you must not fool yourself—and you are the easiest person to fool." When you succeed in conditioning yourself and your behavior to be 99% faithful to yourself, as a result you will become trusted by your environment, i.e. you will create a conviction in others: 'He's a person who fulfils his promises and his tasks.' In other words, you will transfer your personal credibility to others and they will start to trust you unconditionally. Setting such goals for yourself could be the best decision you make in order to become your better self.

Start small

When you succeeded in adopting this pattern, your communication will have an air of congruence and honesty, and when you spread such communication toward others, even those people who have a consistency problem will try to be consistent to you and the promises made to you. We can only expect from others what we give ourselves. Consistent communication means to be completely true to your (better) self.

Great story that seems to drive this lesson home:

One mother brought her young son to Mahatma Gandhi. She begged him saying, "Mahatma, tell my son to stop eating sugar" Gandhi paused, and then said, "Bring me the child in two weeks." Astonished, the woman thanked him and promised to do as he asked. And so it was. After two weeks she returned with her son. Gandhi looked at the child in the eye and said, "Stop eating sugar." Grateful, but confused, the mother asked, "Why did you ask me to come after two weeks then? You could have told him the same thing two weeks ago. "

Gandhi replied," Two weeks ago, I was eating sugar. "

You get the point.

After you install and condition that pattern, you're ready for greater goals, i.e. setting larger tasks for yourself. You're ready for personal grand promises to yourself in order to achieve all the things that will make you the person you want to be.

The story with my book started exactly on February 1, 2012. I sat at my computer and started writing. The goal wasn't to write a book in the shortest possible time, but to develop a pattern of writing – a pattern of putting ideas on paper. Occasionally I wrote an article, but there have been interludes of up to 18 months between them. So, the first step is to develop writing, which I included in my 100 day sheet for 2012. That was the hardest pattern with which I ever tasked myself. Not one field was as black as the field of DW (daily writing).

There were weeks when I wrote 30-40 pages, and I would put checks there, but the biggest struggle was when I had no idea how to proceed, where to start, when I had no inspiration. On those days, my goal was only to fill out the form on the sheet. I would sit at my computer and write a sentence or a title and close the document. If I had no idea what to write, I could just fill out the form, which was the premise… and a good thing that it was.

I'll admit I often put off writing with the excuse: 'I'm not inspired today. I can't write because I don't have any inspiration.' With that conviction/state a few years ago, before I'd started training digital patterns, I wouldn't even try to sit at my computer and open a document. But, I knew that eventually if I wanted to be a writer I would have to train my writing pattern.

That conviction was further confirmed by the author of *On Writing Well*, William Zinsser. At the beginning of his book, he described a situation where he had been invited to a college to tell students about writing. When he arrived, he realized that he wasn't the only speaker. There was also a doctor who had lately been writing great articles in some magazines and achieved great results. The doctor went first and told the students that he wrote in situations when there is an inspiration, and when there isn't any, he goes for a walk or does some other activity. Zinsser said that that wasn't the case with him. 'I think you should write no matter the state you're in.'

If your profession is writing, you should write and that's it. If you're a teacher and you have your own class, you wake up uninspired but you don't say, 'I'll teach tomorrow, when I find inspiration, and now I'm going for a walk,' before you go to school and do the class despite the lack of will or inspiration.

If I work as a communication coach and have an appointed seminar, I cannot postpone it. There is no room for that - my job is to act professionally. No matter how I feel; I have to find positive resources within and make the best seminar. Now I have to apply this to writing. After training the wanted patterns you can trust yourself in setting much larger goals which arise from those patterns, goals which are created by those patterns.

I stopped writing this book on June 6 2012, and removed the writing pattern from my sheet. I felt that I wasn't ready yet. Over the next few months, I read a lot of books and mostly passively developed the final concept. During that time, people who were familiar with my goal would often ask me when it would be finished. I would reply, 'I don't know. When I'm ready.' I didn't have a winning strategy yet. I was looking for it, and it wasn't showing up. On Saturday night, the 26th of January 2013 I realized: I have the patterns, I have the parts of the strategy and I've been trying to find the most ideal, the best and most perfect strategy for this book, and it will not come on its own. Instead of trying to become my better self through writing and learning through that experience, for months I tried to be my perfect/best self in my head.

The way to define a formidable goal

The quote that hit my first trigger was:

"People have impotent goals / that is, goals that do not inspire them."
Anthony Robbins

On January 27, at 1 AM I decided to write the book within 5 days. I sat at my computer and went searching through the existing files. I realized that most of it was useless. I would have to change the concept. This discouraged me because I had assumed how much writing I would have to do in the following days in order to finish it… but I remembered a quote by Ferris: 'Impossible is more possible than possible.' That gave me a trigger. I started writing and creating a new concept.

I knew that if I gave my best, although it seemed impossible, the book would be ready by February 1, 2013. I made a firm decision and a conviction that it was possible. I wrote until 4 AM and decided to go to bed in order to give my best the following day. I went to bed, closed my eyes and started thinking about what was ahead and what strategies I could use in order to achieve this great goal which I set for myself. About ten minutes after I had gone to bed I heard a voice: 'Sasha, you now believe that you'll write the book in time and you made a firm decision, but this decision comes from the state you're currently in – a state of powerful motivation. And now remember some of those situations from your past where you were also psyched before going to bed and woke the other day and it was gone. You found excuses to justify quitting. How honest and consistent is your current decision? If you manage to do this you will surely be satisfied, but if you fail to meet your deadline you will lose nothing.'

And everything I said was true. How will I solve this problem? Should I stay awake and keep writing or what? How do I keep this state until 4 PM Friday? How do I break every barrier that could stand in my way and prevent me from doing this? I know myself enough to know that I could find an easy way out. How should I condition my behavior to strengthen my decision and keep my motivation? I know, I have to condition myself, and for now I only have the positive reinforcement – the feeling of pleasure when I will have finished the book. Is positive reinforcement enough? Now I understand that it's not. I must also condition myself with a negative reinforcement –a punisher.

I started thinking about Napoleon Hill and his story about warriors who burned all their ships, thus removing every possibility of retreat. By burning the ships the commander didn't cause the win over their opponents, by burning the ships the commander killed every soldier's idea that there's even a hope to return home. And now, how do I put myself in this situation? How do I burn all the ships?

The way to burn extra options

In the next moment I realized the answer – a solution that would burn all my ships, all my options. I remembered a famous hypnotist. This hypnotist claims that he made more people quit smoking than any other person alive. Before you come to his treatment, you have to fulfill one condition. This condition is to announce to everybody you know: 'I have an appointment with a hypnotist on Wednesday, and I've made a firm decision to quit smoking. After this appointment I will never again light a cigarette,' several days before the treatment.

What is the goal of this action? The goal is to reinforce the personal decision (positive motivation) to quit smoking and to create expectations in others that this person will quit smoking. If that person doesn't announce this, they will only have responsibility towards themselves, but if they make this announcement and don't quit smoking, they lose personal credibility because they failed to fulfill their own promise, not only to themselves, but to others as well (punisher – negative motivation). This hypnotist honestly says that by doing this, people solved 90% of their own problem, and he just gave them a little push with his 10% on their way to change themselves.

It was 4:50 AM and I decided to act. I got out of bed, opened my Facebook profile and wrote the following status:

With this status I'm using a strategy of a famous hypnotist in order to increase personal responsibility by creating environmental pressure. My first book will be finished in 131 hours. More accurately, it will be done by Friday, February 1, 2013 at 16:00. If it isn't finished by then, everyone who sees this status will have the right to call me out for personal inconsistency and not keeping my word, which is wholly unsuitable and intolerable for someone like me since I do the work I do. This status serves the purpose of eliminating extra options and destroying my personal manipulative nature. So in the words of Napoleon Hill, with this status I'm burning all the ships or knocking down all the bridges.
 As I am writing this sentence, it's Friday, February 1, 2013, 1:32 PM.

Go for it!

In conclusion, choose your own values, things that are important to you. Choose the behavioral patterns that will bring you closer to achieving those values. Train them, train them until they become a part of you, and train them until the moment or day when you realize that you can completely trust yourself. When you've achieved that, define an outcome that breaks all the boundaries of your map, all the frameworks of something you considered impossible only months before. Remove impotence from your goals, because by training patterns and new inputs you created a model based on which you can believe that you are ready. And in the end, digitally specify that goal (time by which you will be done, 15:59:99), spread the word and do what you have made yourself do. Go for it!

So, Raymond...still here? What are you going to do first?

INSPIRATION FOR THE BOOK & RESOURCES

During my personal transformation and the formation of this work, I was influenced and inspired by many life events, situations, people around me, but also wise authors, leaders and their books. I would like to share and recommend with you these resources:

Bandler, Richard & John Grinder (1975a). The Structure of Magic I: A Book About Language and Therapy. Palo Alto, CA: Science & Behavior Books.
Bandler, Richard & John Grinder (1975b). The Structure of Magic II: A Book About Communication and Change. Palo Alto, CA: Science & Behavior Books.
Buzan, Tony: Use Your Head, Pearson Education, 2006.
Clason, S. George: The Richest Man in Babylon - The Success Secrets of the Ancients, Signet, First published in 1926.
DeLozier, Judith & Dilts, Robert, Encyclopedia of Systemic Neuro-Linguistic Programming and NLP New Coding, NLP University Press, Santa Cruz, CA, 2000.
Dilts, Robert, Changing Belief Systems with NLP, Meta Publications, Capitola, CA,1990.
Dilts, Robert, Sleight of Mouth: The Magic of Conversational Belief Change, Meta Publications, Capitola, CA, 1999.
Faulkner, Charles; Robert McDonald, Tim Hallbom, M.S.W (2003). NLP The New Technology of Achievement. Nightingale Conant.
Grinder, John; Richard Bandler (1979). Frogs into Princes: Neuro Linguistic Programming. Real People Press
Grinder, John & Bandler, Richard DeLozier, Judith & Dilts, Robert, Neuro-Linguistic Programming: The Study of the Structure of Subjective Experience, Volume I, Meta Publications, Capitola, CA, 1980.
Hallbom, Tim & Smith, Suzi & Dilts, Robert, Beliefs: Pathways to Health & Well-Being, Metamorphous Press, Portland, OR, 1990.
Hill, Napoleon: Think and Grow Rich. Chicago, Illinois: Combined Registry Company (1937).
Katz, Lawrence; Manning Rubin: Keep Your Brain Alive: 83 Neurobic Exercises, Workman Publishing, 1999.

Korzibsky: ^ R. Diekstra, Haarlemmer Dagblad, 1993, cited by L. Derks & J. Hollander, Essenties van NLP (Utrecht: Servire, 1996).

Lipton, Bruce: The Biology of Belief - Unleashing the Power of Consciousness, Matter & Miracles, 2005.

Maltz, Maxwell: Psycho-Cybernetics, Wilshire Book Co (1960).

O'Connor, Joseph and John Seymour: Introducing NLP. London: HarperCollins (2002).

Rosen, Sidney: My Voice Will Go With You: The Teaching Tales of Milton H. Erickson (WW Norton & Company: New York, 1991).

Smith, Julien: The Flinch, Kindle Edition, 2011.

Welch, Jack and Suzy: Winning, HarperCollins, April 2005.

Online resources:

Likens, Sylvia: http://en.wikipedia.org/wiki/Sylvia_Likens

Milgram experiment: http://en.wikipedia.org/wiki/Milgram_experiment

Pavlov, Ivan: http://en.wikipedia.org/wiki/Ivan_Pavlov

Skinner, Burrhus Frederic: http://en.wikipedia.org/wiki/B._F._Skinner

Watson, John: http://en.wikipedia.org/wiki/John_B._Watson

Watson, John; Little Albert experiment: http://en.wikipedia.org/wiki/Little_Albert

About the Author

Sasha Tenodi is speaker and trainer dedicated and passionate about helping people to take control of their lives. With a Faculty of Education and Rehabilitation Sciences degree from the University of Zagreb and many years working as an expert in the field of Neuro-linguistic programming (NLP), Sasha is able to draw on his own diverse background - rich with experience and hard won lessons - in order to provide strategies and inspire others to become better, more successful versions of themselves. He believes that we all have the ability to become exactly who we've always wanted to be, no matter what conditions or failures we have gone through in life. He shares his knowledge by offering a hands-on approach to learning the basics and complexities behind life design.

His strongest value in life is time. Time for his wife Ana and a new born son Ivano. Time for education, learning and developing new skills. Just about anything that can improve his mind map and mind maps of people he cares for.

Contact Sasha

Sasha speaks on the topic of personal growth, communication and presentation skills. Depending on the needs of the group he can deliver a lecture, a workshop or 5 to10 days of training. If you are interested in finding out more, please visit www.sashatenodi.com

You can connect with Sasha on Facebook and/or Linkedin.

Printed in Poland
by Amazon Fulfillment
Poland Sp. z o.o., Wrocław

52759981R00096